T0113154

PILLOW TALK

PILLOW TALK

What's Wrong with My Sewing?

CRAIG CONOVER

with Blake Dvorak

GALLERY BOOKS

NEW YORK   LONDON   TORONTO   SYDNEY   NEW DELHI

G

Gallery Books
An Imprint of Simon & Schuster, Inc.
1230 Avenue of the Americas
New York, NY 10020

Copyright © 2022 by Craig Conover

Afterword © 2023 by Craig Conover

All rights reserved, including the right to reproduce this book or portions thereof in any form whatsoever. For information, address Gallery Books Subsidiary Rights Department, 1230 Avenue of the Americas, New York, NY 10020.

First Gallery Books trade paperback edition January 2023

GALLERY BOOKS and colophon are registered trademarks of Simon & Schuster, Inc.

For information about special discounts for bulk purchases, please contact Simon & Schuster Special Sales at 1-866-506-1949 or business@simonandschuster.com.

The Simon & Schuster Speakers Bureau can bring authors to your live event. For more information or to book an event, contact the Simon & Schuster Speakers Bureau at 1-866-248-3049 or visit our website at www.simonspeakers.com.

Interior design by Jaime Putorti

Manufactured in the United States of America

10 9 8 7 6 5 4 3 2 1

The Library of Congress has cataloged the hardcover edition as follows:

Names: Conover, Craig, author. | Dvorak, Blake D., author.
Title: Pillow talk : what's wrong with my sewing? / Craig Conover ; with Blake Dvorak.
Description: First Gallery Books hardcover edition. | New York : Gallery Books, 2022.
Identifiers: LCCN 2021049010 (print) | LCCN 2021049011 (ebook) | ISBN 9781982187484 (hardcover) | ISBN 9781982187491 (trade paperback) | ISBN 9781982187507 (ebook)
Subjects: LCSH: Conover, Craig. | Television personalities—United States—Biography. | Southern charm (Television program) | Reality television programs—United States.
Classification: LCC PN1992.4.C6676 A3 2022 (print) | LCC PN1992.4.C6676 (ebook) | DDC 791.4502/8092 [B]—dc23/eng/20220104
LC record available at https://lccn.loc.gov/2021049010
LC ebook record available at https://lccn.loc.gov/2021049011

ISBN 978-1-9821-8748-4
ISBN 978-1-9821-8749-1 (pbk)
ISBN 978-1-9821-8750-7 (ebook)

For Tim and Alex, who left this world much too soon.
And for Mom and Dad.

CONTENTS

PILLOW TALK

HOW DID I GET HERE?

*F*ew sights have the power of transporting me backward in time as do the beaches of Delaware. Those very beaches passed by me out the window of my parents' Jeep Wrangler as I drove down Coastal Highway toward Bethany Beach, a city whose streets and boardwalks I could walk blindfolded. I had spent my summer vacations in those waters right outside my car window, learning to surf and chasing girls. Just a few miles from my childhood house in Ocean View, I was soon overwhelmed by that feeling that I was suddenly *home*, in a way that no other place on earth feels like home.

But why was I home? How did I get here? More than a decade after leaving Delaware, I was back. It wasn't the first time I had been back. But it felt like the most important.

Although I had been home many times since starting my life in Charleston, South Carolina, where—as you probably know—I now live and work, this time was different, because I was different. Charleston is where viewers of *Southern Charm* have watched me . . . well, grow up for the last seven years; it's where I headquartered my company, Sewing Down South, and it's where I plan to stay. But while I have adopted that most beautiful of southern cities as my own, at heart I will always be that kid from the beaches of Delaware. It was here that I learned the meaning of hard work from my parents, especially my father, who had started his own remediation company. It was here that I learned to play baseball. It was here that I learned the power of family, and gained the knowledge that no matter how far away you might stray from your roots, *home* will always be there to remind you who you truly are and what truly matters. It was here that I learned to sew.

Sewing was the reason I was here on a hot summer's day in August 2019: to launch the next phase of Sewing Down South with the first "pillow party"—the first of what became twenty-three pillow parties that took SDS pillows (and me) on a multi-state tour and ended up generating $200,000 in sales. Of course, I didn't know that then, driving down that highway on my way to the first pillow party, fighting off intense feelings of nostalgia and extreme anxiety. Truthfully, I was a nervous wreck. While early sales had been strong, I couldn't shake the feeling that maybe up here no one cared about my pillows, or *Southern Charm*, or a hometown boy trying to start a business.

When I reached the store—a little boutique an old high school friend had inherited from her grandmother called Perfect Furnishings—my first thought was that I had the wrong place. What were all these people doing here? But the tall purple sign on the side of the road confirmed what Siri was telling me: This was it. The store was right off the highway, a simple beach-inspired building painted sky blue, only with a line of people running down the block as if it were an L.A. nightclub. I kept driving. I wasn't ready for that, not yet. A few hundred yards down the highway, I spotted a familiar restaurant, Cottage Café, and pulled in, smiling. This was where I used to sit and eat with my grandparents, and where I had gone on my first date in high school. The restaurant has a porch overlooking the highway, which I thought was the perfect spot to grab a beer, relax, and collect myself.

As I sat there sipping my beer, with Perfect Furnishings just across the way, I saw that the line continued to grow until it stretched down the highway. It was a moment I'll never forget. The next few hours would fly by in a flurry of laughter, pictures, autographs, and shaking hands, and it would be impossible to stop and take it all in. But here, I could. For a brief, blissful moment, my anxieties, my fears, my near-paralyzing self-doubt lifted from my shoulders and I was able to appreciate just how far I'd come. I wasn't about to declare Sewing Down South a success just yet, nor that I had "made it" as an entrepreneur who had followed his passion, despite the naysayers. I knew there was still a long road ahead of me. But at least I was finally on the damn road.

Few thought I'd even get to this point. I certainly hadn't made it easy on myself. There were plenty of people, some very close to me, who assumed that all I'd ever amount to would be another face on reality television. I don't necessarily blame them. Given what they saw and what they knew, they were right to doubt, because time after time I had dashed their faith in me. I would say all the right things, but do all the wrong things. Then, slowly, I started to do some things right. Hell, I started to do things *period*. And somehow, I managed to string together enough right things to get here, watching my fans—no, my *customers*—form that line outside Perfect Furnishings.

I was home, and I was on my way.

When I finally finished my beer (or maybe it was my second), I met my friend and business partner, Jerry Casselano, outside the restaurant. He, too, had seen the line, and the look he gave me was priceless. I smiled and shrugged, and we drove the short distance to the store, where the owner, my old friend Courtney, had reserved a spot for me. The crowd surged around the car as I parked, then cheered when I got out. Being on a hit show, it wasn't the first time I had encountered cheering fans before. But this was different. This was for something I had created, something that was truly *mine*—mine in a way that a massive production like *Southern Charm* simply can't be. And the sheer satisfaction I felt at the accomplishment, which I shared with Jerry and our other partner, Amanda Latifi, is one that will stay with me forever.

Courtney met me in the parking lot and had to shout over the cheering. "What the hell is going on?" she asked. I laughed. I had no idea what to say.

We ended up doing $13,000 in sales that day, while I sat behind a table for three and a half hours signing autographs and talking with my customers. It all went by in a haze, except for a few stand-out moments. I remember my parents arriving with our golden retriever, Fenwick, and my mother giving me a hug and whispering, "This is crazy." I remember seeing my younger brother, Christopher, a soft-spoken guy who inherited our mother's seriousness and work ethic. (I inherited my father's outspokenness and procrastination.) He didn't say much, but he did smile at me, and that was all he had to do. Of all those who had lost faith in me over the years—including sometimes myself—Christopher never did. His smile was his way of saying: "I knew you could do it, Brother."

But perhaps the most powerful moment came from a complete stranger—or rather, a mother and her teenage son, an athletic kid in a football jersey. They had been standing in the hours-long line with the rest. When they finally reached the table, I assumed that the mother was the fan and customer and that she had dragged her poor kid to some ridiculous furniture store to meet someone she liked watching on television. I know my fans, and teenage boys just aren't them.

Then the most remarkable thing happened. The teenage boy set down on the table a sewn tote bag. Embroidered on the side were the initials "IRHS," which stood for Indian River High School, my alma mater and (clearly) his as well.

"He made this and wanted you to have it," the mom said to me. "His father taught him to sew. He was always embarrassed by it, until he started watching you on the show. Now he's proud of his sewing." She shrugged. "Now he knows that it's okay to do something you love."

How did I get here?

That was the thought that kept running through my Adderall-saturated brain as I sat beside a dumpster at four o'clock in the morning in Jacksonville, Florida, hoping that my friend Gaber would come pick me up. Hoping, really, that anyone would come and save me.

Roughly six months before the first pillow party, I had traveled to Jacksonville from the Bahamas, where I had had a terrible final night with one of my best friends, Graham Hegamyer, who is the husband of my assistant, Anna Heyward. A year earlier, I had spent the summer in the Bahamas, where the Hegamyers had a house and were treated like locals. I had fallen in love with the area and was able, during my time there, to break out of the vicious cycle I had created for myself in Charleston—a cycle of Adderall, booze, nights that never seemed to end, and mornings that came far too soon. I would clean up in those tropical waters, only to fall back into my old ways when I returned to film in Charleston. I went back to the Bahamas often, visiting with my friends, but I was still stuck in those destructive ways. During one visit in March, I was scheduled to fly to Jacksonville to meet my friends Shep Rose and Austen Kroll for a golf tournament. On the night before I flew out, I had dinner with the Hegamyers and another friend, a girl who had flown down to the islands. I was on Adderall, and when mixed with booze, I became the worst version of myself during dinner. Sadly, it was the version that was swiftly becoming the only version of myself.

To Graham, I had committed the sin of taking this little corner of the Bahamas for granted. I had turned it into my playground, a place to bring women and party. It's not like Graham had put a bunch of restrictions on me when I visited, but he did expect a level of decorum. I had broken his trust in me, and had my brain not been clouded with booze and Adderall, I might have been able to see that disappointment in his eyes that evening.

The next morning, as I was walking to the plane on the tarmac, I remembered enough to know that I had made an ass of myself. So I called Graham to apologize.

"But you're not sorry," he responded sharply. "You've turned into this person that I don't like." I stopped walking and just listened. "Craig, if you come back, you must understand that things will be different."

What he meant by that, I didn't exactly know. And while he *said* we could still be friends, I realized I might have just lost one of my best. Panicking, I promised that I would change; that I wouldn't act that way again; but in my heart, I was terrified. It was a promise that I feared I couldn't keep.

Nor did I when I touched down in Jacksonville a few hours later and proceeded to numb the guilt and embarrassment the way I always did: with Adderall, booze, and the validation of strangers. Shep and Austen had already called it a night, but I stayed out. I kept going. Which was how I found myself at a random party with random people well after midnight. I didn't know a soul, but everyone there thought they knew me—a fact of life for those on reality TV shows. I'm usually very cordial and open with fans. I enjoy meeting them and learning their thoughts about the show and how they connect with certain cast members. But that night I was well beyond the cordial phase, and the need to leave—the need to get the hell out of there—suddenly took over every other thought in my head. A girl suddenly reached for my phone, for what reason I don't recall, but I panicked, and in my agitated state I managed to smash my phone. I literally ran from the house, hoping the crowd wouldn't follow me.

That's how I ended up beside that dumpster, staring at a busted phone, and asking how everything had gone so wrong for me. This wasn't where I was supposed to be. At age thirty, I was supposed to have *done something* by now. Instead, I numbed my feelings and sought validation from strangers at parties. I had started making pillows but didn't have the discipline to make my passion anything more than a hobby. I was hooked on Adderall, again, and I had just estranged myself from one of my best friends. Something had to change.

1

- - - - - -

A BOY FROM DELAWARE

*I*n the second season of *Southern Charm*, I brought my friends Shepard Rose and Whitney Sudler-Smith to my home in Ocean View, Delaware. We played golf, they met my parents, and during dinner one evening, Whitney told my mom and dad that he was worried about me.

"He's wasting his talents, staying up and partying all night," said Whitney. "He goes out every night. How do we give him a kick to get his life in order?"

I was horrified. I managed to keep it together in front of my parents, but the next morning on the links, I let Whitney have it. I was furious that he would reveal these things to my parents, especially after I asked him not to.

"It's out of concern and love, man," replied Whitney. "You're a bit of a mess right now."

He wasn't wrong. I was falling deeper into the "Neverland"

world of Charleston, living like a celebrity, and losing any drive I once had. I'd recently been fired from my job as a law clerk for repeatedly coming in late. Hell, I hadn't even graduated from law school because I was still shy one credit—though no one, not even my family, knew that yet. And I blurted it all out in a moment of frustration and clarity.

"Every day I'm stressed out as fuck," I finally said to them. "My rent's fucking sky-high. I'm spending too much money. Half the time I'm embarrassed to tell you guys because I don't want you to look down on me. You guys are doing great right now. I'm running away from the truth. This is the first time I'm admitting to myself out loud that, yeah, something needs to change because shit's not going right right now."

It would be some time still before I used these words to change myself. I had a long journey ahead of me . . . and it would get much worse before it started to get better. But while I could at least admit that something was wrong with the direction of my life, that's not why I had exploded at Whitney.

I wasn't pissed because what he said was inaccurate; I was pissed because there was no good reason *why* I was failing and miserable. Maybe I had just been a spoiled brat as a kid, indulged by indifferent parents. Maybe I had always been kind of a failure, struggling through grade school and always the last picked for sports. Maybe I just hadn't ever been taught hard work or discipline, coasting through childhood without consequences.

Whitney and Shep didn't see that. Instead, they saw my bedroom with my many awards and trophies, both athletic and academic. They saw my parents, tender and good-hearted, whose love and devotion to their children was just as strong that day as it had been when my brother and I were first born. In just twenty-four hours, they had caught a glimpse of the boy I had been, surrounded with love and gifted with so many of the blessings that really mattered in life: family, values, intelligence, and a sense of responsibility.

What happened to this boy? Why did he grow up to be this wayward and lost young man they knew in Charleston? There was no reason, no evidence, that explained the difference between man and child. I had been given every opportunity to realize my potential, and yet I was wasting them all. Why?

It wasn't a question I was prepared to answer at that moment, but I also wasn't that interested (yet) in answering it. My little outburst on the golf course was real, if also a bit disingenuous. I believed all these things; I just wasn't ready to fix any of it.

At the time, I was upset because I didn't want my parents to worry. I had tried very hard to keep the truth of what was happening in my life concealed from them. I would straighten myself out, I just needed time.

Looking back, I can admit that I was just terrified of my own shame. In fact, I was riddled with shame—and guilt. All the things that Whitney saw in Ocean View, I saw too. I saw the enormous love of my parents and the sacrifices they had made for my brother and me. I saw the accolades and awards that seemed to foreshadow success. I saw the comfort and safety of a home that encouraged me to dream big and reach my potential. I saw the person I was supposed to be. And every day I looked in the mirror at the person I had become. To avoid seeing that person, to save my ego from the debilitating guilt, I had learned ways to hide from myself. I became very good at it, to be honest. But those methods—the partying, the drinking, the staying out late—were also what intensified the guilt in those terrible moments of clarity.

Going home to Delaware forced me to stare at that boy in the mirror. The boy who had been given everything he needed to succeed and realize his dreams. I had left my home in Ocean View to conquer the world on my terms. I had returned exhausted and broke.

So who was that boy? Where did he come from, and how did he grow up?

LOWER, SLOWER DELAWARE

When I was two years old I started talking, and, as my mother, Marty, says, I never stopped. The polite term would be "precocious," although I believe it's more accurate to say that I was a talkative know-it-all. This isn't unique to me. The gift of gab was handed down to me from my father, Craig, just one in a long line of Conovers who say what's on their mind—often. By the time I reached school, my hand was up constantly, always ready with an answer, correct or not. One of my elementary school teachers one day mentioned to my mother, who was by then also a teacher, that she was pretty sure little Craig knew more than she did. Growing up Catholic, I went to church every Sunday, but being a Conover, I questioned everything I was told, to the consternation of my religious mother and the approval of my skeptical father. In fact, as the years passed, and Christopher and I grew up, it became clear that he had inherited most of the traits of my mother—reserved, disciplined, and serious. Whereas I am more like my dad—outgoing, restless, ambitious, but also cursed with procrastination.

My father started out in the restoration business before he and my mother married. He was the one going on the calls, cleaning the houses and buildings after a flood or other catastrophe, and I think he enjoyed being away from a desk. When they got engaged, my father got an office job, ordering parts and whatnot. By this time, they had moved closer to the beach and my father hated every minute of being stuck behind that desk. "It wasn't me," he once said. (It's not me either, Dad.) Within one week, he'd quit that job and started his own carpet-cleaning company with a few friends. Four months later, the money had run out and one of the partners had left. But my dad stuck with it, and after he and Mom married a few months later, he was able to pay back the investment money, leaving him the sole proprietor of the business. My mother would eventually become an elementary school teacher, but at this time, before I was born, she worked with my father full-time on the company. Those first five years, as they now tell it, were tough, and keeping both themselves and the company above water was a constant struggle.

On February 9, 1988, two years into the business, I was born. Although money was tight, I never experienced want or deprivation. My parents made enough to pay the mortgage and provide my brother and me with what we needed, but there was little left over for any type of luxury or extravagance. I didn't notice—

except when I wanted a gumball from the machine at the grocery store. My future drive to make money had everything to do with my own ambition and almost nothing to do with any painful childhood memories of going without heat or other necessities. As a child, I distinctly remember going with my father on emergency cleaning calls, which I loved. It wasn't the work I enjoyed—I have always hated manual labor—it was being with my dad and feeling like I was an important part of his life. My father eventually grew the business to the point where my mom could start working as a teacher, and the business continues to thrive thirty years later, with Christopher now running the operations.

Meanwhile, my own early childhood was happy. I excelled at school and sports, and quickly grew to love the world in which I lived. My parents eventually bought a second house in Fenwick, closer to the beach, and I spent my summer vacations in those waters, learning to surf and appreciate the quieter life in "lower, slower Delaware," as we call this little corner of this little state. I took to this lifestyle, and for this reason, I never encountered any kind of "culture shock" when I eventually left for Charleston. As southern cities go, Charleston is pretty damn cosmopolitan, but there remain vestiges of the old southern way of life that can sometimes annoy transplanted Yankees. I never experienced this—or, if I did, I was drawn to it as a reminder of home.

And home was and remains my place of comfort. Both my parents worked very hard, but they always had time for my brother and me. They never missed a soccer game, a baseball game, or a wrestling match. They never were too busy to help with homework. They always listened to our worries and troubles, and they didn't act as if our childhood dramas were unimportant. Every night we would have dinner together, no matter what. It was our time together as a family, sharing stories of our day and working together as a single unit. These family dinners were so much a part of my upbringing that I just assumed that's how everyone lived. It wasn't until I was off on my own at college and later that I came to realize how precious and important those times around the table truly were. No, not everyone grew up like that. No, not everyone had a mom or dad who was around to listen to them, to enjoy their company, to build and grow a family into the strongest bond a person can have. There's a reason why in later years, when the weight of my struggles bore down on me, that I often retreated to the comfort of home, to the relaxing and restorative presence of my family around the dinner table.

All of which is to say that of the many blessings I have had in life, none stand out as strongly as the life my parents provided to me growing up. I know that traumatic events that happen in childhood can often lead to severe internal problems in later years, but I can't point to anything like that from my own early years. There was a time when, in the third grade, my aunt on my father's side was killed in Baltimore. It was the first time I ever saw my father cry—a moment that stays with a child forever. It's the moment when you first glimpse your parents, especially your father, as an actual person and not a marble icon. Some years later, when I was a sophomore in high school, my dad underwent heart surgery, and his recovery lasted several months. My father's stay in the hospital had a profound effect on my future. At the time, I had very vague notions of becoming a doctor, but this was based on little more than trying to tie my academic performance to a successful profession. I had no real medical passion, a fact made painfully obvious when I visited my father in the hospital after his surgery. I never made it to his room in the ICU. There was something deeply unsettling to me about being in the hospital, and I found myself running outside before ever seeing him. So that knocked "doctor" off my list of possible careers.

A non-drinker, my father hated taking his pain medication, which made for a very sour patient that the rest of the family just had to deal with. Because I took over a lot of his home care, he directed much of his externalized anger and frustration toward me. Being older and aware of the reason, I took it in stride. But aside from these moments, which hardly rise to the level of traumatic memories, my childhood growing up in Ocean View, spending summers in Fenwick and Bethany Beach, was about as idyllic as a middle-class kid could ever want.

A NEW PASSION AND DEEP SCARS

What this safety and comfort instilled in me was self-confidence from a young age. I pursued my interests and hobbies without the typical adolescent worrying of what others might think. For the most part, these interests were your basic American boy interests, especially athletics. I loved all the sports that are popular on the East Coast, including soccer, lacrosse, and baseball, and I was good at them. Though skinny, I wasn't yet at the level where my size worked against me, so I couldn't even be self-conscious about that yet. But I also wasn't *that* typical. When I'd come home from practice, I would turn on Emeril Lagasse and help my mother make dinner. My mom was a full-time schoolteacher by then, and she was more than happy to have a little help in the kitchen. For me, though, I genuinely enjoyed it. I even started to put together my own cookbook full of my favorite recipes. I suppose I was aware that this wasn't what most boys my age did when they got home from school, but I didn't care. Never much of a video-gamer, I simply loved to cook.

I started to recognize that I had an appreciation for the more domestic hobbies usually associated with girls, especially when I first learned to sew. Neither of my parents were particularly adept or interested in it, as far as I can remember. I first came across sewing in the seventh grade, in Mrs. Hurley's home economics class. The classroom was divided into two sections, one half dedicated to the kitchen and cooking, the other to sewing, with several electronic sewing stations set up. As is typical for that age, most of the boys laughed their way through class, while most of the girls enjoyed it. I was with the girls. While I do think it's true that these interests roughly break down by gender, I think far more of the boys enjoyed it than they were willing to admit. If it wasn't sports, then they weren't *allowed* to enjoy it. But I did, and I had no problem showing that I did. I remember making my first pillow in Mrs. Hurley's class and feeling a sense of tremendous satisfaction at having created something. Using my hands, I had turned what had been some fabric and thread into something real and beautiful (to me, at least). I didn't realize it at the time, but I had stumbled upon something that had given me joy. It was an amazing feeling, similar to what I felt when I sat down to a dinner I had helped prepare. I was too young to realize how precious that feeling really is, and perhaps for this reason I abandoned these hobbies as I got older. It wasn't because I would grow self-conscious about these interests; rather, because my childhood was full of joy, I never expected to find myself in a place where I would need joy to get me through dark moments.

And those moments would strike soon enough. As a child and adolescent, I rarely experienced true cruelty. There was the typical teasing that boys and brothers inflict on one another, but nothing that rose to the level of outright viciousness. But if my childhood could be divided in half, much like Mrs. Hurley's classroom, one half, the earlier half, was full of sunlight, happiness, and love. I had nothing to fear and had been able to develop my abilities and interests free of any outside interference. This would come to a swift end when I reached high school.

There's no need to recount all the episodes of bullying that happened to me as a teenager. The best way to describe it is that it was just this persistent state of being for me, something that I had to deal with every day. Most of it originated with the older players on the school soccer team. *Why* did they target me? I was small and skinny, so I suppose that had something to do with it. I also believe that the self-confidence I had acquired and built throughout adolescence made me a target too. Bullies hate seeing what they lack in others, and their efforts are, above all, an attempt to make the target feel as bad as they do. In that, they were successful. I lost much of my confidence because of what they put me through, and I started to become painfully aware of my own inadequacies, to the point that they were all I focused on. I still carry these scars with me today. I developed a need to be *liked* by everyone, accepted as an equal. If I wasn't good at something—or if I outright couldn't do something—I chose to hide it rather than accept it. I just couldn't bear the idea of anyone having a lesser opinion of me.

One particular moment stands out as emblematic of the bullying. I was a freshman on the junior varsity team, which shared a bus with the varsity players. I got off the bus one day and realized I had left behind my bookbag. The next day I retrieved my bag and reached in to take out one of the books for my English class. It was a thick, heavy book. Well, the older kids had used a whole roll of athletic tape on it, which I had to tear away. And when I finally got the book open, I realized that they had also smashed Doritos between the pages, leaving an oily residue that completely ruined the book, which I had to pay for. To some, it might seem that it's just a book, so what? But I was a good, serious student. I appreciated my books and considered them valuable beyond their monetary price. For those players to deliberately destroy my book affected me deeply. To this day, I don't understand that level of mindless cruelty. What didn't they like about me? What had I done wrong?

With the benefit of hindsight, I sometimes look back on this episode and others like it and wonder if it was really that bad. But then I quickly remember that this was the same thing I had told myself back then. I wasn't getting beaten up; I was just the mark for this group's senseless viciousness. I wasn't afraid for my safety or my life, but I was made to feel like there was a problem with me. Maybe it was my stature. Maybe it was my teeth, which weren't the best before I got braces and whitened them. Maybe it was because I was a little geeky. Whatever it was, their purpose was to make me feel like garbage. And, like I said, they succeeded. I internalized their bullying to the point where I felt that something was wrong with me if *they* didn't like me. This obsession with what others thought about me—by no means abnormal for a teenager—made me turn from a confident kid into someone who sought validation from others. I couldn't be happy with myself unless others were happy with me. This was the bullies' deepest cut, and the one that left a lasting mark. At the same time, I knew that one day I would prove them all wrong. I didn't know how then, but their cruelty was motivation for me then and later.

Despite the prevalence of the bullying, I never got used to it. Some days were better than others, when the bullies simply forgot to make me a target, but that only led to agonizing uncertainty and paranoia. When I'd leave for school in the morning, I girded myself for what might happen. If I was bullied, then I had to deal with it. If I didn't get bullied, then I was left with this pent-up anxiety that started to affect other aspects of my life. It was during these years when I developed some obsessive-compulsive tendencies. I don't think I can attribute all of it to the bullying, since OCD definitely runs in my family, but like many mental health conditions, my OCD needed a trigger—and bullying was the trigger. For instance, my bedtime routine started to take forty-five minutes, because I had to look under my bed three times; I had to check the closet; I had to shut the doors just right; I had to turn off the lights just right; and I had to brush my teeth in a certain way that made me gag. In the mornings, I would repeat this process, and sometimes throw up my breakfast.

One day I had to serve an in-school suspension for an incident that was a result of the bullying. Before school, I had already thrown up my breakfast because of my OCD, and so went to serve the suspension on an empty stomach. For lunch, the school served only cheese sandwiches, which I couldn't eat. Don't ask me why. The single-slice Kraft cheese makes me nauseous. So I went without lunch that day. After the suspension, I had a wrestling match that just so happened to be against one of my main antagonists. I had never lost to this kid. In fact, I was undefeated. Everyone expected me to win—including myself. Except I hadn't eaten anything all day and had no strength going into the match. I lost. On the way home that evening, my father could tell that something other than losing was bothering me, and I finally broke down. With tears running down my face, I explained why I had lost; I explained what had been going on at school; I explained why it took me forty-five minutes to get to bed each night, and why I left for school hungry that morning.

This was the first time I had ever tried to explain the impact of the bullying to my parents. There was so much shame that came with it, like I had let my parents down for becoming the bullies' target. Again, this is the effect of the bullying itself, since it suggested I wasn't strong enough to handle a little teasing. I don't think that way anymore, and I remember feeling tremendously better after telling my father all the things I kept hidden from him. The reason I had not said anything before then was because I didn't want to worry them. Listening to me spill my guts, my father understood the dilemma. He knew that, as a teenager, I wouldn't want Dad and Mom coming to save me. But he also made it clear to me that he was always there to support me and help me through difficult moments in my life, no matter what. It was an offer that I would accept more than once in the years that followed. Still, it wouldn't be until I started talking about the bullying on television that my mother finally understood the extent of it. I know it crushed her to hear how badly those years affected me, and that she blames herself for not seeing it at the time.

Eventually, as those older kids graduated, the bullying slowed and then stopped altogether. I went on living my life, playing sports, getting good grades, and otherwise enjoying my high school years. By the time I graduated, I felt like those years were behind me, that I had survived them, and I wouldn't have to worry about the bullies ever again. I was right in some ways, but terribly wrong in others. The bullying might have stopped, but the scars would stay with me for many years.

A BUSINESS CHAMPION—KIND OF

I don't want to leave the impression that my high school years were defined only by bullying. There were some pretty remarkable moments too, not just in sports but also in my academic pursuits. In particular, and quite relevant to this book, I was a member of the Business Professionals of America, which seeks to empower students with business and leadership skills. Several friends and I were members of BPA, and as juniors we had competed at the state championship in the category of small-business management. Much to our own surprise, we won the state tournament and had a chance to compete in the national competition at Disney World in Orlando.

There was a bit of a "David vs. Goliath" atmosphere to the national tournament, which was dominated by far wealthier private school teams. The other teams all showed up in matching uniforms; we were dressed in our plain clothes, just four public school kids from Indian River High School. Our feeling was that we were just along for the ride, happy to be there and enjoy a mini vacation at Disney. We didn't go expecting much, and so wouldn't have been terribly disappointed if we left with nothing. In fact, as we presented our business solution to the judges—it was based on revamping an ice-cream shop—they stopped us repeatedly and challenged several of our assertions. We all got the sense that the judges were trying to intimidate us, although I won't go so far as to say that it was because we were public school kids from lower Delaware. I just think the judges felt we wouldn't be as prepared as some of the more serious teams. But we didn't back down. Two of our team members, Chad and Tom, had even worked at an ice-cream shop in Bethany Beach during the summer. That didn't necessarily make them ice-cream professionals, but it certainly gave them far greater insight into the business than these judges had. The back-and-forth got quite heated, to the point that when we left the room, we felt that that either we had just earned the tournament win . . . or last place.

The next day was awards time, and we filed into a huge auditorium with five thousand other people. The organizers ran through each category, inviting each of the finalists onstage before announcing the winner in that group. When they got to the small business category and started calling up the top ten finalists one by one, the speaker announced, "Indian River High School," and the four of us started smiling. We walked toward the stage amid the glares of the other teams who were furious that this ragtag group of public school kids had bested them. Onstage, looking out at this sea of people, the judges said they'd announce the top three, leaving the winner for the last. Third and second place were announced, and we all looked at one another. Holy shit, we'd won! So when the speaker once more said, "Indian River High School," we just started laughing. Perhaps the best moment of that day was seeing our advisor, Mr. Murray, jumping up and down in his seat as the spotlight came to rest on his winning team.

Now, I don't mean to suggest that our crushing victory at the BPA Nationals foretold any future business success. It's not like I saw my career path as an entrepreneur or anything. But I've always been struck by how four kids with a little bit of street smarts were able to take down teams that were steeped in theory and formal business education. (The looks on their faces were pretty priceless.) I'm reminded of that triumph every now and then when debating future decisions for Sewing Down South. Sometimes all the education in the world simply exists to tell you why your idea is a bad one. You've learned enough to know that you don't know anything, and you become paralyzed or guided by fear. You don't pursue the chances you should because all the business books tell you they won't work.

Well, sometimes they do work. Sometimes listening to your gut and going off your own experience is the right path forward.

COLLEGE AND CHARLESTON

By the time I was old enough to start thinking about college, I only knew this much: I was ready to leave home. I didn't know where yet. I just knew that my path was beyond the confines of Delaware. I wasn't running away, either. Yes, the bullying had left a deep and lasting impression on me, but it wasn't the reason I wanted to leave home. It was more like I was running toward something. I felt I had done all that I could in this little corner of the world and that it was time for a fresh start (and independence) elsewhere. I guess you could say that I had the same feeling the early American settlers had had when they looked out across the expansive West. There I would find my fortune.

I applied to several colleges but had no strong feelings about any of them. That's when my friend Sean told me about the College of Charleston. It wasn't like Charleston was any sort of destination for me. I didn't have thoughts about the city one way or the other. But then I went down for a visit. I realized, *Yes, this is where I'm going to go to school.* I was close to my beloved Atlantic Ocean; I was in a culture and a lifestyle that wasn't frenzied or manic. (The sight of the southern women didn't hurt either.) And while there was a feeling of familiarity with Charleston, coming from "lower, slower Delaware," there was also a vibrancy that excited me. The city was in the middle of a cultural renaissance, with the Old South—and birthplace of the Confederacy—giving way to this younger, more socially aware wave of outsiders. In other words, Charleston had become a destination for those who appreciated the city's beauty and wanted to help it move beyond its more traditional roots. There was also a pretty kick-ass partying scene that certainly impressed a kid like me.

In trying to place my college years in the narrative of this book, there are two points that stand out. The first was coming to some understanding of what I wanted to do with my life. I had mentioned the idea of being a doctor earlier—only to learn that hospitals were horrible places for me. I had left behind any notion of pursuing sewing or the other domestic crafts that I had fallen in love with as a child. Those were personal interests, but hardly career-worthy pursuits, or so I thought. I was smart, but I had no firm direction toward a specific intellectual passion. Looking back now, I regret that I wasn't introduced to the field of engineering at an early age. The mathematics and the science inherent in engineering were two fields I had always excelled in, and was even passionate about. But I came to this realization too late in life, certainly if one wanted to be an engineer, whose career path begins freshman year in college.

But then there was the law.

On *Southern Charm*, viewers were right to question my commitment to the law, especially in those earlier seasons. Lawyers must necessarily be hardworking, disciplined professionals—the very qualities I lacked in my mid-twenties. I can laugh at the joke now, even if I want to correct the record a bit. I did fall in love with the law in college. There were a couple moments that are worth mentioning. The first is that during my junior year I was arrested for public intoxication. It was, in fact, a case of mistaken identity (they later caught the real culprit), but it left a lasting impression on me. My father called a friend of his who was an attorney to ask for his advice. After hearing my story, he decided to represent me in court and got the charges dismissed. The whole process fascinated me, not least because I felt like I had been wronged by the system. Being punished for something I didn't do opened my eyes to the harsh reality of the judicial system. Yes, it often works as it's supposed to, but it also sometimes doesn't. And to say that no system is perfect doesn't do much for those wrongly accused or convicted. Even as a child, and especially as an adolescent or teenager, injustice affected me deeply. I still remember being on that soccer bus when the bullies had turned their sights on another kid, and sticking up for him. I knew what it would (and did) lead to, but I can't stand watching others suffer unjustly at the hands of bullies.

This growing passion and fascination with the law was also spurred by a course I took on federal courts in my junior year, taught by a federal magistrate. My eyes were opened to the inner workings of a system whose roots stretch back centuries. And the ones who have knowledge of this fascinating system, and know how to navigate it, are lawyers. Their job is to seek justice—and put down the bullies. I was in.

That's the righteous part of my decision to go to law school. There remains a more banal and unflattering one. Law school seemed like a surefire way to become wealthy and successful. I didn't have a driving need to make money because of the circumstances of my upbringing, although my brother's and my love of good food and travel continually perplexes my parents, who rarely experienced either. I wanted to make money because I wanted to "make it." I wanted to feel successful by having all the trappings of success. I also saw the law as a way to achieve financial freedom, to live the way I wanted to, and even to give back if I could. I felt like becoming a lawyer would prove to all the bullies back home that I had succeeded, despite their best attempts. My revenge was my success. While this isn't the best reason to go to law school, I also don't think I'm unique in having less-than-savory motives for choosing a profession like the law. But I will admit that I was very much responding to the scars that the bullying had left on me.

Besides, for a procrastinator like me, law school offered a structured path forward. I could delay my entry into the real world another three years and come out of it with a six-figure associate's salary. Yeah, I was definitely in.

THE BEGINNINGS OF ADDICTION

The other point I should make about my college years is that this is when I first started taking Adderall, and that's because my procrastination didn't start to become a problem until I went to college. Then it became a big problem. In high school, I was sheltered by the structure of my family life. When one was home on a school night, there wasn't much else to do other than schoolwork. That structure disappeared in college, and I often found myself overwhelmed by the plethora of distractions. There was always something else I could be doing besides studying. I went from getting As in high school to getting four Ds one semester during my sophomore year in college. It was toward the end of my first semester junior year that my roommate gave me an Adderall, telling me it would help me study. I had never taken a pill like that before. But, damn, did the little thing work. It was like a light went off in my brain that said, "THIS is what we've needed all along!" By the end of my junior year, I was taking business administration and finance classes, which I loved, and got on the Dean's List with a 3.8 GPA. Not surprisingly, I gave all the credit to my new friend.

Which isn't to say that I spent all my time in the library. I did go to the library, where I would pop a pill and study for several hours. But Adderall keeps going even if you've finished the task you took it for in the first place. So, whether it was nine o'clock at night or one in the morning, I'd go from the library to a bar or a party. I had grown into myself while at college, and the girls had noticed. I had always been shy, but I learned that I transformed into this new charismatic person after just a few drinks. I quickly became very acquainted with the Charleston social scene, befriending all the bartenders and club owners, who often extended invitations to my friends and me to exclusive openings because they knew we'd bring the girls. I stopped being an outsider and carved out my own place in this young, vibrant town. Everywhere I went, I knew someone, whether they were a student or a local. One of the students a few years ahead of me, Jerry Casselano, bounced at a favorite bar of mine and would let me in even though I wasn't twenty-one. Jerry would remember me years later when he was running his own sports marketing firm, and he would make a call that would change both our lives.

Adderall helped me study, but it didn't solve my procrastination. For instance, I realized quite quickly—and this would become a major problem in law school—that I could avoid doing most of the work during the semester if I pulled some all-nighters at the end. For most people, this is an unsustainable behavior, but with Adderall, I could do it. I could study all night, night after night. While I still wasn't taking the drug recreationally—by which I mean, for partying—I started to use it whenever I needed to accomplish anything. Suddenly, I found reasons to drive home to Delaware, instead of fly, because Adderall made the trip fun. The little pill would focus my mind in a way that felt superhuman.

I eventually approached my parents about it, since I wanted them to know I was doing something about my academic decline. Taking it without their knowledge had felt shady, and I hated that feeling. And to be honest, Adderall is a bit of a truth serum. Once I started talking, I just kept going. I was still nervous to tell them, for all the reasons I was nervous to tell them anything, because I thought they would worry. Both my parents had stopped drinking when I was born, and to this day they remain absolutely sober. Taking a pill, even one that has appropriate medical uses, seemed like something they'd be against. Except my mother wasn't. "Oh, Craig, I've known you should have been on something since grade school, you just never needed it," she said when I spilled. As a schoolteacher, my mother was well aware of ADHD, and she had long suspected that I suffered from it. She wasn't wrong. My father was supportive, too, but he also saw the early stages of what was to become an addiction. When I was home from school, I'd typically wait to pack until the very last moment, then I'd stay up all night packing. These are behaviors that parents catch on to. So while they were supportive of me getting a prescription to combat my ADHD, even then my father was aware that I wasn't always taking it for the right reasons.

"I KNOW JUST THE GUYS"

Still, it would be some years before I started to really abuse Adderall. I had come to rely on it more and more, but I also attributed all my later academic success to it. How could something so helpful to me be bad for me? In any case, with my grades greatly improved, I was accepted into the Charleston School of Law, with a partial scholarship, which I entered a year after graduation. I was excited. I was also confident. College had given me a much-needed dose of validation that seemed to sweep away the nightmares from my high school days. I was no longer just a geeky kid. I was still skinny, but I had also grown into my body. I had made lifelong friends and had become popular, not just in college but in the city itself. People knew me, and I was treated like a local at bars and restaurants. Charleston had become my home. And I had no intention of leaving. Three more years of nothing but school seemed about right.

It was during my first year in law school that I received a Facebook message from a friend, a girl named Lane. She was a local, a true Charleston girl who I knew from the bar scene. She said she was working with a television producer, a guy named Whitney Sudler-Smith, who was in town to cast a new reality TV show. Whitney had asked her if she knew any young guys who were fun, charismatic, and keyed into Charleston's social life.

"I know just the guys," she replied.

2

THEN, EVERYTHING CHANGED

I stared down at the pile of papers on my counter, pen in hand. All around me swirled the commotion of a party in progress, with people yelling, laughing, and enjoying life. My roommate Paul and I had decided to have a little late-summer get-together at our rental house on Bogard Street in Charleston. Perhaps it wasn't the best moment to make a major life decision, but in my head, I had already made up my mind months ago. This was just a formality. As friends mixed drinks in the kitchen, I continued to look at the contract on the counter, the papers that would take my life in a vastly different direction than I had planned. A year earlier, I was just a law student, happy in my choice to pursue a legal career, and confident that I was setting myself up for a lifetime of success and wealth. Then everything changed, not all at once, but gradually over the course of 2012 into 2013. It was now August, and I had given lots of thought to those changes this pile of papers portended, and what they might mean, and whether I wanted them. I did—well, most of them anyway. I couldn't help but think of the friend who wasn't at this party. He was somewhere in Europe, or maybe back in his hometown of Greenville, South Carolina. I didn't know, because we had stopped talking. If I was taking stock of the changes that would occur in my life, then I had to include those that had already happened. Changes like losing my best friend. Of course there would be more changes that would come, many just as unforeseen and unwanted.

But at that moment, drink in hand, surrounded by friends, the adventure of a lifetime staring me in the face, I banished all such negativity. Then a thought made me smile. I imagined what all those bullies from high school were doing at that very moment. I imagined the looks on their faces when they saw that the skinny kid they had teased with such cruelty was now on television. He had made it.

Smiling, I signed the contract.

A "FUN DOCUSERIES ON CHARLESTON"

In her Facebook message to me dated July 11, 2012, Lane wrote: Hey Craig! I hope your summer is treating you well. One of my close friends, Whitney Sudler-Smith, producer and director of *Ultrasuede*, and an upcoming Bravo TV show, *Southern Gentlemen*, is looking for three established, young, professional, attractive guys for his pilot. I personally couldn't think of two better guys to tell this about than you and Kory. Whitney works between LA and New York City but has a house in Charleston. He would like to meet with you before he heads back to LA. I will attend the meeting with you if you would like. Can you guys meet tomorrow? This isn't a reality show, but more of a fun docuseries on Charleston. Call me if you're interested.

My first reaction was to call Kory Keefer, my roommate and best friend. I had known Kory since college, when he and I were in the same fraternity. In fraternity parlance, Kory was my "little brother," which meant I was like his sponsor and mentor. The big brother/little brother relationship is a close one in the Greek community, and often leads to lifelong friendships. We also had been born in the same hospital in Salisbury, Maryland, even though Kory was from Greenville, South Carolina. We only discovered this during a college trip to Canada, when we had to present our birth certificates at the border crossing. Well, look at that! Our friends laughed along with us. It was just too perfect.

When Kory was still a senior, he had moved in with me on Bull Street during my first year in law school. The next year, we rented a house with my friend Paul on Bogard Street in downtown Charleston. For years, we were inseparable. In our adventures gallivanting around Charleston, we had developed a bit of a reputation as the same guy, just in different bodies. We talked the same. We told and laughed at the same jokes. We even look alike. Women had problems telling us apart. We were both terrified of making the first move on a woman out of a fear of rejection, if you can believe it. Whatever this Whitney guy was looking for, it made sense to us that if one of us "had it," then both of us "had it."

But when I told Kory about Lane's message, he sighed and said, "Here we go again."

What he meant was that this wasn't our first encounter with reality TV producers. In the fall of 2011, while I was in my first year of law school and Kory was a senior in college, we took our families out to dinner. At one point, as Kory got up to head to the restroom, a woman approached him. It was an odd enough moment that those of us sitting at the table took notice of this stranger who had suddenly started chatting up Kory. We were too far away, however, to hear anything of the conversation, so when Kory returned to the table, we asked what that was all about.

Kory just shrugged. "I'll tell you later."

When he did, confiding in just his mother and me the next day, he said that the woman at the restaurant was a talent scout for CBS's *Big Brother* and had been in town casting for the upcoming season. She had been watching Kory interact with those of us at the table, especially me, and determined that Kory fit the look and personality the producers wanted on the show. The scout even told him that her casting efforts had failed to find anyone the producers liked, but that Kory fit the bill perfectly. That being said, Kory couldn't tell anyone about their conversation. He had to keep his potential involvement in the show a secret. Oh well. Kory told us the next day, and given what would end up happening, I'm glad he did.

Neither of us watched the show or knew anything about it. So we sat down and streamed a few episodes and learned that it was not just a reality show but also a game show, sort of like how CBS's other hit, *Survivor*, was a game show. I knew all about *Survivor*, since it was one of the shows I watched with my father, our weekly bonding moment in front of the TV, along with *24* and *Alias*. The premise of *Big Brother* is that a bunch of house-guests live together and have their every moment recorded for the audience. One by one, the other contestants are evicted from the house by being voted out by their fellow roommates. The last one left wins $500,000. I asked Kory what he thought, and he told me he was going to pursue it. I didn't think about his reasons much at the time. I probably would've done it too. It seemed like an exciting opportunity, and who knows what doors the show might be able to open?

But looking back—and understanding my own reasons for pursuing a reality TV show—I now understand better what was going on in Kory's head. He was still a senior in college, soon to graduate, and while he was a smart, good-looking guy who could succeed at anything he tried, Kory was a bit lost. In the same way I was also a bit lost at that point in my life. Yes, part of it was that Kory didn't know what he wanted to do with his life, but that's only a very small part. Most college graduates are a bit unsure about their future and scared about which career is best. Kory's inner turmoil was more about our very peculiar life in Charleston. To outward appearances, both of us had the "look" of success, without the actual substance of it. A lot of our friends and those we hung out with in and around town did have money (if not success). We were surrounded by it, we lived in it, we talked about it, but we didn't have it. It's like we had been invited inside this exclusive club not because we met the membership requirements, but because those inside just enjoyed our company. Only we weren't members.

Our age, our status as students, and our social life—which in so many ways was our entire life—allowed us to ignore this reality. We played make-believe with the idea that just because we consorted with those who had money and just because clubs invited us to exclusive openings, we were living the fairy tale. But in Kory's quieter moments, away from the buzz of the bars and the attention of women, he felt an emptiness. He could see behind the facade we had both built and what he saw depressed him. He wasn't rich, he just hung around rich people. He wasn't successful, at least as he had defined the term. And, perhaps most dispiriting, he had no plan for achieving either one of those aims. As he later explained to me, he felt like he was always "chasing coattails" instead of taking control of his life.

So when a chance came along that provided if not the solution, then at least an opportunity, Kory jumped at it. Here, at last, was *something* for him. He called the casting scout back and was invited to an interview, where he was told that he did great. A couple weeks later, Kory flew out to Los Angeles for the final casting interviews and the "wellness check," which is when a potential cast member is put through a psychological evaluation to determine if they can handle the mental rigors of reality TV and potential celebrity. While Kory was in L.A., the producers confirmed that he'd been selected. So Kory returned to Charleston and quit his job at the local gym. On the morning he was scheduled to fly out to start filming, I said my good-byes at the house we shared and wished him luck, assuming I wasn't going to see him for several months. Then I left for class, while Kory waited for the car that was going to pick him up and take him to the airport. When I returned a few hours later, Kory was still there.

"What are you still doing here?" I asked him.

It was a question Kory couldn't answer. He didn't know. No car ever showed up, and he hadn't been able to get in touch with the producers. Since his flight was well on its way to the West Coast by then, we decided to grab some dinner. While eating, a producer called Kory. The conversation was quick, with Kory barely saying anything other than "Okay." When he hung up, I asked what happened.

"They decided to go in a different direction," said Kory.

"That's it?" I asked incredulously. It didn't make any sense to me. How could they simply pull the rug out from under him?

Kory shrugged. "That's it."

I knew the rejection hurt Kory, as it would hurt anyone. Even if one never had a dream of being on television (which Kory certainly didn't), getting so close to it only to have it yanked away is a painful experience. While we both understood that the entertainment industry is a cutthroat world, this seemed especially harsh. There had been no warning from the producers that they might, at the last moment, decide to withdraw the offer. Actors whose lives are spent in the audition room likely have the mental toughness to endure this kind of disrespectful behavior, but Kory wasn't an actor. The scout had approached *him*. Even now, having been in the industry for nearly a decade, I still consider what happened to Kory to be slimy. I mean, they didn't bother calling him until after the flight took off. I don't care what business you're in—you don't do that to someone.

Looking back, I can finally appreciate just how much this episode affected my friend. It's not that *Big Brother* was taken away from him; it was what *Big Brother* might have led to that bothered him. Those doors that were about to open had slammed shut, and he was back in Charleston, living with me, and doing what, in his heart, made him feel worse. But we still did it. We all went back to the life we had been living together, doing a lot, but accomplishing very little. I wish I had seen all this at the time. I wish I had been able to understand what was going on in Kory's head. But he never told me, and I, regretfully, never asked. It was back to the bars; back to the drinks; back to the women.

When I told Kory about Lane's offer, he was excited like I was, if a bit more realistic about where it might lead. He thought he knew what he was getting into and, more important, that he shouldn't get his hopes up a second time. Little did either of us know that the casting for *Southern Charm* would prove to be altogether different than the casting for *Big Brother*.

Living in Charleston, you hear all sorts of bullshit stories. Everyone is doing something amazing, even if most of them aren't doing anything at all. I mean, they're at a bar at one a.m. on a Tuesday night. How amazing could their day job be? Whoever Whitney Sudler-Smith was—and I had never heard of him before—I was excited (and flattered) to be presented with an opportunity that would open up that world to me. And yes, I was excited about the possibility of fame and fortune. I would be lying if I said that these things didn't motivate me. But, of course, what does that mean exactly? What did I know about fame and why did I want it? The short answer is that I didn't know a damn thing about it, but still felt that very natural human pull toward it. I was twenty-three at the time, just starting my life. Concerns like wealth, women, and popularity were my driving ambitions, all of which I wrapped together in this idea of success. I think wealth and women are easy enough to understand; they're pretty much what most young men want, for better or worse. Popularity is a bit more convoluted, and my yearning for it goes back to my high school days, when I was so often the mark of the bullies. I had grown out of my adolescent awkwardness while in college and discovered that women liked me, but there was also this bottomless need for validation. Because the bullies had stolen my self-confidence at such an impressionable age, there is some part of me that will always be trying to recapture it.

I know this now, and my focus has shifted from seeking validation from others to self-validation. It's still the force that allows me to survive in this crazy world; if I'm happy with myself, then I'm happy. But I didn't know this then. In 2012, I saw an opportunity to achieve popularity on a level I had never dared dream possible. It was an irresistible temptation, easing (or so I thought) that pain in the center of my heart that had never fully healed. Fame was validation, and I wanted it.

Then again, maybe Whitney wasn't legit and there wasn't even a show. In that case, if it was bullshit, then it was bullshit and we walk away. Kory agreed, and we called Lane back.

"THE NETWORK REALLY LIKES YOU GUYS"

A couple days later, Kory and I were walking up to this magnificent house in the heart of old Charleston, a few blocks away from the Ashley River. The gated mansion belonged to Whitney's mother, Patricia Altschul, a well-connected Charleston socialite.

The house was built in 1854, and is celebrated for its Roman and Italian villa architecture. The southern facade looks like a damn Roman temple, with six Corinthian columns holding up an imposing pediment. The house is an artifact of Charleston's bygone age, when slaves worked the grounds and the southern elite dined on the portico. Neither Kory nor I had any connection to that tragic era of Charleston's past—and neither did Patricia or Whitney. But part of living in Charleston is being in this (sometimes combustible) maelstrom of the modern, progressive city crashing against the memories and relics of the antebellum South. The city and its people have for the most part embraced a new identity as a cosmopolitan destination for those who love the warm weather, the beautiful scenery, the good food, and the nightlife. Charleston is still a southern city, but it's moved well beyond its historic designation as the birthplace of the Confederacy. Vestiges, often beautifully built ones like Patricia's house, of that legacy remain, however, offering both the locals and tourists glimpses into an age long past.

And sometimes, for Kory and I, memories of a wild night a few years before when we had jumped the gate of this very house and swum in the pool. We were on our way back from the bars and had passed the house, where it looked like no one was home. The pool is visible from the street, even though high brick walls protect it from ruffians like us, and the thought came to us, drunk as we were, to go for a swim. Fortunately, no one caught us. If we had been, then I doubt either of us would have been considered for the show.

At the door, Patricia's butler, Michael, greeted us and led us into the living room where we met Whitney, a middle-aged man with a boyish face. My first impression of Whitney was that he was a talker, and a good one. He was friendly, personable, and seemed genuinely interested in us. This wasn't the formal interview Kory had experienced with *Big Brother*. Whatever this was, Whitney wanted to get to know us, two guys almost twenty years younger than him. Over cocktails, Whitney talked to us about his idea for the show, which mostly involved following a group of locals who personified both the old and new Charleston, southern gentlemen and ladies with roots in the city mixing with, well, guys like Kory and me. A kid from Greenville and a kid from Delaware. Even though his mother lived there, Whitney explained how he was still trying to get acquainted with the social scene in town. Which, to Kory and me, sounded like he wanted to meet some girls. Whatever. We could do that, we offered. Then we went swimming. And that was our first introduction to Whitney, a rather casual afternoon at a ridiculous mansion that ended how our first visit to this mansion ended a couple years earlier: with us in the pool. Only this time we had been invited.

Over the next month, Kory and I showed Whitney our version of Charleston. We went to dinner; we had drinks; we partied; and we usually ended up back at Patricia's house in a haze of booze, girls, and late-night swimming. Somewhat strangely (or not), the topic of the show rarely came up. When Kory and I did remember it, we sort of chuckled, since we were quite sure by this point that Whitney was absolutely full of shit. Perhaps he was a producer or filmmaker of some kind, but we thought he was mostly interested in hitting the town. Not that we minded. All of it was a far cry from what Kory had experienced with CBS and

Big Brother. We remained somewhat guarded, but we never felt like Whitney was "casting" us; he was just hanging with us, and we acted as we normally would—or as normally as two guys in their early twenties could act with the entire city of Charleston as our playground. Show? What show? We were young and this guy was kind of fun.

Had we been a little older and wiser, then maybe we could have deciphered the logic in Whitney's strategy. Looking back, he certainly was "casting" us, but he was also meeting the city of Charleston—its people, its bars and restaurants—through us. But Kory and I never caught on to that part. If there was even a show, we concluded, we definitely weren't going to be in front of the camera. Our "job" in the production was to let Whitney live through us, this older guy hanging with the recent college graduates. Still, we were convinced by this point that there wasn't a show at all.

After about a month, Whitney told us he wanted to get us in front of the camera. The request came as a bit of a shock. Until that moment, neither of us had seen a camera, a production crew, nor anyone other than Whitney who might be remotely connected to a television show—and we had both decided by this point that he might not even *be* a real producer. But we were told to dress well and swing by Patricia's house for a chat, where Whitney would interview us on camera.

I've been living my life on camera for eight seasons now. But for anyone who finds themselves in the situation Kory and I suddenly found ourselves in, there is a moment of inner debate. A mental barrier needs to be breached to agree to be on camera.

We've all grown accustomed to living our lives on social media via the pictures and videos we take with our smartphones. But *we're* the ones doing it, so it's okay. In other words, there is a fine line between having your picture taken by friends or family and posted on social media and being in front of the camera. One is for personal consumption; the other is for mass consumption. And for this reason, most of us balk at "being on camera," or at least feel uncomfortable with the idea. I'm not saying that Whitney's request was a major stumbling block for either Kory or me, but it represented a turning point in my life, one that had until that moment been lived outside the public eye, privately. To say yes to being interviewed on camera was one small, but significant, step toward entering a whole new way of living for me.

The actual interview itself wasn't a very big deal. In fact, that was part of the source of my continued disbelief that Whitney was who he said he was. I showed up at Patricia's house and was greeted by Michael, who asked if he could make me a drink. Of all the things I would start having to get used to, being served by Michael was one of the hardest. I just have this aversion to being waited on by anyone, especially in circumstances when I'm quite capable of pouring a drink myself (although not the way Michael poured drinks—that guy is a master). Outside on the deck, Whitney had set up what can only be described as a camcorder. I was a bit underwhelmed. I thought I had agreed to an actual, professional interview, with television cameras and a crew. Instead, I was greeted by Whitney and his camcorder. Once more, I saw those red flags waving in my head that not all was as Whitney wanted me to believe.

Whitney's questions were mostly benign, asking me to talk about myself: who I was, where I came from, what I did, and why I liked Charleston. He wanted me to play up my nascent legal career, as someone with ambition and drive. The whole thing was over in a few minutes, and while it wasn't much, it was the first moment during the process that was unfolding when I felt like I was being duplicitous with the other parts of my life. I was in law school and working at a law firm. My family and friends, aside from Kory, all assumed and expected that that was what I was doing with my life. Yet here was this other part that was taking up more and more space. What's more was that I hadn't sought it out. It's not like I went to a casting event. I had simply agreed to talk to a random guy about a show, and now here I was, on camera, and wondering if this was what I wanted. Was I just wasting my time? Was I setting myself up for some massive embarrassment that would ruin my legal career and disappoint my parents? These questions started to weigh on me, even as I continued to walk down this path.

Kory also did an interview with Whitney, but I would learn later that the behind-the-scenes conversations Whitney was having with the actual production company had started to focus on me. Like I said, Kory and I were the same guy, just different bodies. No show needs two of the same character. One will do. And I had been identified by people I had never met to be the one they wanted. Nothing was said to Kory and me. At the same time, Kory and I had sort of an understanding that neither would go forward with the show without the other. While this wasn't an official agreement, we had started this together and we would do it (or not) together. We never stated this explicitly to Whitney, but we thought we had made it apparent with our actions. With the exception of the interview, Kory and I were always together. Whitney seemed fine with this; indeed, he never tried to pull me away or divide us at all. Everything we did with regards to the show, we did together.

Even when Whitney told us that the next step in the process was to film an actual pilot at a plantation a few miles outside Charleston, he was speaking to both Kory and me. "The network really likes you guys," he told us one day, not long after filming the interviews at Patricia's house. "We're going to have a party at the Millford Plantation with a camera crew, and I want you guys to be there." Except for the addition of the camera crew, nothing particularly stood out about Whitney's request to either of us. We had been partying with this guy for over a month. What's one more party? Nevertheless, it was one more step along a very long journey. The plan was to show up at Patricia's house dressed in our best, then take a bus with the other guests to the plantation where the cameras would be rolling. Kory and I brought along our other friend Trevor, expecting more of the same type of intimate gatherings we had been used to at the house . . . only to discover that this was no small gathering. When we walked out to the backyard, we saw at least twenty young women there, and one woman in particular named Naomie Olindo. I knew most of the women, including Naomie, just from the city's nightlife. When Kory and I saw Naomie, we both shouted: "Ponytail!" It was a silly nickname we had given her from the first night we all met, at a bar, when Naomie had been wearing a ponytail. She hated the nickname and thus rolled her eyes when she heard it from across the lawn.

Even though Patricia's house was supposed to be just the pre-party, Whitney and his mother had spared no expense. We were waited on by a whole team of butlers and servers, and had all varieties of food and drink from which to choose. At one point, I wandered into the kitchen where I saw a tall guy stuffing his face with finger sandwiches. I introduced myself, only to be more or less ignored by this new face. "Shep," he mumbled, barely interrupting his chewing. Kory and I weren't impressed, Shepard Rose showed no particular interest in us, and we returned the favor.

Then it was time to get on the bus. Before long, we pulled up to the Millford Plantation, which was nearly two hours outside Charleston. The plantation itself is gorgeous, tucked away in a region known as the High Hills of the Santee River. Built in 1840 in the Greek Revival style, the house sports six Corinthian columns along its front facade, not unlike the columns on Patricia's house. While we got to tour the mansion, the real party was on the lawn out back. And there were cameras. A lot of them. And all of us were miked up. Whitney warned us that the cameras would be following us around the grounds, sometimes getting right up close to us. If this was what a "fun docuseries," as Lane had originally called it, was, then I was all in. The only one who was very much opposed to appearing on camera, especially talking to producers on camera, was our friend Trevor. But he had a good excuse. His father was an elected official, and Trevor didn't want to embarrass himself or his family in any way. Fair enough.

Out in the backyard, away from the party, there was a place where guests could shoot skeet. Before long, I was on a team with a friend named Sam, firing skeet against our opponents, Shep and Naomie. The details are a bit hazy, but I know that Sam and I won; that Naomie was a crack shot; and that Shep couldn't hit the broad side of a barn. After the contest, I was walking back to the mansion grounds when I spotted a camera crew surrounding one of the guests, who was speaking very freely and openly with the producer. I recognized Trevor. I wandered over, smiling, because the one guy who had vowed to not appear on camera was now the one guy mugging it up. But as I listened, I was horrified to hear that Trevor was spilling all the dirt. Not only was he breaking his pledge, but he was also discussing his father's political career, as well as the scandals, such as extramarital affairs, that had plagued him. It was my first taste of the strange transformation that comes over us when, plied with booze, someone thrusts a camera in our faces and we start talking. Eventually, the party ended and all of us hopped back on the bus, exhausted and drunk. And maybe because of my inebriated state, I found the courage to sit down next to Naomie on the way home. I knew she had a boyfriend at the time, and our talk wasn't anything more than reminiscing about the party and the absurdity of the situation. Still, a seed had been planted. I wanted to know more about Ponytail.

THINGS GET REAL

"Okay, I guess this Whitney guy is real."

That was the thought I finally had when executives from the production company Haymaker began arriving in town to meet those of us in Whitney's casting. For several more weeks, sometimes on camera, sometimes off, Kory and I spoke to the producers. What had been an extremely informal process suddenly took on the weight of seriousness. We still were having fun, but we now understood that this wasn't bullshit anymore. And something came over me when that realization hit: I suddenly started to want this. Now, there was a distinction between wanting something in the way someone wants to fulfill an ambition or a lifelong dream and wanting something simply because you don't want it taken away. Kory and I had been going through this "casting" process for months now, and I'd be damned if it had all been for nothing. And this feeling began to disrupt the bond Kory and I had formed when we entered on this journey together. I had by this point recognized that the producers were focusing more on me than on Kory. They were constantly calling me down to film at a restaurant, at the beach, at Whitney's house. But Kory wasn't getting those calls. I could have said something, if not to the producers, then at least to Kory. I could have asked him what he thought about the attention I was getting. I could have, but I didn't. I wanted this.

Kory saw what was happening as well. He didn't say anything either, but at least his reason was better than mine. He didn't want to appear jealous. I didn't want to do anything that might upset my chances at being chosen. A separation had set in, and it led to several arguments between us, often late at night when he and I had had too much to drink. We'd argue, pass out, then wake up as if nothing had happened. Kory later told me that he thought things might have been different if we hadn't lived together. I see his point. Our closeness, our bond, so long a source of joy between us, had suddenly become the thing that was driving us apart.

Our arguments were never about the show itself. They were the arguments two people who spend nearly every waking moment together have when something comes between them. If that sounds like a marriage, well, that might be the best way to describe what was going on with my best friend and me. We never confronted the real issue head-on; instead, we sniped and bickered at each other over smaller offenses. Kory would hear about something I'd said about him from others and he'd confront me with it; and I did the same to him.

The show, while a recurring source of pain for Kory, wasn't the only reason for our growing estrangement. There were several issues that were eating away at what once had been a rock-solid friendship. The problem was that we never talked about those issues. We let them fester until our frustrations came out over other, pettier moments. Had I been a little older, a little wiser, and a lot less hooked on booze and Adderall, then I might have had the clarity to see what was going on. I might have at least been able to talk to him during our sober moments. But neither of us did so. We were drifting apart as friends, and the show provided the final slice to sever us entirely.

And it came in the worst possible way.

In the spring of 2013, the producers from Haymaker invited a lot of the people involved in the casting to a special dinner at Rue de Jean, a swanky French eatery in downtown Charleston. Most of the people I had gotten to know over the past several months were there, including Shep and Thomas Ravenel. Whitney explicitly invited both Kory and me, explaining it was just an informal dinner to get to know the producers. But when we arrived, it was obvious that the dinner was very formal in the professional sense. This wasn't one of those carefree nights out we had been having with Whitney. The whole tenor of the evening screamed that the courtship was over. It was time to get down to brass tacks. And I felt extremely uncomfortable. The producers started talking to those of us who would eventually appear on the show: Shep, Thomas, and me. They mostly ignored Kory, as if he wasn't even there. The only time they addressed him at all was when they told him he wasn't going to be a part of it, not even as a supporting cast member. This was a blindside not just to Kory and me, but to Whitney as well. It was my first indication that Whitney was just a piece of a large puzzle. I even think he was a bit taken aback at the loss of control over a project he had initiated.

"You're just too young," said one of the producers to Kory. "Maybe in a few years."

Staring down the barrel of another rejection, Kory asked, "What do I need to do? Tell me what I need to do or the person I need to be."

But the producers had made up their mind. They turned their attention to the rest of us. Kory had been dismissed. And that was that: I was going to be on the show and Kory wasn't. He eventually got up and left. I was shaken by the episode, and despite Whitney's assurances later not to "worry about him," I felt terrible and somehow responsible for what had happened. But I wasn't equipped, and wouldn't be for many years, to be the friend that Kory needed at that moment. It wasn't the show that proved to be the final straw; it was that Kory felt I had abandoned my role as his older brother, not the big brother from the fraternity, but the one who would always look out for him. That pain went deeper than anything the producers could inflict.

The fights with Kory would continue, but perhaps the biggest and most painful sign of our separation was that we just started to avoid each other. We still lived together, but after that dinner and his expulsion from the casting process, we saw less and less of each other. Then, near the start of summer and toward the end of the lease on our rental house, Kory told Paul that he wouldn't be coming back. He was going to leave, maybe go back home to Greenville for a bit. I wish I could say that this news roused me from my senses and made me try to salvage the friendship with someone who had been my brother for the past four years. But it didn't. The previous six months had done serious damage to our friendship. I was a constant source of frustration and irritation to him, and he was the same to me. I can't say that I was glad to see Kory leave, because that wouldn't be true. But I didn't ask him to stay. Too much had happened, and my life was about to change.

So Kory left. He did go home for a time, and then to Europe, where he remained for several months. I knew he'd dreamed of traveling across Europe, and that he had been saving his money to make it a reality. But I didn't know at the time that that's where he was heading.

When my best friend walked away, our friendship ended then and there. And I wouldn't talk to him again for several years.

QUESTIONS AND ANSWERS

Meanwhile, I had some serious decisions to make. What started as a farce, a random Facebook message from an old friend, had suddenly become a major life moment for me. The producers had sent me a contract to sign. This was it. I knew in my heart I wanted to pursue this opportunity, but I also didn't trust my heart. I needed some other reassurance, a more concrete form of validation to convince me that what I wanted to do, I should do. I remember one particular moment, sitting in class at law school, when I pulled up Google on my laptop and typed: "Should I go on a reality TV show?" Seriously. That's what I wrote, and what I discovered didn't help my decision-making. There was nothing on the entire internet that helped my decision. Not a single blog entry; not a single article; nothing that revealed the true nature of living one's life on television. Blocked from one avenue of inquiry, I pursued another, which proved much more useful.

The best way to describe Cameran Eubanks at this point in my life is that she was a sort of mythical creature in Charleston. This is a small town, and everyone knows everyone else, so of course I knew Cam, but I didn't *know* Cam. In fact, I remember the brief moments when I'd catch a glimpse of her . . . out at a bar, having coffee with friends, even crossing the street. I'd point at her and say, "That's Cameran!" Then sigh. Like every other heterosexual male in town, I had a crush on this elusive woman. She lived in her own world, and that world just hadn't intersected with mine. But it was about to. The one thing I knew about Cam was that, in 2004, she had been on MTV's *The Real World* in San Diego. Leaving aside *Survivor* and the episodes of *Big Brother* I had watched with Kory, *The Real World* was my only experience as a reality TV viewer and I, like millions of other boys who stared at the screen back then, was mesmerized by this woman. That fascination hadn't dissipated even now that we lived in the same city.

Under normal circumstances, my innate shyness around women would have prevented me from what I was about to do. But I was desperate. I needed answers, and Cameran, at that point, was the only one I had a remote chance of getting them from. So on March 23, 2013, I hopped on Facebook and sent her a message:

ME: Hey Cameran. I know this is super random, but I have nowhere else to turn. I've tried googling this, but you're the only person I can think of to ask. I've been contacted by this reality show and I don't know whether I should do it or not. Is there any way I can ask you about your past experience?

CAM: Hey Craig. Funny enough, they've approached me too. I'd love to get together to chat.

Casting was like that. In any case, she and I exchanged a few more messages and decided to meet. Cam also reached out to Shep, who would join us for lunch a few days later at (once again) Rue de Jean. Cam and I got there first. Then Shep walked in. He and I had gotten to know each other more after our first meeting at Patricia's house, but our interactions had been mostly booze-fueled, and hardly the stuff from which strong friendships form. In any case, I was about to be on a show with these two people, and we wanted to get together to discuss our thoughts and feelings. And it was fun. We discussed the show, the ridiculous nature of the casting, and how Cameran, whom none of us even knew was being considered, had been approached. Cam being Cam, she wasn't one for all the wild parties, and she had even vowed to never go on a reality TV show again, but was now seriously considering the offer. Shep was as excited as we were, but he didn't agonize over it the way I did. It was a great opportunity, and he was going to do it. We also learned that none of us knew much more than the other about the process. It's not like we had been given a guidebook about how our lives would change or what filming would look like. We had been told almost nothing.

But the lunch provided something that I hadn't considered. Even at this early stage, the three of us formed a bond during that afternoon. We were able to talk through our concerns, our hopes, and our expectations, and that helped tremendously. I no longer felt like I was about to go into something without a single good friend beside me. Our lunch meeting might not have answered all my questions, but it certainly eased a lot of my concerns. As, I believe, it did for Cam and Shep as well. We decided that we would do this, together. I walked out of that lunch feeling much better about the show, and life in general. Then, a few days later, I woke up and my mind was made up: I wanted this. I saw it as one of those rare moments in life that I would regret not pursuing. I would always wonder what might have been. I didn't want to feel that. I wanted to know that I took the chance when it was offered, that I didn't shrink from it. What would I regret more? Not doing it and wondering what if? Or doing it and dealing with the consequences later on? An opportunity like this would never come again.

You might have gotten the impression that I forgot all about my burgeoning legal career throughout all this, but that wouldn't be true. I had only realized that this whole "fun docuseries" was even a real thing in the last couple months, and even then I wasn't sure I would be selected. My studies had continued, even if my method of studying was more than a little unhealthy. Nevertheless, I made law review and the trial advocacy team in my second year. But it wasn't just law school that I had to consider. Earlier that spring I had been accepted into an internship that functioned more like a season of *The Apprentice*, in that I was competing against other students for a spot at Akim Anastopoulo's law firm. I had made a good enough impression that I was now working as a law clerk for Akim, in addition to pursuing my law school work. And all this was happening while I was being cast on the show. Far from abandoning my legal career, I was rushing full steam ahead toward it. (Which also explains my growing use and dependence on Adderall to finish all my tasks.)

Naturally, I talked to my parents about it too. In unison, they both asked, "What's Bravo?" When I explained that it was a network known for its reality TV shows, they asked, "What's a reality TV show?" This wasn't going well.

My mother's main concern was my law studies. "Craig, you're in law school," she said. "Why are you doing this?" I know she would have preferred me to maintain my focus on my studies and passing the bar, even after I had explained that I thought I could do both.

But it was my father whom I talked to most about my decision. He was worried that the show would damage my future legal career. "In twenty years, if someone wants to make you a judge, they're going to have to go through everything you said on this show. You cannot be on national television drunk, making stupid comments."

I didn't have a great answer to that concern, except to say that perhaps I didn't want to be a judge. Much to every child's annoyance, parents always take the long view. What my father was really saying was that the show might open doors, but it would certainly close some as well. I understood that, or thought I did. We went through the positives and the negatives, but in the end, the decision depended on my wishes. Did I want this? I said I did. And to that, both my mom and dad said they would support me. So I got their blessing, if not their encouragement.

But my parents had raised a point that I needed to answer in some way: How would appearing on a reality TV show impact my future career as a lawyer? To get the answer, I visited Margaret Lawton, the associate dean of academic affairs at the Charleston School of Law. I explained my concerns that the show might be detrimental to my career, to which Dean Lawton responded:

"Craig, if you do this, you probably won't be able to work at a big defense firm. They won't want the attention. But you also live in a different age. These types of things are becoming more normal. As long as you don't do crack or heroin on TV, you're going to be fine."

Could I tolerate having the doors to a large defense firm shut to me?

Sure.

I don't know if Dean Lawton could have said something that would have made me rethink my decision. Perhaps if she had warned that all chances of a legal career would be destroyed the moment my face appeared on a television, then maybe—just maybe—I might have walked away. But anything short of that wasn't going to change my mind at this stage.

I rushed home from Dean Lawton's happier than I remember being in a long time. My roommate Paul was there as I burst through the door.

"Get up," I said to him. "We're having a party."

A couple of hours later, I was staring at the contract on my kitchen counter, those good feelings augmented by a Bud Light. I picked up my pen, smiling, and signed my name. Putting the pen down, I wondered: Now what?

"WE'RE GREEN-LIT!"

About a month later I got a call from Whitney. It was now summer 2013. I had signed the contract but I hadn't heard a peep from anyone about anything in the meantime. My life had continued as normal, as if the previous six months had been a dream.

But no, Kory wasn't there. It wasn't a dream. It had all been very real.

I picked up the phone. "Hey, man," I said.

"We're green-lit!" Whitney cried on the other end.

"What do you mean, 'We're green-lit'?" It was an honest question. I didn't know what "green-lit" meant.

"The network decided to pick us up," explained Whitney. What the hell? I thought the network had *already* decided that. Why had I signed a contract if we hadn't been green-lit?

"Are you serious?" I said. "Do you know what I've gone through the last few months? I thought the show was already a go!"

"No, the network had to agree first," said Whitney. "And they did!"

Clearly Whitney expected me to be just as excited as he was, but once more I felt like I had been deliberately kept in the dark. No one had explained that after all the negotiations, after all the casting, after all the personal drama and agony I had gone through, that in the end, the show might not have even happened.

Did it matter? I guess it didn't—the show was going forward. But it was one of those moments when I felt like I wasn't entirely in control of my own fate; that others were making decisions about my life and telling me only when it suited them. It was uncomfortable, but, I thought, maybe this is just how it goes. There would be many things from now on that I would have to get used to.

"Okay," I said to Whitney. "Well, what happens now?"

"They'll be in touch," he said, then hung up.

That week, I got a call from one of the producers. They were coming over to film at my house.

"When?" I asked.

"Right now," came the response.

Moments later, a camera crew was in my house and I was being miked up. One of the producers looked at Paul and asked him how he wanted to be miked up and if those were the clothes he was going to wear.

Horrified, Paul said, "I'm not going on camera."

The producer then looked at me, as if I could convince Paul. But that wasn't my job. If Paul didn't want to be in front of a camera, he didn't have to.

Me, on the other hand? I had to.

3

TRYING TO HAVE IT ALL

I sat across the kitchen table from my parents and laid out all my outstanding credit card bills. This was part of the deal. In exchange for helping me get out from under the crushing debt, I had to show them everything—and promise to stop using my credit cards. That wasn't all, though. I would also pay off my debt to them by working for my father's remediation company. It was a typical nine-to-five deal, which I can't say excited me. But at that moment, I wasn't exactly in a position to do what I found exciting. I was broke. I was also homeless, having been unable to keep up with my rent. I was unemployed after leaving my job as a clerk at the law firm. I was without a law degree, despite three years of law school, and because of this, I couldn't take the bar exam. So even if I wanted to find a job as a lawyer, I couldn't. I was also tired. Two seasons of filming *Southern Charm* while managing law school as well as the responsibilities of working as a law clerk at a busy firm had drained me, physically and emotionally. *Life* in Charleston had drained me. The endless nights; the booze; the struggle to keep up; and, yes, the Adderall had kicked my ass. The consequences of living like a celebrity had finally arrived and beat the hell out of me.

Which was how I found myself back in Ocean View, Delaware, sitting across the table from my parents, trying to come up with a plan to get my life back on track. Although exhausted and staring at seven thousand dollars in credit card debt, I have always been an optimist. Especially if there's a plan. At that moment, my father was setting out that plan, and suddenly all the problems that had overwhelmed me started to seem manageable. I just needed time. And rest.

"THE NEXT ROY"

Roughly two years earlier, in the fall of 2013, I was sitting across a different table, talking with an altogether different person. His name was Akim Anastopoulo, owner and partner of the Anastopoulo Law Firm, which handles personal injury cases in Charleston and several other cities and states. He was my boss. He was also a friend and a mentor. I had first met Akim during an internship in the spring, although his wife, Constance, had been a law professor of mine. As I mentioned, the internship was more like a competition; it had pitted me against other law students for a chance to work at Akim's firm. I won, and had been accepted by this most generous and intelligent of people. Akim had taken great interest in

my promise as a lawyer, and I, in turn, looked up to him as someone to emulate. Not only a successful lawyer, Akim was respected
in the community, where he had practiced law for almost thirty
years. He had wealth, prestige, a thriving legal practice, and had
even had his own television show. Running from 2003 to 2009, *Eye
for an Eye* was a pseudo-court show in which Akim played Judge
"Extreme Akim," known for issuing tough and often strange sen-
tences on the guilty party. Given that the show was produced by
National Lampoon, you can understand that this was all in good
fun, and Akim, by his own account, had a blast living this alter ego
on camera.

In my few months of working for Akim, I felt like he had
taken me under his wing. This was someone who didn't put a lot
of stock in credentials and top-tier schools. He looked for hungry,
street-smart people. On several occasions, Akim had compared
me to another associate at the firm, a former classmate of mine at
Charleston School of Law, Roy Willey, a guy who was crushing
it at Akim's firm. "You're the next Roy," Akim would say to me.
He also once called me his "secret weapon," by which I think he
meant that I had a reservoir of untapped talent that other firms
would have overlooked, but that he, good judge of talent that
he was, saw immediately. Although not yet a full-time lawyer,
I was doing real legal work helping out the other lawyers and
had started to focus on pharmaceutical law. Rounding out the
mentor-protégé relationship, Akim often took me to conferences
so I could learn and meet people who specialized in this area of
the law.

Within the firm, I was treated as an equal, and often voiced my opinions (which clerks often don't do) on important cases. I spent many late nights at the firm strategizing with the other associates and partners and was responsible for preparing PowerPoint presentations that they would need for mediations and other legal proceedings. The work was grueling at times, but I loved it. I was doing what I felt like I should be doing. I was able to grasp how lawyers interpret law and serve their clients, and that logic-based thinking appealed to me greatly. My future as a lawyer looked bright.

There was no way of knowing whether the show would be popular, and if so, how long it would last (or if I would last with it). I needed something else—something that was my own and that I was passionate about and committed to. The show's producers were excited about it too. Heck, half the reason I had been cast was because I was supposed to be this up-and-coming lawyer. But it was for me as well. In any event, I found what *I* wanted working for Akim.

As the show started filming, there was just one problem: I hadn't told Akim about it yet. Even though Akim was no stranger to reality TV, I was afraid it would tarnish his impression of me, an impression I had worked hard to cultivate, since it suggested I was splitting my focus. Akim was grooming me to be the "next Roy," after all, and I didn't want the show to ruin that process. But it's not like I could keep the ruse going forever. Eventually, after filming had been going on a few weeks, I had to come clean and tell Akim what I was doing. I needn't have worried. Akim was overjoyed to hear about it, even declaring that we were going to skip the rest of the day and celebrate at Juanita Greenberg's, a downtown Mexican restaurant.

Over margaritas, Akim offered me plenty of advice. My main concern, I told him, was how much of my "true self" to reveal to the cameras. We had had one or two group gatherings with the whole cast so far, including the party at Patricia's house where we all (especially Thomas Ravenel) had first met Kathryn Dennis, the youngest member of the cast, whose relationship with Thomas, a man nearly thirty years her senior, led to some of the most dramatic moments of those early seasons. That moment would come to dominate the next several seasons of the show, for all the obvious reasons. But Thomas wasn't the only one who had been smitten by this young, outgoing woman. At this early stage of filming, four of us—Thomas, Whitney, Shep, and I—had all tried our luck with Kathryn. In the end, fate put Thomas and Kathryn together, setting the stage for epic showdowns, not just between the two lovers, but between the whole cast.

It was at Patricia's party that I realized how quickly I could forget the cameras were rolling, not that I did anything embarrassing. But it scared me that I might do or say something that would look bad later on. I was guarded, in other words, and it wasn't a comfortable feeling. I didn't want to spend possibly years of my life having that feeling that I was on the verge of losing everything I had worked toward because of one bad moment on camera. Such a mistake wouldn't just reflect poorly on me; it could humiliate Akim and the entire firm.

But Akim waved away my concerns. "Be yourself," he said

bluntly. "Screw everyone else and just be yourself." Coming from my boss, and someone who stood to share in any embarrassment I might inflict upon myself, I couldn't have been happier. I realized that Akim was telling me that short of committing a crime, he wasn't going to be watching my performance like a hawk. As long as I continued to put forth the effort at the firm, he wanted me to relax and enjoy my television career.

Our talk continued for a couple hours and more than a couple pitchers of margaritas. I felt like a weight had been lifted hearing Akim's encouragement. Best of all, Akim said he would help me juggle my responsibilities in any way he could. How many bosses would say that? Their employee comes to them with news that they are involved in what for all intents and purposes is another job and they slap them on the back and say, "Tell me how I can help."

Somewhat wobbly, I left the restaurant feeling much better about everything. I felt liberated in a way. Perhaps I could have a law *and* a television career? Perhaps I could have it all? Coincidentally, I had to film that night at Thomas's house. Episode 6 would go down as one of the more dramatic episodes of that first season, with Thomas's dinner party being remembered as "The Glass Menagerie" night. I would remember it as the first time that I arrived at filming already drunk. Not blackout drunk, but I had enough margaritas in me to show up a lot less guarded than normal. Perhaps for that reason, and given what Akim had said to me, I didn't hold back when the moment came. And it came big-time.

The whole purpose of Thomas's dinner party was, as he said,

to "impart some wonderful words of wisdom." He proceeded to reveal way too much information about his past mistakes and old loves, with his girlfriend, Kathryn, sitting beside him. It was a comical moment for the rest of us. Sitting across from me was Cam, and we passed most of Thomas's speech kicking each other under the table and trying not to break out laughing. Tying together the loss of an old flame ("I threw her away like yesterday's trash") with the Tennessee Williams play *The Glass Menagerie* (apparently, he felt he was trapped in his own "glass menagerie"?), Thomas went around the table imparting advice one-on-one. I somehow managed to escape Thomas's font of wisdom, but Whitney didn't. "I know you to be intolerant," Thomas said to Whitney, whose rage was clearly rising. "Very close-minded, narrow-minded. Very judgmental."

Thomas, for obvious reasons, was a polarizing person to be friends with. But I have to admit that I always got along well with him. Besides, who other than Thomas would say that he likes the smell of cocaine in the very first episode? We were able to have honest discussions from time to time, especially about his relationship with Kathryn. During a hunting trip we took on episode 7 in the first season, I had a chance to talk to Thomas about her. The cameras didn't capture what I said, but my main point to him was that Kathryn hadn't exactly been faithful during their brief relationship. I told him to be careful about falling head over heels.

Thomas appreciated my advice. He always had this way of listening to someone to make them feel like the most important person in the moment. He even mentioned to me how he felt like he was being used. Nevertheless, he stayed with Kathryn. Oh well.

I did my best. I'm not going to defend Thomas's many transgressions, but I will say that he never once turned his sights on me. Perhaps that's small praise, but I believe he had respect for me for going about life my own way. I won't go so far as to say he was my first cheerleader, but given how Shep and Whitney would come to lambaste me for all my supposed failings, Thomas's respect was a very nice exception.

In any case, after Thomas's speech, the first course came out. Most everyone took Thomas's critiques lightly, knowing perhaps that he wasn't quite sober at the time. All except Whitney, who was very upset. Yes, there was what Thomas had said, but I also think Whitney was fuming because the show he had imagined was turning into something he didn't enjoy. The conversation around the table had turned to commitment and dating, specifically in Charleston. Then Kathryn and I got into it a bit. The argument itself was silly. I simply made the point that, while times have changed, chivalry in dating isn't dead. Kathryn disagreed.

"The way you're talking to me shows that chivalry is kind of dead," she replied. A bit later she, in conversation with Shep but loud enough for the whole table to hear, including me at the far end, said: "I'm not going to have a conversation with people who have zero class and think they do."

Shep, sitting next to Kathryn, responded with a "Shut up."

But I wasn't going to be so demure. Be myself. Screw everyone else.

"Sleeping with three people at this table in the course of three weeks isn't class, so please don't make comments about class," I said.

"Oh really," Kathryn replied. "Name them."

I didn't. I was going to walk up to the line, maybe dance on it, but not cross it. Viewers of course knew the three people by then, and so did everyone else at the table, but I didn't need to say more than I already had. I had been myself. I had spoken the truth.

While Kathryn and I would make amends and become friends soon after this moment, it was the first time in filming that I had truly said what was on my mind. I was the truth teller. Now, this wasn't a reputation that I had necessarily sought out. While close friends and family know that I have inherited the Conover gift (curse?) of speaking my mind, I didn't realize that this was a trait that I wanted to show off. But in the moment, fueled by Akim's words and a good dose of tequila, washed down by Thomas's excellent wine, and stung by Kathryn's barbs, I had blurted out the best possible comeback I had in my arsenal.

In the episodes and seasons to follow, there would be more moments when I spoke the truth. But then, so early in the show's production, I simply was myself. As the rest of that first season of filming continued, I would go from guarded to open, depending on my situation and mood. Besides, most of that first season revolved around Thomas and Kathryn's relationship anyway.

I only realized much later that I was learning how to be more comfortable in front of the cameras. But I was still fearful of the repercussions on my legal career and sometimes held back or played it safe. My talk with Akim, a man I deeply respected, gave me the freedom to separate these two halves of my life. He gave me the encouragement to *have fun* with this unique opportunity. And by fun, I don't mean to party and act like a fool; I mean fun in that I could use my personality to good effect. Simply by being me, I had created a memorable moment. My first memorable moment. Far from being a liability, my big Conover mouth was an asset. It was my talent, just as much as my skill with the law was a talent.

BALANCING ACT

My first season on the show was strange for many reasons. Whitney had always told me that I was the up-and-coming big-time lawyer, someone who typified the new Charleston: young, handsome, and ambitious. Charleston was a place where one could have it all: success and money. As someone who came from a far more humble background than a lot of the cast, I was meant to embody this new look for a city historically known as a refuge of southern genteelism. The problem was that the cameras rarely captured this side of me, the side where I was working toward my dreams. There are a few snippets from the first season of me in the office, but nothing . . . well, interesting. And that was part of the issue: Watching someone practice law outside the courtroom, where I wasn't allowed anyway, is boring. It's just me reading, taking notes, and putting together PowerPoint presentations. The other part of the problem was that cameras often weren't allowed to capture those moments in the office, where it would have been illegal to film us discussing cases or clients, or in the classroom, which might have been interesting. In the end, production gave up altogether.

I don't blame them, but the version of me that viewers saw that first season was distorted. While a lot of the cast got to film during the day, most of my filming, with the exception of the weekends, occurred at night. So it's no wonder that many viewers just assumed I was a party guy. I mean, I did party—and my partying definitely picked up as the seasons wore on—but I was also holding down a demanding job and trying to finish law school. This continued into season 2, although the focus had changed to my struggles at the job, and that I hadn't yet taken the bar exam.

Not only was I very much working and going to school at the same time, but I was also doing a very good job at both. In school, I had made the law review. For those unfamiliar with law school lingo, what that means is that I had been invited to be a member of this prestigious journal that publishes scholarly articles from professors and other luminaries in the legal profession. Not just anyone can join; your grades must show a standard of excellence above the average. Traditionally, only first-year students who are the top of their class get an invite. And I got one.

Then there's the perception that I was little more than a glorified secretary. While some aspects of my job at Akim's firm were your typical entry-level administrative duties, that is entirely normal for the industry. But I was also helping out on cases. Between the first and second season of the show, I was put on a potential case that involved a tragic story of poisoned water in a rural South Carolina town. Essentially, the firm's argument was that sewage had seeped into the water supply of the town and had caused brain damage in a lot of the inhabitants. This wasn't a new issue, either. The reason behind the poisoned water goes all the way back to the Jim Crow days of South Carolina's past. Akim sent Roy and me to the town to gather support for a class-action suit to be brought against the town on behalf of the sick residents. What we encountered was a splintered community where neither side wanted much to do with the other. Long-simmering racial tensions had created a distrust among the black and white sections of the town, which hindered our attempt to bring the class action. But Roy and I persevered and spoke with the leaders of each side—both pastors, incidentally—to try to unite the town against this historical injustice. During a town hall meeting in an auditorium, where Roy and I had brought the pastors together and set forth our case, the community united behind the suit. To this day, it remains one of my proudest moments.

Viewers saw none of this. What they did see was what my schedule allowed me to show them: out at night partying. I learned to live on the edge, going out at night and working during the day. It was a balancing act that a lot of my friends, who were independently wealthy, didn't have to achieve. I thought I could balance these two halves of my life. I wanted both the law and the fun.

But the cracks started to appear. Going into the second season of filming, the atmosphere around the show—and me—had changed dramatically. We suddenly were part of a hit. I'm not saying that everyone in Charleston loved *Southern Charm*, but everyone in the cast had, seemingly overnight, become a local celebrity. We had an invitation to some party somewhere every night of the week. And our filming schedule only increased. I was still working full-time for Akim, having graduated law school (well, not officially). In between seasons, Akim even got me my own office space downtown, and so my presence at the North Charleston office became rarer and rarer. Akim was trying to be helpful and accommodate my increasingly hectic lifestyle, but the ultimate result was that no one at the office saw me very much.

It was during these frantic months, with filming for season 2 having begun, that my abuse of Adderall kicked into high gear. I had been abusing it already, I admit, but nothing on the scale that I started to in 2014. Looking back, I should have gone to Akim and told him I needed a lighter workload. He would have understood, but I was too proud. I thought I could do it, even if "doing it" meant I stayed up all night to finish my work. It was a way of living that wasn't sustainable for any duration, as events would later show.

In the second episode of season 2, the cameras showed a conversation I had with my brother, Christopher, who had come to town to visit. As we tossed the lacrosse ball in a park, I opened up a bit to him, describing the frenzy of my new life.

"I'm surprised you can still get up in the mornings and balance all your law and work and social life," said Christopher.

"I'm just good at getting my work done on my own schedule," I replied. "I just can't wake up in the mornings sometimes. But I always get my work done; it's always done on time, above par. It just makes the owner a little uneasy that sometimes he's in the office and I'm not there. It's really hard to tell your boss that it's pointless for me to waste my time to come in during those hours."

What you hear in this conversation is my attempt to justify the slippage that was going on. But I had little choice except to justify it. If I confessed that my solution to the problem wasn't working—if I admitted to staying up all night to finish work at the last minute and failing to make an appearance at the office the next morning—then I also had to admit that my attempt to balance my law work with my personal life was doomed to fail. I couldn't do that. I still very much believed—and still desperately wanted—to have both. I was good at the law; why should I give it up?

The other factor was that, by season 2, the fans had arrived, and I learned I was very good at talking with them. Few things gave me greater pleasure (even today) than spending just a few moments talking to a fan and helping to utterly transform their opinion of me. Instead of meeting this self-entitled, lazy party boy, they encountered an articulate, charismatic guy (at least I like to think so) who was genuinely interested in their views of the show. I love hearing what fans think. I've always believed that being on the show carries a certain responsibility when the cameras are turned off. It's not required to be good to fans, but I always saw it as part of my responsibilities, and it made me happy to meet with my supporters.

I was also fast approaching a moment when I would have to make a choice between the two worlds that I loved. It's like having two families: both demand so much of your time, more than you can possibly give. If you had just one, then it would be manageable, but not two. Two is an impossibility. There was no balancing act. It could only be one or the other. This was a truth I was going to learn the hard way.

FINALLY FREE

It wasn't long into the filming of the second season that I started to realize balance wasn't possible. My absence at the firm had started to become a problem. In my head, I thought that since I got my work done, it shouldn't matter whether I was in the office or not. But that's not how the real world operates. In the real world, face time is important. The boss and colleagues seeing you at your desk is important.

So I had a disciplinary meeting with a fellow lawyer at Akim's firm. The cameras caught the lawyer, Casey, telling me I had to get in on time in the mornings. It was nothing I didn't already know or hadn't already been told. Most of my work at the firm was on behalf of other lawyers, whom I helped on their cases. They relied on me for research and for PowerPoint presentations that they would use for legal proceedings, like mediations. But because the cameras often didn't capture me working, they missed a moment that was far more devastating to my law career than a dressing-down from a lawyer.

In addition to Roy, one of the other lead lawyers at the firm was Eric Poulin, whom I was helping prepare for a mediation. The mediation was scheduled for a Wednesday morning at eight thirty a.m. I stayed up all night working on my PowerPoint presentation, delivering it at seven thirty. But Eric didn't need it on the morning of the mediation; he needed it two days before the mediation so he could use it to prepare his argument. I had procrastinated on it. Even as Eric was blasting me with text messages, asking for it, I couldn't get it done until an hour before the meeting. By the time I did deliver it, Eric didn't need it anymore. He had given up on me and had to use other materials for his presentation. I was crushed, and humiliated. I had pushed the work off until it was too late. I hadn't done what I was supposed to do, and it had hurt the firm and made life harder for a colleague. I met with Eric later, when it was all over, and he expressed his disappointment in me.

"I've lost trust in you, Craig," he said.

There were other moments also not caught on film. I recall staying up all night working, then making it into the office the next morning for a boardroom meeting. My eyes were bloodshot from the lack of sleep and from working on a computer screen all night, and I was still hopped up on Adderall. I tried to keep my sunglasses on to hide my state, but that only brings attention to the very thing you're trying to hide. So I took them off, and everyone saw I was a mess. While it wasn't a moment that led to any direct action, it stands out for me as one where I had to admit that I was screwing up. I was clearly not doing this job the right way, and it was being noticed. I certainly saw what was happening. I could no longer convince myself that I was doing good work or that I could do my job and live the lifestyle I was living.

Viewers saw the ax finally fall on episode 7 of season 2, when I sat down with Akim in his palatial mansion and was fired. I think the show had shown enough of what came before to make my termination mostly expected. But there's more to the story. First of all, there's the relationship that Akim and I had. We had had conversations before the meeting where we both agreed that I couldn't handle my workload with my other responsibilities. Akim told me that I always had a place at his firm. He told me

I was one of the best employees he'd ever had. He told me that I would be a superstar attorney one day. I suppose I was "fired" in a strict sense, but it was a firing that I had agreed to. Whatever you want to call it, I knew by then that I couldn't have both the firm and the show. I had to make a decision, and I made it with Akim. My (and his) reasoning was that the show was a unique opportunity that was happening *now*. My legal career could happen *later*. Focus on the show now, and then, when I was ready, come back to the law.

At the time, I was disappointed that things hadn't worked at the firm, but hardly devastated. In fact, I was relieved. I no longer had to balance these two halves of my life. I could focus on the show while knowing that my law career would be waiting for me when everything was over. I was free. The anxiety; the struggle; the late nights working—I felt these things were finally behind me. My life was about to get a whole lot easier.

Or so I thought.

FREE-FALLING

Addicts often blame their addiction on outside forces. The typical way this is expressed is: "You'd be an addict, too, if you had my problems." In those early seasons, I often blamed my internal demons on the outside pressures I was facing. Thus: The stress of work caused me to party a lot. The need to finish my work caused me to take Adderall. The anxiety of needing to "be on" when I went out to the bars caused me to take more Adderall. And so on.

For those just starting to abuse substances, these things might be true. Stress, anxiety, depression are all triggers that cause some of us to self-medicate, whether through alcohol or pills. Our solution seems to work—we find relief and discover that the substances help us get through the day. Out, at a bar, surrounded by friends and fans, I could forget about everything else that was going wrong. Isn't that the point? To get away from it all and just relax? Well, going out was my daily stress relief, where I could forget the parts of my life that I wasn't happy with and revel in what I did well. But forgetting is more like ignoring; and ignoring doesn't solve the underlying issue, whether it's the abuse of substances or my failure to achieve my professional goals.

There comes a point when our solution to our problems becomes *the problem*. My lifestyle, going to law school, had set in motion a pattern of living that I couldn't break once I had "freed" myself from the rigors of law school and the firm. I don't know if I thought things would be magically better for me when I was fired, but I certainly felt like a big weight had been lifted. Now, I had thought, I could focus on the show. What happened, as events would prove, was that I was merely unmoored from anything that could have put a check on my worst habits. The release from work didn't solve a problem; it allowed me to dive deeper into my real problem.

I need to make a distinction here. I worked hard at law school and the law firm. I was good at the law. The impression that many viewers had of me in those early seasons was flawed because the show rarely gave viewers my side of the story. However, I'm not blameless in the matter. No one said I had to go out as much as I did. No one made me spend as much money as I did. And nothing other than my own procrastination prevented me from finishing the PowerPoint presentation Eric needed. More important, it was procrastination that stopped me from officially graduating from law school. This last problem would be one that would hang over me for the next two years.

When I finished law school in the spring of 2014, I was one credit short of earning my JD. I had failed to turn in my upper-level writing requirement—essentially my final paper—before time ran out. There's no one to blame for this except myself. I simply didn't get it done. My school still allowed me to walk during graduation, and I was still gainfully employed at Akim's firm, but I didn't have the degree. And I wouldn't have the degree until I finished the paper. I was given until the end of that summer to finish, but I still couldn't manage to do it. Procrastination runs in my family. My father suffered from it as a young man, and I inherited this trait. To someone who suffers from it, it's not enough to simply say: "Get it done!" The more we need to "get it done," the less we can. Because procrastination is really anxiety, crippling anxiety. My use of Adderall helped this anxiety when I was in school, but the more I abused it, the less it worked for the moments when I needed it to work. Oh, I'd get stuff done, just not the thing I needed to get done. By the second season, I was using Adderall daily, often right before filming, and when I went out at night. When you're using a drug that frequently, especially one that is supposed to treat a specific problem, it simply stops working. I'd still get the high, but I got none of the benefits.

My procrastination now threatened to undo everything I had worked toward in law school. This was my own fault. What happened next wasn't my fault, but it's emblematic of how things start to spiral for an addict. As I was trying to finish my paper, I started to hear rumors that a private company called InfiLaw was attempting to buy the Charleston School of Law. It was unclear what the buyout would mean for me, but I didn't want to find out. My anxiety spiked, and I reached out to my professor, who was also sponsoring my paper, asking what I should do. He told me he would work with me to get it done, but that I should hurry. And then my professor, as well as several others, got fired because of the buyout.

Oh shit.

Suddenly, over the course of a few months, the status of the school I had gone to was in limbo. No one knew what would happen, although a lot of the Charleston community was against the buyout. The professors who knew me and wanted to help didn't work there anymore. I didn't have a diploma and I didn't have a way of obtaining it. My attempts to find answers led nowhere. The only solution I could find was that I might have to enroll at the University of South Carolina Law School to finish up my final credit. This, in any case, was the background for much of what viewers saw in season 2, especially my friends' constant questioning of why I hadn't taken the bar. I hadn't taken the bar because I couldn't take the bar, not without a diploma. But I was too embarrassed to say that to anyone—not my friends, either on the show or off, and not my parents. So the impression to others was that I hadn't taken the bar because I was just too lazy or too uncommitted to take it.

This was also the background for my trip home to Delaware with Shep and Whitney. I had been looking forward to it, even if I was a little uneasy about the cameras invading my parents' world. Home had always been a refuge for me; a place where I could reset and find some solitude within the comforting presence of my parents. I yearned for that feeling now, even though I was coming back not just with a camera crew but also a whole bag of problems that I didn't know how to resolve. And I didn't expect or want to resolve them there, with my parents. I should have expected that Whitney would cause trouble, but his revelation to my parents during dinner that I was "wasting my talents" led to the very conversation with them I wished to avoid. Such as questions about my job, which caused this exchange:

Mom: "How's work going?"

[*Pause*]

Me: "We're not talking about work. I don't talk about work when I come home."

Mom: "Okay. So how's getting ready for the bar?"

Me: "That's fine. I got my application in."

My first answer was an evasion; the second was a half-truth. I had sent in the application, but it was incomplete. My belief at the time was that I wanted to fix these problems on my own. I didn't want my parents to think I needed their help, which, looking back, I did. There was an answer to these problems; I just needed time to figure it out.

What I would only discover later is that my own behavior and actions were sabotaging my search for answers. I thought my problems were only these outside forces; but my real problem at this time was that I was caught in a cycle of living and substance abuse that I just couldn't break. But I didn't see it then—or perhaps I didn't want to see it, even when my father pressed me on that point. During dinner the next night, I had this exchange with him:

Dad: "So you go out a lot?"

Me: "Thursday, Friday, Saturday. Happy hours on Sunday."

Dad: "The drinking and all that stuff, you got to watch. It runs in our families. Mom's, mine."

My parents see more than they say, even when I don't tell them the whole truth. I was going out a lot more than the days I mentioned. A fact, I believe, my father intuitively knew. Regardless, I was able to finally talk to them about *some* of my problems, such as "transitioning out of work." They were understanding, as always, and nonjudgmental. I left Delaware with a sense that I could, perhaps, dig myself out of the hole. I had even come to an understanding with Shep and Whitney, who both had expressed their belief that I would turn things around. I truly believed that. I was going to start working on my problems. I just wasn't going to work on the right problem.

Of course, leaving the comforts of home and heading back to Charleston, where the temptations and distractions swirled around me, I felt like I had experienced enough soul-searching to deserve a break. And so the cycle continued. As it would year after year. I simply wasn't able to see that the things that were holding me back were the things I turned to when my anxiety spiked and life got hard. I still saw them as the solution, the medication I needed, while I tried to figure out how to deal with these *other* problems. If I was concerned about my substance issues—and, look, my father's warning did reach me—I always imagined that I could control them once I controlled the rest of my life.

And so, that's how you get this line, when the whole cast got together at Jekyll Island, Georgia.

"I'm aware of how wrong it is to go to Jekyll Island right now," I said during an on-camera interview, thinking back to my departure from the law firm. "But I think I've done enough facing reality in the last few days. I'm finally just ready to go have fun again."

Back to the medication. It was so much easier to just ignore my lack of diploma, the bar, my unemployment, and direct my efforts entirely on having fun, to spend time with my friends and get into all sorts of crazy shenanigans. But the money I was earning through my various endeavors wasn't enough to satisfy my lifestyle choices, and those financial decisions had started to add up. I was in an apartment with two other friends, Paul and another roommate. Paul and I had left our house on Bogard Street that we had shared with Kory, but the new place wasn't working out. We had missed rent several times, perhaps because none of us had a day job. We were up all night, which upset the tenants below us. And our landlord was getting pissed.

Amid all this, the cast headed to Jekyll Island to spend a weekend at a resort. Of course drama ensued, and I played my part as the truth teller, mostly on behalf of Kathryn. Over the year since she and I had had our blowup at Thomas's house, a friendship had formed. It had mostly happened because Kathryn was so often the target of the rumors and the barbs from others on the show. Because of the bullying I had experienced, I never could tolerate standing by while someone was singled out. So I started to stick up for her, especially since I saw her as the victim of other men's games. Kathryn had certainly brought a lot of her problems upon herself, but that's no excuse for older, supposedly wiser, people to take advantage of her. We were also two of the youngest members of the cast, and I think that also brought us closer together. Not to mention that we both had a love for style and fashion.

So after dinner, as was starting to be the norm, Whitney and Kathryn got into a fight. I admit I played a part in starting it. While Kathryn was in her room, I mentioned that we, as a group, should be more welcoming to her. Whitney didn't take kindly to that and asked, rhetorically, when I had started to become her confidant, reminding me and everyone else how I had been one of the first to call her out for being an opportunist.

"And suddenly now you're her friend?" said Whitney. "You're so disingenuous."

I had been hard on Kathryn, but that was before I got to know her. People change, opinions about people change. I don't like using first impressions to decide my relationship with someone for the rest of our lives. Not to mention that I had spoken those things to Kathryn and Thomas before they had a child together, before they had a family. "It changes the situation," I shot back to Whitney. And then I snapped: "You don't talk to her unless you're sleeping with her."

At that moment, Kathryn walked in and sat down. Then the fireworks started between her and Whitney. It wasn't the first time their animosity toward each would escalate into a shouting match, but this night was particularly fierce. And of course I stuck up for her. Later that night, as things died down, Kathryn and I were still awake, and we made the kind of decisions one does when it's late at night and you're drunk. We took one of the golf carts for a spin around the island. Production had shut down, so there were no cameras, just Kathryn and I out on the cart as the temperatures started to drop. Then the cart died. We decided to walk back to the resort, only we had no idea how to get back. Our phones were dead, and we realized we were walking in circles. I then noticed that Kathryn was freezing, so I decided that the best thing to do would be to hunker down for the rest of the night and try to keep warm. So I dug a hole beside some pine trees and covered Kathryn with pine branches. Fun, huh?

The next morning we got up with the sun and tried to find our way home. We were hungover, walking miles on barely any sleep. Eventually we found another hotel and walked in to use their phone. With Kathryn asleep on the lobby floor, I called a producer, who came and got us. We both collapsed on our beds to get a little rest before heading back to Charleston. When I woke up, I learned that the rumor had started that Kathryn and I had hooked up. I can understand why the rumor started—I mean, Kathryn and I were nowhere to be found all night—but it was just so opposite of the truth that it upset me. To think that sometime during that hellish night either of us thought it would be a good idea to make out is absurd. In any case, it's what viewers talked about for months later, and I've had to deny the rumor several times. So let me deny once more: No, Kathryn and I didn't hook up.

If anything other than tawdry rumors came out of the night,

it was that Kathryn and I became better friends. We started to support each other, maybe because we believed we were misunderstood by our friends. When I started my sewing and pillow-making journey, I turned to Kathryn for advice. And Kathryn, unlike so many of my other friends, never teased me about my passion; quite the opposite, she was a supporter from the very beginning.

The other notable occurrence from the Jekyll Island trip was my deteriorating friendship with Shep. I had grown increasingly annoyed at Shep's constant sniping at my career and especially my failure to take the bar. Like a dog with a bone, Shep just couldn't let it go, and while I know he claimed he was helping, it only pissed me off. I suppose, like two roommates who are continually in each other's presence, a lot of our disagreements simply stemmed from mutual annoyance. We saw each other's flaws, and there were moments when that's all we could see. But rather than supporting me through this tough time, I felt Shep's comments only served to bury my face in my own shame. And I suppose like Kory and I a year earlier, this growing frustration came out in silly ways, as was the case in Jekyll, when Shep embarrassed me while I was trying to give a toast to the group. Rather than stay silent and let me thank Landon for bringing all of us to her childhood vacation place, Shep interrupted me again and again. Why? Well, I have a theory . . .

Things between us came to a head at the bachelor auction for the Wounded Warrior charity event in episode 11 of season 2. Shep was auctioned off first, and it didn't go well. Cam ended up "buying" him for about $1,750. Then it was my turn. And I went for $5,001 to country singer Kelsea Ballerini. It was all in good fun, but after the event, Shep was visibly annoyed—not just at the embarrassment of going to a friend, but also of losing to *me*. Afterward, as we had drinks outside, Shep and I got into it again. Only this time he attacked me for being a loser.

"What do you have?" he said. "A girl who fake bought you?"

Viewers probably wished I had stuck around and accepted the challenge, but I was growing tired of Shep's constant attacks on my character and professional life. So I walked away. While Shep would always say that he was just worried about me, his actions throughout season 2 reveal someone who was constantly trying to prove he was better than everyone else. I wasn't part of the world that Shep, Whitney, and Thomas inhabited, where family money and connections had given them wonderful opportunities. But I never had a chip on my shoulder about it. I would make my own way. Shep seemed to think that I *should* have a chip on my shoulder; that I should look up to him and the others with important, wealthy families. So any time I got the better of him—or even any time he was just feeling like being a jerk—Shep made a point of reminding me who he was and who I was.

There were times when I believe Shep truly was trying to help. When the show started, he was far more comfortable about the person he was and the life he had chosen; I certainly was less secure. And when he approached me in the right way, I tried to listen—even if I still followed my own path. But we've both moved on from those early seasons, and now we've found a genuine friendship with each other.

LANDING IN DELAWARE

Season 2 wrapped soon after Jekyll, with Thomas's defeat in his Senate primary providing the capstone. The end of a season is always an exhausting time. The rigors of filming are hard on everyone. When the cameras finally turn off, it's like you've been traveling at 100 mph only to suddenly come to a complete stop. There is a whiplash effect. The need to get away from it all takes hold.

I was exhausted. Unlike the first season, where everything was new and exciting, I had fallen into a cycle that had utterly drained me. The constant nights out; the constant drinking; the constant drama; and my own personal failures had taken their toll. What made the end of season 2 especially difficult was that I had left the chaos of filming to enter the chaos of my personal life. As I said, my living arrangement with my roommates was spiraling downward. Paul, who had been going through a bad breakup, decided to split for California. Our other roommate left soon after. I got stuck with the rent, which was sky-high, and I was unable to stay at that apartment. Fortunately, our landlord, who I think just wanted us gone, agreed to let us out of the rest of the lease. Meanwhile, my credit cards—I had several—were entirely maxed out. I was making minimum payments on them, further eroding not only my credit but my entire financial situation. I could barely afford gas by this point. I was in a bad place. I had no job. I was in a state of purgatory with law school and the bar exam. I heard the sudden call of home, and I found it irresistible.

The time I went home with Shep and Whitney had done more than expose me to all the ways I had failed to live up to my parents' and my own expectations. It had also reminded me that I had a home, a place where I would be safe and could find the support and comfort that I was so desperately lacking in Charleston.

My intention was to go back home only until I found a new place to live in Charleston. I packed up my stuff, put it all in a U-Haul trailer, left the trailer at Shep's beach house, and drove home for about two weeks. I came back to Charleston once to put my stuff in storage—and to pay the U-Haul bill, which had ballooned to nine hundred dollars, entirely because I hadn't read the fine print on the insurance coverage. That settled, I drove back to Delaware again, expecting to stay through the holidays, only to end up staying much longer.

It was then that I told my parents everything. We were at the kitchen table, and I admitted what was going on, including all the things I had left unsaid the last time I had been home. But my biggest fear was my financial troubles. As I spoke, my dad took out a bunch of papers that he put on the table, most of it records of my past financial difficulties going all the way back to college. My dad had kept a record of it all. My father is meticulous with records, so I guess I wasn't surprised when he dumped out my life in the form of bills onto the table.

"Craig, I've known you've had these problems," he said. Which was another way of telling me that I hadn't been hiding anything from them. They knew. If not the particulars, they had known that I would likely run into these problems someday. It wasn't the show; it was just who I was. I was my father, who had all the same characteristics I did. Whereas I was learning these things about myself, he had seen them early, because he had the same qualities—the good and the bad ones, especially the procrastination.

Why had I ever felt like I could hide from them?

I spent the next four months at home, working for my father's remediation company. I wish I could say that I overcame all my bad habits, but that would be a lie. I still struggled to get into the office on time. I still struggled with procrastination, often staying up at night to finish my work. But I also did a lot of things right too. I stopped drinking the whole time I was home. I helped bring my father's company into the twenty-first century in terms of upgrading his computer systems and software—a necessity which my brother, who would soon take over the company, greatly appreciated. I also was able to help my mother during a particularly scary health crisis. Not long after I came home, my mother was diagnosed with thyroid cancer. She started to receive a radioactive iodine treatment, which meant that she couldn't have iodine (salt) in her diet. I was able to fall back on my culinary knowledge to cook meals for her that were iodine-free. I was useful again.

I had made a lot of bad decisions during that year, but going home proved to be one of the best decisions I ever made. I was able to get back some semblance of a normal life. I had been living as this celebrity for so long that I had forgotten what it had been like to rest. To enjoy the simple comforts of family. I wasn't spending money I didn't have to keep up with a lifestyle I hadn't earned; a lifestyle that was slowly killing me. I found happiness again sitting on my couch at night watching *other* people on television. I was part of something special, helping my mother through her bout with cancer and my father with the company that had provided me with everything I had needed growing up. I was able to finally give something back, and the joys of doing so gave me some sorely needed perspective.

In all these ways, my time home allowed me to reset and consider what I wanted. It wouldn't be the last time I needed a respite, but it reminded me that there were people and places that mattered more to me than anything else. My one regret is that I didn't use that time home to wean myself off Adderall. That was still the demon waiting over my shoulder . . . the one I wasn't ready to give up.

Then, in February 2015, as I was preparing to leave the office with a heavy snow falling, I got an email:

Hey loser. I have two tickets for Fashion Week next week and I was wondering if you wanted to go.

It was from Naomie.

4

A LOVE FOUND...

Shortly before the third season of *Southern Charm*, in the summer of 2015, I was having dinner at Naomie's parents' house outside Charleston when a producer from the show called me. I excused myself and took the call outside on their gorgeous patio.

"We hear you have a girlfriend now," the producer began.

I confirmed that I had by then been dating Naomie for roughly six months, most of it long-distance.

"We're going to want to see her on the show," said the producer.

I had anticipated this. Naomie had been part of the original group of local Charlestonians whom the show's producers had invited to the Millford Plantation. As with me, a friend had connected Naomie with Whitney, although she didn't go through the prolonged casting experience I did. All she did was attend this party, more out of curiosity than anything. The show's original name, *Southern Gentlemen*, was enough to turn her off from wanting to be part of it, which I get. When we started dating, she of course knew that at some point her life—our life together—could intersect with the show. It was *almost* unavoidable, even though Cam had been able to shield her husband from the cameras. When we discussed the show during those early months together, Naomie wasn't against being on it, especially if it helped me. It would have.

The problem was that most of her social circle at the time was against it, including her parents. In the two years that the show had been on the air, a divide had settled over Charleston regarding the production. As much as Charleston has moved on from its southern roots, it is still a city where a wealthy local elite, many with historical family ties to the city, hold sway, like de facto gatekeepers of what is considered welcome and unwelcome in *their* city. Those of us on the show of course knew this divide existed, but I rarely came into contact with it—or opposition to it—aside from the occasional run-in with non-fans. By dating Naomie, my life suddenly straddled the divide, and I witnessed firsthand the contempt that many felt for *Southern Charm.* I had to overcome this bias with many of Naomie's friends (who did accept me in the end).

Now, I don't want to give the impression that the Olindos, Joel and Carole, were against me; they were against the show and wanted to protect their daughter. Nor, I should add, were the Olindos representative of this city society as I have described; they had been welcomed into the city, but they were not "gatekeepers" in any sense. Nevertheless, they were concerned that their daughter's boyfriend might pull her into this world that they couldn't control. I think their worries were justified in many respects.

Which was why I pushed back against the producer that evening on the Olindos' porch. I made it clear that I didn't want Naomie on the show if she didn't want to do it. Eventually, my desires made clear, I hung up without a decision being made.

When I walked back into the house, Naomie, Joel, and Carole were standing in the kitchen. Uh-oh. Then Joel began to speak, while Naomie translated from his native French. They had overheard the conversation, he said. He had listened proudly as I had fought to protect his daughter. He said he now believed that I would protect her just as strongly as he would. And then he gave his blessing: If Naomie wanted to film, he and Carole would support her decision because they knew I would look after her.

In time, I would learn that however much I was able to protect Naomie from the cameras, I couldn't protect our relationship. But in that moment, I was grateful and overjoyed.

FINDING MY HAPPINESS

But let's flash back to that fateful night. Naomie's message to me that snowy February evening in 2015 came as a complete surprise. She and I had not seen each other in over a year. In fact, as I scrolled through our old conversations, I saw how often I had messaged her only to receive quick replies, if I received one at all.

I would usually send her a message on her birthday, or on holidays like Easter. Eventually, I took the hint and stopped reaching out. But the truth was that "Ponytail" had never been far from my mind. She had become "the one that got away," and I had accepted that reality.

And yet, here she was, asking *me out*—kind of. Perhaps it was only "as friends," but I would learn later that Naomie had just broken up with her longtime boyfriend, which explained why she had two tickets to Fashion Week. So I was the rebound. Whatever. The girl I had had a crush on for years had snuck into my DMs and I wasn't about to get all virtuous or technical about what it meant. I immediately replied before heading home for the night, accepting her invitation and kicking off several weeks of flirty banter back and forth.

The funny part was that I was already going to Fashion Week in Charleston, which started on March 17, having agreed to emcee one of the nights with Shep. Which I suppose meant I might have run into Naomie anyway. Not that I believe in fate and all that, but clearly our life paths, so long diverged, were meant to cross again. A few weeks later, I packed up some things and made the nine-hour drive back to Charleston, where I had not been for several months. In that time it was amazing how unconnected I had become from the city. I had no home. I was still working at my dad's company. I occasionally talked to Cam or Shep on the phone, but otherwise I had entirely separated myself from that former life. Except now I was returning to go out with Naomie. That was enough. That, to me, was everything.

I ended up staying at a friend's house, and on the day of

the event, Naomie picked me up. I'll never forget how beautiful she looked in her gray-and-white knee-length dress. Better than her appearance, though, was the way we naturally fell into a comfortable rapport with each other. I hadn't seen Naomie in over a year, and even then, it wasn't like we had chatted all that much. She had come in and out of my life as a lot of people from Charleston did. It's a small enough city to feel as if you know everyone around your age. But seeing someone at a bar or restaurant doesn't mean you're best friends. Those are the surface-level friends, and however much I crushed on Naomie, I can't claim she and I had ever been more than that. Which was why that drive was so special. It was as if we hadn't been *ready* to be close before; like we had been on different paths and pursuing different dreams. But now we were ready, now we were on the same path, now we could discover who the other truly was. We didn't only become friends in that short car ride to the show; it was like we had *always* been friends.

And thank God, given what happened at the show itself. Because I was an emcee, I had backstage passes to the event and took Naomie behind the curtain to see the production. It was then that Naomie's dress split down the middle . . . of her backside. With one hand covering her butt, Naomie grabbed me with her other hand, a look of embarrassment on her face. I think if the chemistry hadn't been kindled on the car ride over, if the date had felt forced and unnatural, then her splitting her dress might have been horribly awkward. But it wasn't like that at all—well, at least for me. I'm sure Naomie was in fact feeling very awkward. I, however, trying to suppress my laughter, jumped into action and ran to find one of the show designers. She hurried Naomie to one of the dressing rooms, and within minutes, the split had been sewn up as if nothing had happened. An awkward moment became a memorable first-date memory that we would laugh about for the next several years. As for the rest of the evening, it went by in a haze of joy and excitement, where memories blur together and leave one with a feeling of happiness. And I realized then how long it had been since I had been truly happy.

The next night of Fashion Week, Shep and I emceed. Afterward, a lot of us, including Naomie, grabbed dinner at Hall's on King Street, then went back to Shep's house for a party.

The next morning, as I was packing up to make the drive back to Delaware, Naomie came by my friend's house to say good-bye. We had our first kiss. Then I left Charleston, a smile on my face, and my phone buzzing the whole way back to Delaware with texts from Naomie. We talked on the phone every day over the next several weeks before we found time to see each other again. I started to visit Charleston more frequently and stayed at her parents' house. Yes, that *was* awkward, but also a bit unavoidable. Naomie came up to visit me in Delaware too. She even traveled with me to New York City when I filmed the reunion episode for *Southern Charm*. While it might seem like our relationship was progressing rapidly, maybe too rapidly, I wasn't ready to return to Charleston full-time. I was still paying back my parents for digging me out of credit card debt and I couldn't just leave my responsibilities at the company. But honestly, I was just happier at home. Far from interfering with my growing relationship with

Naomie, it seemed to help things tremendously. I wasn't in that Neverland world, pulled and pushed by all manner of temptations. I wasn't constantly on the hunt for the validation I previously looked for at parties and bars, out among strangers. For the first time in a long time, I felt in control of my life. Until there was a reason to return to Charleston full-time, I was quite content to nurture and grow this relationship with Naomie.

In fact, some of our happiest moments were when she visited me in Ocean View. How many times did she and I, clad in pajamas, sit on the floor in my living room, nuzzling with our retriever, Fenwick, eating junk food, and watching movies? Or riding bikes together to the beach, where we would grab an Orange Crush and watch the waves? When I think about us together, these are the memories that elicit the strongest emotional response. There's a reason for that too. I quickly noticed that Naomie seemed happiest at my parents' house, an odd thing perhaps for someone who had been raised in the elite social life of Charleston. Ocean View, and my childhood home, are humble places. We were always well-off, and I don't want to give the impression that I or my family ever wanted for anything. But my parents are informal people; they work hard, they laugh hard, and they love hard. Our family doesn't follow strict social etiquette, but rather is bound together by traditions. Our idea of entertaining is throwing a few steaks on the barbecue and some Bud Light in the cooler. We don't do "cocktails" at five p.m. and we don't care about the latest restaurant or club opening, and not because there aren't really any "openings" of clubs or restaurants in Ocean View. It's because my parents, and the home they created for my brother and me, were utterly devoid of pretensions. What mattered was the family, not what others thought about our family.

This, for Naomie, was a wholly different world than the one she had grown up in. The Olindos emigrated from France in 2000, when Naomie was only eight years old. Their first few years in Charleston were tough, not least because Joel and Carole barely spoke a word of English. To succeed in Charleston as restauranteurs, especially in those days, required being accepted by the local gatekeepers. Locations, permits, liquor licenses, and employment were all obtained by those who had ingratiated themselves with the "gatekeepers" of the city. Imagine the obstacles that faced Joel and Carole as they struggled to build a life and a successful restaurant career: A hostile local elite, no connections, and a language barrier were just a few of the challenges they had to overcome. But, hardworking and ambitious as they were, the Olindos persevered and prospered. They carved out their own place in Charleston society and became firm fixtures in the happenings of the city. Even if they were from a different Charleston than I would come to know and love, the Olindos earned every ounce of their success. They had found their American Dream.

But far from spurning the humble roots of her boyfriend, Naomie embraced everything that Ocean View represented—or at least, part of her did. I don't know if she would have accepted that kind of life forever; heck, I haven't even accepted that kind of life. But she was able to find some measure of solace and happiness in a home that didn't ask her to be anything other than who she was. There were no expectations; there was no judgment. You walked in, you kicked off your shoes, you put on your sweats, and you ate snacks while watching a terribly cheesy romantic comedy. We *slept in*—which for Naomie, who was expected to be up early every morning, was amazing. In lower, slower Delaware, Naomie had found an escape. And I had fallen in love for the first time in my life.

A NEW HOME, A NEW LIFE

In the summer of 2015, I got the call that filming for season 3 would begin in the fall. The eight months I had spent in Ocean View had successfully rid me of the debt and the depression that had caused me to flee Charleston in the first place. I had had a lot of time to think about what went wrong, and my conclusion was that I had been careless and reckless. I had dropped my guard and gotten crushed by life. I'm not putting the blame on the show, of course. Admittedly, I dove face-first into the waters of celebrity and almost drowned. My search for validation, always strongest when I'm depressed or lonely, had found easy targets in every bar, club, or party I walked into. Even if the cameras weren't there, the fans were. And the fans had helped me forget that I was still without a law degree and without any real path toward becoming a lawyer.

Entering season 3, I was determined to take control of my own story. For the first time in a long time I had something very valuable in my life that I had no intention of losing. But would I be entering the new season with Naomie by my side? I wanted her to be with me, not because of the optics, but because I was simply happier when she was around. If Naomie had to hide when the filming started, then I worried it would drive a wedge between us. Regardless of her decision, I was still determined to protect her, and us, from the consequences that came with the cameras. And I never pushed her to do it. In the end, Naomie decided to film because she wanted us to be together. With her parents' blessing, we would be a single unit on the show—or so was my hope.

As I was preparing to move back down, Naomie told me that her parents wanted to help with my living situation—which at that exact moment was undecided. I knew that I didn't want to live downtown anymore. Well, really, I knew that I *couldn't* live downtown because I would constantly be bombarded with the temptations of the city. Removing myself from that world was one of the decisions I had made while back home in Delaware. I had to get back to Charleston because my life was there, but I didn't have to deliberately put myself in a bad situation. The Olindos provided a solution. They owned a house in West Ashley near Edgewater Park that they were trying to sell. They wanted me to stay there while the house was on the market. As viewers saw in season 3, the house was gorgeous. Located on a sprawling lot beside the Stono River, the ranch house came fully furnished and was completely renovated. Who wouldn't want to crash there for a time?

I accepted the offer, at least until I could find my own place, as long as they let me pay (although they never cashed the checks). The Olindos lived close by, which meant Naomie was often with

me at the house. Before long, she all but moved in, and thus we
made our first mistake: We started living together in the first year
of our relationship. Much as Kory and I discovered, Naomie and
I grew apart the closer we lived together. Of course, at the time,
we didn't realize this. We were in love and very happy. Naomie
was working as a real estate agent, a job she hated, and I encouraged her to find other opportunities, perhaps even go back to
school to earn her MBA. This greatly appealed to her, but not
only for reasons of professional happiness. Her past relationships
had been very controlling, much as a lot of her life had been very
controlling. It came as a happy shock to her that she could be
with someone who encouraged her to do what *she* wanted. I urged
her to forge her own path, for the very same reasons that I wanted
to forge mine: We can never truly be happy unless we follow our
passions. My passion at the time was still the law, even if that path
seemed to be closed to me for the moment.

For several months, our life together was a sense of comfort
and joy to both of us. We stayed up late watching movies and slept
in while our cats nudged us for attention. We never fought. The
hours I kept, which would soon become such a source of resentment for her, were hours we kept together. Looking back, I took
this very simple, but also powerful, sharing of sleep for granted. I
didn't realize how important it was for our relationship—for any
relationship, really—to go to bed together. When that stopped
happening is when things began to fall apart. But that was all in
the future. During our first months of living together at the West
Ashley house, we settled easily into a life that probably didn't look

much different than if we had been married. Yes, marriage. I had already started to think this way, although one moment in particular brought it home to me.

As we often did, we were watching a movie together, just the two of us. It was *The Notebook*, a movie I had never seen before. I've always been a sap for romantic films, comedies, or, in the case of this film, serious dramas. At the end of the movie, the elderly couple die together peacefully in bed, holding hands. I turned to look at Naomie and remember thinking, *This is the woman I want to spend the rest of my life with*. I wanted to grow old with her and do the very thing we were doing at that moment: sitting together on the couch watching a movie, for the rest of my life. Carried away? Perhaps. But isn't that the joy of being in love?

BLINDSIDED

Before season 3 started filming, J.D. Madison approached me with a proposition. As a guest cast member, J.D. had been introduced to viewers in the previous seasons as one of Thomas's friends. He and his wife, Elizabeth, swiftly became regulars on the show, often joining the main cast at parties and getaways, even if they never were full-time cast members. In any case, J.D. proposed that I join his hospitality company, Gentry, as an equity partner. He said that eventually I would be put in charge of his new bourbon division.

It was an intriguing offer. I was unable to take the bar until the situation with my law school graduation got sorted out. I didn't have any idea when that would happen, but I couldn't just stay home all day. I need a job; I needed income. The tagline for the start of the season had been a funny play on my old ways: #new-craig. I accepted this tongue-in-cheek moniker because I *was* trying to be a newer, more mature version of myself. I accepted that I had gone astray in so many ways—professionally, personally, and emotionally. I had left the previous season utterly drained and depressed. Gentry offered me something to do, with an interesting opportunity in the bourbon industry. I know that my friends ended up mocking me relentlessly for my belief that I could run a bourbon company. But it wasn't me who raised the idea; it was J.D. I would not have agreed to join Gentry if the only offer on the table was to run one of J.D.'s hotels; that kind of work had never interested me. And in the end, I never really did much for J.D.'s hotel.

My focus, because J.D. had promised me that it would be my focus, was on the new bourbon business. I played along only because I had been led to believe that it would culminate in something I really did want—running the bourbon division. Except that J.D. never planned on putting me in charge of the bourbon. It was all a ruse. So while I waited to be brought into the bourbon division, I ended up not doing much of anything at all, really. But this didn't bother me so much at the time, and there's a very simple explanation for why.

Going home had gotten me back on my feet, but it was meeting Naomie that gave me purpose. I'm no different from a lot of people out there who might feel adrift or unfulfilled in their current life or career. We seek passion and purpose, without which we wither. The law had been and still was my passion, but it felt further away than ever. My job at my father's remediation company, while necessary, hadn't exactly been a passion pursuit. I did it because I had to do it; but I also did it because I wanted to help. And if I'm not passionate about what I'm doing, or if I'm not helping someone, then I don't prosper. I grow listless and turn to other distractions to occupy my mind—oftentimes bad distractions. In a word, I get bored.

I fully appreciate that a lot of people don't have the luxury of being bored. They work, not because they love what they do, but because they must. They have families to feed and bills to pay. They don't have the privilege of searching for their passion as I did in those days. I took the show very seriously, but I always wanted something more for myself. And even though I know I am and have been incredibly blessed, it doesn't make it any easier for me to simply put my head down and slog through a job I don't enjoy. I already struggle with procrastination; putting me in a situation where I don't particularly care about the work I'm doing is a surefire way to get me to check out.

But once I found Naomie, I experienced a sense of purpose stronger than I could ever remember feeling. I still wanted to find my own professional passion, but it was so I could be in a position to build a life with her. Nothing else really mattered. I understand that this isn't necessarily a healthy thing. You can call it professional apathy, and plenty of my friends believe it was, but it was more a question of focus. My focus was on her, and that left little room for worrying about a nine-to-five job. I had purpose, but I lacked balance.

So it's little wonder that I went along with J.D.'s offer; and perhaps equally as unsurprising that I thought I could run a bourbon division. Of course, my confidence in this regard wasn't wholly unreasonable. It was J.D. who first suggested it; it was J.D. who made me think that this was more than a possibility. Back in college, I had even tended bar and served for several summers. Why would I turn it down? If J.D. thought I could do it, he was the expert; he should know. I simply jumped at what looked like an easy opportunity to get a quick job that could lead to something more. By doing so, I opened myself up to the exact blind side that J.D. had planned for me. The moment went down at Gentry's North Charleston warehouse, which viewers watched in episode 6 of season 3, where J.D. had organized a tasting for cast members and other friends.

I walked into the tasting expecting to be given more responsibility—if not control—of the new business, only to learn during the event that it was never in the cards. At one point, as J.D. separated the group into tasting tables, I asked him if I could lead one. Rather dismissively, J.D. responded: "You can help." It's like I could see the humiliation happening in slow motion. Later, I was talking to Shep and I confided that I "thought I was a bigger part of the bourbon than I really" was. Shep, for once being his best self, didn't throw my embarrassment in my face but listened sympathetically.

Later, J.D. pulled me aside to reveal what he had kept from me all along.

"You're not in a position with the historical knowledge to lead a bourbon division," he said. "And you know that, right?"

My rejection—and humiliation—was absolutely real. I was crushed. I don't know why J.D. set me up like that, but discovering he never had confidence in me in the first place was a true embarrassment. Naomie and I stayed behind after the event, and she could sense the degree of my dejection. Naomie felt just as terrible as I did, maybe worse. She, too, had been led to believe that this was a viable path for me. We hadn't yet reached the point where my professional inertia had driven a wedge between us. She just wanted me to find my "thing," whatever that was. And I had told her that this was it; or, to be fair, could be it.

But there was one silver lining. If I had received this kind of humiliation, which I hadn't felt since being bullied in high school, without Naomie by my side, I know exactly what I would have done. I would have gone out to drink away the pain. But here again was the power that Naomie had in my life. I didn't want to do that. I just wanted to go home and be with her. She was, after all, my focus. Her presence, and the simple joy of just enjoying our time together, calmed me.

I played out my time with J.D. for a while longer, at one point angering him because I traveled to L.A. with Shep to party and film with Whitney. But without the bourbon division holding me at Gentry, there wasn't anything for me to do, and it was time to end this little charade. I would go back to focusing on the law, even though my status with the law school remained in doubt. But before that happened, Naomie and I had our first real fight—and it happened on-screen.

The background was the ongoing feud between Whitney and Kathryn. I had always suspected there was something more to

Whitney's dislike of her, even though I understood that Kathryn often simply rubbed people the wrong way. My suspicions were confirmed when I talked to Kathryn about it, and she told me that Whitney had had much stronger feelings for her back when they first hooked up in season 1. I kept this bit of information in my back pocket, waiting for the right moment to confront Whitney. Importantly, I had told Naomie all about this, even that I was going to confront Whitney with it. She understood and agreed that the full story should be told. That moment came when the whole cast traveled to Shep's family's magnificent home in North Carolina. Kathryn didn't attend, although Shep had extended the invitation. The first night at the house, while I was outside on the deck grilling steaks for everyone, I decided that if the conversation turned to Kathryn, with the usual snide remarks directed her way, I would defend her. I knew exactly what would happen when I did that, and was prepared to deal with the fallout.

As usual, the conversation around dinner turned to Kathryn, and why no one wanted her at the group events. With Naomie sitting next me, I looked at Whitney and said that the only reason he was still so upset with Kathryn three years later was because she had chosen Thomas over him. Oh boy. The shit hit the fan. First Whitney freaked out. Then Cam, who was always close to Whitney, freaked out. But I didn't back down, maintaining that all of Whitney's animosity toward Kathryn was because of hurt feelings and wounded pride. That's when Naomie turned to me and said, "Would you just quit?"

And that, I believe, is the moment when our relationship started to fall apart. Because Naomie knew all along what I was about to say if the conversation turned to Kathryn. She didn't know *when* I would say it, just that I would. So when she turned against me at the dinner, I was utterly blindsided. J.D.'s little scheme was nothing compared to the sense of betrayal I felt in that moment. Instead of supporting me against the storm, she added to the storm. I felt alone and hurt.

Later, after things had calmed down, Naomie and I were alone in the kitchen. "What you did was low and embarrassing, and I just wish you would not have cornered Whitney in front of all of us," she said. "And what you did ruined everyone's night."

"No one's night is ruined," I said.

"Well, mine is."

"That's why I'm sad," I said. "And I'm sorry. I really am."

I was hurt and confused. And so was Naomie, who, soon after the cameras caught us talking alone, took off her mike and cried in the bathroom.

Later, away from the cameras, we talked about the moment on the deck, and I asked her why she hadn't supported me. She explained that the confrontation between Whitney and I made her extremely uncomfortable, as it would any normal person. She said that she went into fight-or-flight mode, almost panicking. I, with two seasons of filming under my belt, had learned to over-come those feelings and stay in the moment. But Naomie hadn't learned those tricks yet. She acted as a normal persona would have acted. The reason she cried later was because she realized that her reaction would look poorly on me. And therein was the trap I hadn't considered when her father allowed Naomie to join me in front of the cameras.

I had had plenty of fights on camera before this. Take Thomas's dinner party that closed out episode 11, the penultimate episode of season 3. The background to the dinner party was that Thomas and Kathryn had gotten back together with the birth of their second child, and were presenting themselves as a united couple. Thomas started off well enough, doing his typical showmanship schtick, before saying he wanted to offer a "few wonderful words of wisdom to all of you." That's when things went off the rails. After offering a quick nod of praise to Kathryn, Thomas turned to Cam and compared her to his sisters: "self-righteous . . . judgmental . . . sanctimonious." I was next, and just like at the last infamous dinner, I got off pretty clean. I was a "great guy," who shouldn't be someone I'm not.

Then Shep got his, with Thomas telling him to stop "f-ing every girl in Charleston" and look to Landon as a woman he could settle down with. And to Landon, Thomas remarked: "You've been a little catty. You've been a little disrespectful toward Kathryn."

After that, the night devolved into a shouting match, with Thomas and Shep almost coming to blows. The party broke up after Thomas literally chased most of the guests out his door. When he sobered up the next day, Thomas made the rounds and called everyone to apologize. For most people that was enough. A sincere apology is usually all that's required—even when one is literally kicked out of a house. Another example is the trip I took with Shep to visit Whitney in L.A., also in season 3. The trip happened after I had called out Whitney over Kathryn. There was real bad blood between us. Whitney was pissed. But I was told that Whitney was fine with me coming out, only to hear from Shep that Whitney didn't know. The whole thing could have been this big dramatic moment, but that's not what any of us wanted. Instead of a bang, my feud with Whitney ended with a whimper. I apologized, Whitney accepted, and we were back to being friends.

Turning this back to Naomie and me, I don't think we were ever comfortable playing this game with each other—fighting, apologizing; fighting, apologizing. I certainly wasn't. I wanted to protect our relationship, and that meant showing the world that we were united on all things. My whole concept of a strong relationship comes down to the "ride-or-die" mentality; you support your partner because that's what you do. But Naomie aired so much of our dirty laundry in front of the cameras, I felt betrayed. I never considered that she would want to play the game with me, and I couldn't help but think that it was me who had brought this on myself. After all, it was I who had wanted Naomie to do the show. She wouldn't have if I'd asked her not to.

After that evening at Shep's mountain house, and everything that came of it, I started to wonder if I had made the right decision. Naomie was starting to wonder too. She even told me she didn't want to keep filming. I said that it would look terrible if she disappeared; that it would do more harm to our relationship than if we stuck it out and tried to find our balance within the show. You could say I was more concerned about the optics of our relationship than our actual relationship at this point, and perhaps that's true. But I also did honestly believe that it was important for us to be together on the show. I was terrified that we would look like a damaged couple. My motivation was to protect our image and thus our relationship.

FINALLY, GOOD NEWS

The effects that the Whitney episode had on our relationship lingered, probably because we never really addressed the underlying issues. We simply carried on. While I might be the guy on the show who is constantly speaking the truth, I have never been particularly good at addressing difficult topics with those I love. I tend to retreat or ignore the problem until I explode, and looking back, neither of us effectively dealt with our growing resentments. On the surface at least, my relationship with Naomie was still strong. We rarely fought, and I was deliriously in love with her. We talked all the time about being together forever. But the show had started to intrude. The pressures of keeping up appearances for the camara stressed out both of us. Naomie wasn't sure how to act and I wasn't sure what to tell her. The irony was that we each wanted to help the other, but by doing so we drifted further apart.

Toward the end of filming for season 3, the West Ashley home sold, and we moved into a brand-new house that her parents had bought for us. It, too, was very close to the Olindos', just a few doors down the street. At first I was against it. I wanted us to buy our house together, not be given one that we didn't choose. In my mind, a gift as large as a house comes with strings, and I didn't want to feel beholden to Naomie's parents. Naomie, however, didn't understand this. She was overjoyed that we suddenly had this wonderful new home to start our lives in. But I felt as if I was losing control.

When filming wrapped for season 3 in the fall of 2015, we did a bunch of traveling together. We went to Monaco to watch the Grand Prix. We spent time at the Olindos' home in Nice. We traveled to Thailand. For the most part, these were wonderful trips, and this was a happy time for us. But again, that was on the surface. Underneath, the small schism that had opened between us was growing wider, and I take responsibility for a lot of it. These were days when I was hopelessly hooked on Adderall. My addiction to it had moved beyond taking it before filming or taking it to stay up working all night. I was simply taking it all the time. My daily dosage included three 15 mg pills, morning, noon, and night. Naomie, of course, knew I took it, even if she disapproved of how much I was using. If only she had known the truth. I had learned that the sound of my opening up the bottle was a dead giveaway to Naomie that I was taking a pill, leading to a conversation I didn't want to have. So I took to the practice that nearly every addict in history has used to hide the true nature of their addiction: I started concealing pills around the house, just to avoid opening up that bottle and alerting Naomie to my out-of-control habit. I had the pills stashed everywhere, just in case.

And my addiction followed me as we traveled the world together. Which also meant that I was staying up far too late and getting up far too late. Naomie would bounce out of bed early in the morning, ready to see the sights, while I couldn't move until lunchtime. It was the beginning of a cycle that would continue when we returned to the States. Our schedules were coming apart. We stopped going to bed together during our travels, and it started to affect our relationship. Naomie's resentment began to grow, and I was too blind to see it. Or, if I saw it, I was too proud to accept that it was my fault. In addition to messing up my sleeping schedule, Adderall also frayed my nerves, and I started to lose my temper a lot. Little perceived slights would get under my skin, and I'd lash out. Looking back, I now recognize these supposedly joyous travels together as the beginning of the end of our relationship. When we returned, it was no longer a relationship that was growing; it was one we were trying to keep together.

One bright spot during these months happened on New Year's Eve 2016, while Naomie and I were in Thailand. I remember lying in bed that night watching the fireworks out the window, and receiving a message on Facebook. It was from my old law school classmate, who had taken control of the school. He was letting me know that the status of the Charleston School of Law had finally been resolved, and that the school would be back in operation. Which also meant that I finally could finish my thesis and earn my degree. I could graduate. I could take the bar. I could become a lawyer.

Naomie joined me in jumping up and down on the bed in celebration, until we both tumbled off the bed, laughing.

See? I said to her. It was all going to work out. I would finish what I had started.

5

- - - - - -

...AND LOST

*I*n June 2017, Naomie and I traveled to Charlotte for the wedding of our mutual friends, Madison and David Nelson. Madison and Naomie had been friends for a long time, and David was a former NFL football player. The four of us had become close over the years, and had all run the New York City Marathon in 2016 to help raise money for David's I'mME orphan care ministry, which helps children in devastated regions of Haiti.

Of course, I was late in getting ready, and we had to rush to Charlotte from Charleston, a three-hour drive. We argued the whole way, as Naomie thought we would miss the ceremony. We didn't, but it meant that when we arrived, we were both very angry. The wedding was absolutely stunning, held beside a lake beneath a canopy of trees through which the setting sun cast shadows over the wooden cross that hung behind the altar. The couple had written their own vows, but I'll only repeat part of Maddy's here:

I promise to serve you and create a home that is full of love, creativity, joy, and freedom. I know that I will frustrate you and I will challenge you. But I promise to make you laugh every single day and I promise to be your biggest fan . . .

When Maddy said those final three words, I turned to Naomie and saw she was crying. That wasn't so remarkable. Almost everyone in the audience was crying by that point. But I saw that Naomie wasn't crying tears of joy for her best friend; hers were tears of sadness. Later, during the reception as we celebrated the newlyweds, she would tell me that she was crying because of us. I asked her why.

"Because I know I will never be your biggest fan, Craig. I can't be that person for you."

After the reception, most of the guests went out in Charlotte to continue the party. I wanted Naomie to come with me, but she was tired. I got angry when she asked me not to go. But I went anyway. At the bar, I spoke to Maddy, and she told me everything would work out.

"Every couple struggles, Craig," she said.

When I got back to the room that night, Naomie was both angry and sad.

Echoing Maddy, I said everything would be fine. "I can't explain it, Naomie, but I know it will all work out. Trust me."

Naomie didn't believe me anymore.

FALLING APART

Up to this point, I have tried to tie the narrative to the seasons of the show. But I'm going to diverge from that structure moving forward for a couple reasons. In my attempt to keep this book focused on my story and what led me to sit down at a sewing machine for the first time in nearly twenty years, I simply don't have the space to give a full account of each season and all the drama and twists that occurred. Even if some of these moments involved me, I'm only going to focus my attention on those that are relevant to my passion and what would become Sewing Down South. In a lot of cases, the most relevant parts weren't captured by the cameras at all, even if they occurred during filming.

My relationship with Naomie, or rather, our deteriorating relationship, was the principle motivation behind my taking up sewing again. Even though I had discovered an interest in it way back in junior high, I couldn't call that interest a passion. It wasn't. I hardly thought about sewing at all, and if I did, it was simply one of many domestic activities that I enjoyed, like cooking or gardening. To be honest, I enjoyed cooking far more than I enjoyed sewing at this moment in life, and I was much better at it too. But cooking and sewing both share one thing in common: the act of creation. I have always experienced so much joy in simply creating something new with my hands, whether sewing, cooking, or carpentry. Sewing won out in the end over all the others probably because it was the most commercially viable, but I dabbled in all of them.

In fact, season 4 began with me talking about my new hobbies, carpentry and gardening. I realized that many of my friends poked fun at these activities to reinforce the notion that I simply was lost. I won't deny that I was a bit lost at this point, but I was also trying to finish up my final paper for law school so that I could graduate. The cameras didn't show that. Most of the cast never believed that I would really graduate, then pass the bar. So instead I was shown to be doing nothing much at all, simply finding ways to spend my hours while Naomie was at business school.

I won't defend the way in which I chose to finish up my law school paper. As I had always done, I stayed up until sunrise working on it while Naomie slept. She would then get up early for school, and we often crossed paths as she left the bedroom and I entered it. That schedule alone was crushing our intimacy, and I was fully responsible for it. But I was doing *something*, at least at night. And during the day, I was finding new ways to use my hands to create. I did so because it brought me a sense of calm and fulfillment. It brought me peace. The maelstrom of filming; my relationship with Naomie; my anxiety over my future—all these pressures rattled around in my head when my eyes opened, and, as a procrastinator does, I dealt with that stress by avoiding all of it.

I was very good at convincing myself that everything was all right. I told myself that I was doing fine. Everything was fine. I didn't care that no one believed I was working on my thesis. It was fine that I didn't have a job that required discipline and a schedule that would match Naomie's. At one point in season 4, while I was helping Naomie organize a fundraiser, I let things go down to the wire as I often did. Naomie got upset with me, as she was doing more and more. I told myself that it was fine because the work got done in the end. "I don't get stressed," I said to the camera. "I'm able to reason any worry out of my brain." I really did believe this. I thought I could shut out all the noise and just do what I wanted to do: study at night and work on my hobbies during the day—or, well, the afternoon.

I should say that, despite what viewers saw on the show, Naomie in private really didn't have a problem with my lack of a viable profession. She knew I was trying to finish my thesis so that I could then take the bar, and it didn't bother her. What bothered her was my schedule; what bothered her was *how* I went about doing what I did. It remains one of the greatest regrets of my life that I couldn't see the damage my late nights were having on our relationship. I can put a lot of the blame on my addiction to Adderall, since I invariably popped half a pill after dinner every night, ensuring that I would be wired until well past midnight. But an addict must also take responsibility for his actions, and I didn't at the time. I always assumed that whatever problems Naomie and I were having, we would eventually resolve. I didn't recognize the urgency that things were swiftly careening toward a point of no return.

She knew that I was working toward the degree. But these were the very things she would bring up with me in front of the camera. In episode 5 of season 4, I am shown cooking a nice dinner for Naomie before she gets home from class. I had set up a table at her parents' place and surprised Naomie when she walked in the door. She knew I had been studying, but she went ahead and sabotaged this romantic dinner because the cameras were there.

"You keep saying you want to be a lawyer, but you don't do anything about it," she said. "That shows people you don't want to be a lawyer."

But I was doing something about it. She *knew* I was doing something about it. It was as if once the camera turned on, Naomie became the girlfriend she thought the audience wanted to see.

Which was probably why I snapped back: "I think you're being silly and ignorant and you're acting kind of dumb."

There are only so many times you can have these "fights" in front of the cameras before they spill over into your real relationship. When someone like Shep would pick a fight with me over law school or whatever, I could usually keep my cool. Those arguments also bothered me, but I wasn't going home with Shep. Naomie was different, and my original plan to protect our relationship from the cameras was coming undone. Instead of arguing that she was only doing what was right for the show, Naomie started to believe that what she said on camera was how it was off camera. In other words, she had convinced herself that that was how she really felt. I never thought it would be Naomie who would be the one driving the wedge between us.

I'm not trying to absolve myself from blame in how the relationship began to fall apart. I know I was blind to many things. Naomie had every right to be resentful of the way I was living my life and how I stopped nurturing the relationship. But I also know that she was able to hit my vulnerabilities in a way that no one else could. I had been able to overcome my search for validation in others because of Naomie. The only validation I sought was hers, and when she began to pull away, she took that with her. What was left were all those old childhood insecurities. What's more, that sense of purpose I had found with her was slipping away.

ORPHANS IN HAITI

You never forget the first time you see a child locked in a cage. In the fall of 2016, Naomie and I had been talking with our friends Madison and David, who were going to be married the following summer. They mentioned to us that they had a few open spots on their New York City Marathon team, which they had put together to raise money for David's organization that helped orphans in Haiti. I knew it was a cause that Maddy and David were passionate about, even if I didn't quite appreciate what "orphans in Haiti" meant. My concern then was that I hated running. I still do, although I do find that it can help me relax. At our friends' insistence, Naomie and I agreed to run a marathon, despite the fact that I had never run longer than three miles.

On October 5, Hurricane Matthew slammed into Haiti as a category four storm, devastating the island and unleashing horrific flooding. Through David's organization, I'mME, he and Maddy were going down to help with relief efforts, and they asked Naomie and me if we wanted to join them for a few days. We wouldn't be doing much work. It was more of an opportunity to see what we would be raising money for, a kind of educational trip. Naomie didn't feel up for it, but I jumped at the opportunity. I have always had what you could call a philanthropic impulse; I find great joy and fulfillment in helping others. I would trade my smile for someone else's in a heartbeat. And since becoming a celebrity, I had wanted to use my platform to raise money and awareness for causes close to my heart. I was also searching for some kind of purpose in my life at this time—or perhaps I should say, I was *still* searching, since I hadn't found it yet. I wanted to be part of something that I believed in and that really helped people. But having that urge to help and actually witnessing true human suffering are two different things. What I saw when I traveled to Haiti shook me and left an indelible mark on who I am and how I want to live my life.

I flew into Port-au-Prince and could see the effects of the hurricane from the air. Whole swaths of the coastline had been destroyed, and you could trace with your finger the high-water mark of the flooding, which had reached miles inland. I deplaned and walked to the pickup lane, and that's when I looked around at this strange land I had entered. There was barely anyone around, aside from a few people a little ways off who started to eye me. I kept my distance and tried to be inconspicuous as I waited for Maddy and David to pick me up, but unfortunately a white American wearing the clothes I was wearing sticks out. The group that was watching me started to heckle. I had trouble understanding what they were saying to me, but I tried to answer back in French—which wasn't great but had improved considerably through my travels with Naomie. So I said something to the effect that I was waiting for my friend . . . I think. They just laughed and backed off, but I still watched them warily. I felt exposed and entirely out of my element, counting the seconds until Maddy and David pulled up. When they did, I literally jumped in the car. I asked them why the streets were so empty.

"Because of the Haitian election," said David as he took us to our compound. "It's disputed, so everyone is afraid to be in the streets. And we're ordered to remain inside."

Great. My first day in Haiti and I arrive in the middle of a contested election. As we drove through the mostly deserted streets, I'd catch glimpses of people, mostly young children, in rags picking through the debris. I asked David why I only saw children. Where were the parents?

"When the floods came, most of them fled," said David.

"They left their children?"

"Many do," he said. "That's why we're here. These kids have nothing left."

We eventually arrived at the compound where we were staying in the commune of Croix-des-Bouquets, about eight miles outside Port-au-Prince. Through David's organization, Under Armour had sent down a team of relief workers who were staying with us. After unpacking, we all hopped in a pickup truck and went back into the city. As we drove through one of the more devastated areas, children as young as five or six began peeking their heads out from under the debris. They must have recognized either the truck or David, because they ran toward us, and David told them to jump in the back. We picked up maybe seven or eight of them this way, lost kids with no home, no parents, and barely anything to eat or drink. David then drove us to a nearby soccer field where we all got out and played with the kids for a bit, kicking the soccer ball around. You would have thought it was Christmas morning the way these kids laughed and screeched with joy. They crowded around me, picking at my clothes, my bracelet, my watch, my hat—anything that wasn't part of my body.

David looked on, smiling. "I hope you don't have anything too valuable," he said.

"Why? Are they going to steal it?" I asked.

Maddy laughed. "No! You're going to end up giving it all away to them."

And she was right. By the end of the trip, I had handed over nearly everything that seemed to catch the children's fancy. How could I keep it? I wanted them to have everything.

The next day, I learned that not all the parents had fled. Other children had joined us in the dirt roads, some with their parents. I found myself playing with this little boy the others called Tin Tin, whose mother was nearby, watching. At one point I had Tin Tin on my shoulders, running around with him, and then set him down. I looked up and noticed the mother was looking at me, not exactly angrily, but definitely determined. I walked over to David.

"Is she mad that I was playing with her son?" I asked.

David shook his head. "No," he said. "She hopes you take him with you to America when you leave."

Tin Tin and I soon started to play with a "toy" that I had picked up. The way he acted, it was like I had given him the most amazing toy he had ever seen. But it was just a plastic bag, and all I was doing was blowing it up like a balloon. Tin Tin just laughed and laughed.

Another boy they had found a year earlier we called Banner, because of the Incredible Hulk shirt he was wearing. Banner had been found in one of the many garbage heaps that were just piled throughout the city eating garbage and using the refuse as his bed. Banner had cerebral palsy and had been abandoned by his parents when he was just two or three years old, as many special-needs children are in Haiti.

David's organization did what it could for these lost children, such as building schools and improving access to basic necessities. But the sheer number of orphaned children was staggering, and most of these children would remain on the streets, growing up as urchins or else succumbing to disease, thirst, or starvation. Especially when I was down there after the hurricane, there was almost nothing for the regular people by way of food, water, and shelter. The Haitian government simply isn't equipped (or is too corrupt) to manage a humanitarian crisis of this magnitude, which is why David started his organization with his brothers in the first place. They do what they can, when they can, even if it's just a drop in the bucket.

The next day, Maddy took me aside before we headed out to visit an orphanage.

"This is going to be one of the hardest things you ever do," she said.

We then drove to the orphanage, although you have to rid yourself of American ideas of what an orphanage looks like. This wasn't a place where kids lived in relative comfort and security until adoption. This was a place where lost children were *stored*. As we walked inside, I saw wooden cages stacked on top of each other, several feet high. Dangling out of the cages were little arms and legs, children as young as three or four years old trapped inside.

We also visited the nursery, where babies with severe mental or physical abnormalities were kept. At least they had cribs, but otherwise these were children who had been rejected by their parents for their differences. Maddy and I were able to hold a couple of them—probably the first time they had ever been held lovingly—before armed officers entered the room and escorted us back outside. I don't remember ever breathing air that felt so free. We had only been inside a few moments, but it was enough to prove Maddy's prediction correct. Even then, nothing could have prepared me for the horror I had seen inside that terrible place.

A feeling of utter helplessness gripped me. I wanted to open those cages and set those children free. I wanted to take as many as I could back home with me, where at least they had a chance at life. But there was nothing any of us could do. David and Maddy wanted me to see it because they wanted me to realize that when we ran the marathon, *this* was who we were raising money for. I had never wanted to run 26.2 miles so badly in my life.

On our last night in Haiti, David took the whole group to dinner at the Hilton, which was a few districts away. During dinner, however, our armed escort suddenly erupted into the dining room and whispered to David it was time to go. They weren't messing around, either. They were literally pulling us out of our chairs and hustling us to the doors.

"We have to go now," said David, looking directly at me.

We all ran outside and jumped into the Land Rover, as our protective detail gunned it down the road. I mean, we were flying through these darkened streets. I was totally confused at what was going on until I looked behind me. Out the back window, the whole horizon was on fire, a reddish-orange glow that seemed to swallow the entire night sky. I would learn later that the towns-folk had rioted because of the election results. They burned down most of the town. And as we were careening through the streets, trying to avoid the mob that would surely have given us trouble if we had stopped, I started to laugh. I was in the back seat with one of the Under Armour guys. We were both laughing almost hysterically. I was scared for my life and all I could do was laugh. Maybe it was just a release of nerves. After several days of witness-ing such horrific suffering, my brain just couldn't take any more. But there was also this dark absurdity to the whole ordeal, as if it couldn't be real. That this level of misery and violence could be considered living was a concept I just couldn't grasp. I still can't. But it was all too real. Those children were real. Tin Tin was real. Banner was real. The cages were real. And those arms and legs that dangled from the cages were real as well.

And maybe that's why, as I laughed almost maniacally, another man in the Land Rover started to cry.

A NEW HOBBY

I spent only four days in Haiti, but when I finally returned to Charleston, it felt like I had been gone months. It's hard to describe the changes that the experience triggered in me; some were immediate, like wanting to help David's organization more directly, while others have matured over time. There was an awakening in me, a realization that my world and my problems were manageable after all. I wish I could say that this feeling stuck with me, but that's not how life works. I've found that you either grow or shrink depending on your surroundings. If your world is small, then your concerns will be small. When you open that world up, you expand both mentally and spiritually to take in the breadth of those new horizons. You can't expect a single experience, good or bad, to change your life. You have to *use* that experience to help you grow, and change will happen over time. So while I might have fallen back into my old ways upon returning home, I held on to that experience, and in time, it would lead me to helping others the way David and Maddy tried to help those lost children.

As filming for that fall continued, and I occupied my time with my hobbies and continued to (slowly) work toward finishing my thesis, a package arrived for me one day. Inside was my first sewing machine. I had purchased a nice model, one that did a lot of the more technical skills by itself, including embroidery. All the user had to do was set it and let the machine work. Now, the question of *why* should be addressed. Unfortunately, the answer is pretty banal, at least for me. I bought a sewing machine not because I wanted to start making pillows or anything; I bought it so that I could embroider. That's it. I enjoyed altering clothes and adding my own design flourishes on them. I love accent-based clothing and wanted to make my own. My love of clothing is no secret to viewers of the show. I am drawn to bright, bold colors that make a statement. Why drape yourself in something bland?

Embroidery, for me, was an offshoot of that love of ostentatious fashion, a way to be the *creator* of my own patterns. I wasn't all that skilled at it, but I didn't have to be. The machine did most of the work. As I played with my new toy, I did pick up some skills that I started to employ. Far from being the start of a new passion, much less a profession, the sewing machine was simply another hobby I added to my growing collection; one that allowed me to work with my hands, as the others did, and create.

But to Naomie, the sewing machine was just another distraction for me. She saw me accumulate these hobbies like a child goes through new toys. On to the next, the old forgotten for something bright and shiny. And look, there was an element of truth to that. My procrastination, a consequence of my ADHD, isn't about doing nothing; it's about doing anything *but* what I'm supposed to be doing. Even Adderall, that special little pill that I had discovered in college that seemed to answer all my prayers, wasn't magical enough to make me focus on what I had to do. It just made me do something with intense focus for a while. There were therapeutic qualities to my hobbies that I can't deny; they helped me relieve stress in a healthy way. But they also added to my stress by giving me yet one more thing to do except for the thing I had to do. All of which is to say that I could have finished my thesis much sooner than I did. Naomie knew this. Which was why she started to get resentful at my hobbies, especially my sewing. She'd come home from a long day, interacting with people who were trying to achieve their professional and educational dreams, and find her boyfriend at his sewing machine. She thought I was wasting my time—and my talents.

I get that. I can't say that my sewing in those early days was all about passion and entrepreneurship. But I have always thought that our hobbies, whether they rise to a passion or not, are also important and useful. They allow us to lose ourselves in an activity that brings us joy. We all can't have jobs that also function as hobbies. I mean, that's the goal, I suppose, but most are not lucky enough to find that. We pursue hobbies because they give us an outlet for creative expression, for knowledge, and for community. This last benefit I wouldn't understand for a couple more years, but it has certainly been one of the greatest joys of my life to meet others who share my love of sewing. We develop a genuine love for these little activities or pursuits that make us happy. Most of us never intend to turn this love into a money-making venture, and that's fine too. But I also know people who make money at their jobs *so that* they can more freely enjoy their hobbies. What they do at work doesn't define them; their hobbies, their home, their family—that's what defines them.

Certainly as a man, I felt that tug of professional embarrassment. I was approaching thirty and still had very little to show for it, aside from a successful reality TV career. While gender roles have certainly matured over the previous decades, I still felt that sting. I'd see other friends who were living their professional dreams *and* making money, and I wondered why I couldn't be like them. Why couldn't I get going? Why did I so swiftly lose my fire over a new professional opportunity? I wouldn't have answers to these questions for many years. But at the time I was deeply bothered by my inability to answer them.

And this helps explain the seesaw of my life that viewers saw in seasons 4 and 5. Even the hobbies that brought me joy also brought me embarrassment. Not because sewing is "unmanly," but because it was just another thing I was doing instead of what I should have been doing. So when Naomie attacked that vulnerability in me, she usually hit her mark. I didn't care what Shep thought or Whitney or any of my other friends. Let them laugh at me at my sewing machine. But Naomie? Yes, that hurt.

A MASSIVE FAILURE

"Successful people don't sleep all day. You sometimes exhibit loser behavior by doing that. I don't want to come home after a fourteen-hour day and you still be in bed. I don't want that."

Naomie said this during a therapy session while the cameras were there. We had made the decision to attend therapy together, although the psychiatrist I saw for my Adderall prescription had helped me see the potential. I often spoke to him about my resentments with Naomie, especially the way she put me down, and he was able to confirm that I wasn't being ridiculous. My hope in going to a therapist was that Naomie would be able to hear from someone else how her words and actions affected me. I clearly couldn't get through to her, but someone else might.

By this point, toward the end of 2016, I had finished my thesis and had earned my law degree. In my mind, accomplishing these tasks, however delayed they may have been, would lead to a natural reconciliation between us. I could finally sign up to take the bar and start studying, finishing what I had started so many years earlier. Instead, things continued to get worse. My dabbling in other pursuits had further annoyed her, to the point that she doubted whether I was serious about the law. I started to think that I could never please her. And I think, looking back, there was some truth to this. The man she wanted me to be—the successful, powerful attorney—just wasn't who I was at the time. I had the potential, but I wanted more out of life than to settle in as a lawyer till the end of my days.

So I grew resentful. I saw her constant badgering about my career as a sign that she was ashamed of me. Instead of a successful, ambitious lawyer with a thriving practice, she had a boyfriend who slept all day and sat at his sewing machine when he was awake. *Yes, he has his law degree now, but he isn't doing anything with it!* During this period, I had started to think that I could start a company, and even spoke with a friend about being my partner. We called it Flawed, and our original idea was to make it an eccentric, accessory-based clothing line. By this point in my sewing, I was experimenting with adding creative accents to my own wardrobe, and I thought this could be the start of a new brand and profession for me. But the clothing line never got much farther than the concepting phase, and so to Naomie, it was just another one of my failures.

And maybe it was. I was still two years away from starting a *real* company, and I only accomplished that after receiving much-needed help. Instead of supporting me, though, Naomie rolled her eyes and ridiculed me, killing my confidence from the very start. Now here's where I want to add that I think we were both right, and both wrong. Naomie was right in that I often failed to follow through on anything, and that these hobbies or business ideas were mostly a distraction from what I *should* have been doing, which was the law. But I was right in assuming that if she loved me, then she *should* support me. She should have been my biggest supporter! But if I wasn't moving forward with a real profession, then Naomie didn't want to hear about it.

I saw her complaints as an attempt to shame me into being this person she was *supposed* to be with. But I didn't think I was any different from the man Naomie had fell in love with a year earlier. I hadn't changed; Naomie's expectations had changed. I constantly reminded her that my schedule used to be *our* schedule, until she had started school. She had had no problem with it then; she had loved our life together. Why, then, should I have to change, since I was the same man? I could never understand this, even if now I can acknowledge that my schedule wasn't conducive to building any kind of life with someone. And however much pressure Naomie might have been getting from the fans on social media to ditch the loser, she was right to want to push me to try harder to pursue my dreams.

These are the kinds of truths that you accept long after the emotion of the moment has passed. In the moment, I was hurt, and I was resentful. I often lost my temper during our fights and snapped at her, which the cameras captured. I regret these outbursts, just as I regret my refusal to change anything about myself that might meet Naomie halfway. The more I felt she wanted me to be this other person, the more I refused to be anyone other than who I was. Granted, who I was then wasn't the best version of me. I didn't care. I wasn't going to change simply because she thought she deserved to be with someone who looked good on paper. I knew what her friends were saying; I knew what viewers were saying; and I knew that everyone was wondering why she was with me. Let them say whatever they want about the guy who likes to sew. What angered me was that Naomie *listened* to them instead of supporting me. She had ceased to trust me and had put her trust in others, believing they had her best interests at heart. I was locked out; these strangers were let in.

So by the time we sat down with the therapist, both of us were carrying this overflowing anger and resentment toward each other. Worse, we both were too proud to back down and hear the other's side. We both accused the other of verbal abuse. To be sure, the cameras didn't help. There's simply no way to have an honest therapy session when you know millions of people are going to see it. But we had no choice with the cameras; they had to be there because we went during filming. And as one would expect, we left the session angrier than when we had walked in. Naomie wasn't even talking to me. I kept asking her what was wrong as a camera crew followed us out. We eventually got home and went inside, only to have the crew show up on our doorstep.

I locked them out, screaming through the door that they couldn't come in. To be fair to the crew, they had every right to be there. They were just doing their jobs. Then Naomie became angry at how upset I was. Eventually the crew left, and our tempers cooled. But it didn't matter. The whole day had been a massive failure.

THE COLLAPSE

In early May 2017, there was a knock on my door. I remember the time. It was 12:57 p.m. I rushed to the door, because I had been expecting this visitor. I pulled it open to see my friend and old law school classmate, Andrew, standing there. I had asked Andrew to monitor the results, since I was too nervous to do it myself. I just wanted to shut it out. When I saw him, he was smiling broadly, but then gave me a weird look. It's only then that I realized I was in my gym shorts with no shirt. Whatever.

Andrew smiled again.

"Did I really fucking pass?" I asked, my voice cracking with nervousness and excitement.

"You fucking passed!" he said. I started to shout with joy. Naomie came running to the door. Saw the two of us shouting and hugging, realized what it was all about, and started shouting and hugging me as well.

I had passed the bar.

About an hour later, after I had put on a shirt and a decent pair of shorts, Naomie's dad, Joel, came by the house with a nice bottle of champagne. He poured everyone a glass, including himself. Naomie and I were stunned. Joel hadn't had a drink in twenty years—not for any substance abuse reasons, but simply because he just wasn't a drinker. But now he was about to toast me. We raised our glasses and celebrated. It was perhaps our last happy memory together as a couple.

A few weeks later, in June, Naomie left to study abroad in Budapest for six weeks. I stayed home and looked after our cats.

There was Gizmo, whom viewers knew and loved, but there was also Zee, a rescue cat we had adopted together. Viewers never saw Zee because, as the producers told us, "everyone already loves Gizmo." The producers thought it would be too complicated for the audience to keep track of two cats. Poor Zee, but Naomie and I loved him just as much as Gizmo, and there was something nice about not having to share him with the world. I also visited the Olindos for dinner a couple of times.

My other task was to keep watch of the construction we were having done to our new house. It was going to be almost an exact replica of our current home, the one the Olindos had bought for us. It was also right next door to our current home, a fact that upset our elderly neighbor, who didn't appreciate all the construction sounds early in the morning. I wasn't too happy either, since the work encroached on my garden in the backyard. Unlike our previous house, I was told by Naomie that I would have more control in the new one, meaning I would be able to make design decisions. That didn't last very long, and soon I was sending pictures of the construction to Naomie in Europe, working as a middleman between her and Joel as they made decisions. It was like I wasn't there anymore.

It wasn't long after Naomie returned that we traveled to Charlotte for Maddy and David's wedding. Despite our joy together in my having passed the bar, things weren't any better. I could tell that far from making her miss me, Europe had only broadened the rift between us. Her words to me that evening, after the ceremony, that she was never going to be my "biggest fan," hurt me deeply, and maybe that's why I went out that night. Or maybe I didn't appreciate just how close Naomie was to ending things.

Later, we were invited to stay at a hotel downtown as a promotional stunt. I thought it was a great opportunity to reconnect and work on us. That night, after I had popped an Adderall, I started to crave a beer and told her I was going to head down to the local store to grab a six-pack. On my way, I saw J.D. and some other friends at his nearby bar. They asked me to join them, but I continued to the store. On my way back, however, passing them once again, they asked me to take a picture with some fans, so I agreed to pop in for a drink. Naomie knew where I was, because she could ping my phone. She saw I was in a bar. I eventually did call her and asked her to come down, but she refused. I should have left right then. Instead, I stayed for over an hour. When I got back to the room, Naomie was in bed, and then she turned in bed to look at me. She didn't need to say anything. I started to cry.

I had thought that her time away would do us both a world of good, but it just revealed how far apart we had grown. We often talked about how the show accelerated things, meaning we had to discuss how we felt and what we thought before we were truly ready. You can't just clam up or walk away with the cameras rolling. You have to say *something*, and this is usually a gut response to whatever drama is going on. And, often, when it's a moment with your girlfriend, saying something is much, much worse than keeping your mouth shut. Because once those half-baked thoughts or feelings are out there, you are kind of forced to talk about them. In other words, working on your relationship as normal people do isn't possible during filming. We both needed time away from the cameras, and, perhaps equally as much, we needed time away from each other.

Despite everything that had been said between us, I still truly believed that we would recapture that happiness we had once known. I had changed, hadn't I? I had my law degree; I had passed the bar; I was going to be sworn in as a lawyer. I could *finally* be the man Naomie wanted me to be. I wanted things to be different, and I believed they could be.

We eventually got ready to move into the new house. And that's when Naomie told me she wanted to let our friend Wilson move in with us as a renter, to help bring in extra income. I had nothing against Wilson, but I felt like this was a move *backward* from where we should be headed. This was our second house together. We should be thinking about starting our lives as husband and wife. And now we'd have a renter?

Of course, I knew what the decision meant. Naomie didn't want to move forward. I was losing her. As we argued, she finally said it.

"Craig, I don't love you anymore."

There it was. The words she had wanted to say to me for months. I slept in the guest room that night and woke up the next day to find a note from her. She apologized, using the pet names we had for each other. *I just want my Craigy back*, she wrote.

Maybe she had said it in a moment of anger. Maybe things could be like they had been.

But no. She'd meant what she'd said. I was tired. I didn't want to play the game anymore with her—and I finally accepted that we shouldn't live together anymore. So I moved out, taking Zee with me for the time being.

This wasn't really the end of our relationship. I ended up staying at the house of our friends, Graham and Anna Heyward, whose wedding we had attended back in April in the Bahamas. They were still there, so they let me crash at their empty house until they returned at the end of the summer. Naomie and I still saw each other regularly, often for dinners.

I wish I could say that living alone helped me recenter myself a bit. But that wasn't the case. I was taking more Adderall than ever, only I really had zero reason to be taking it other than to numb my own sadness. I was stressed and felt lost. Now I realize why. Naomie had given me purpose, and I felt that purpose was slipping away. I had to start looking at a life that didn't have her in it. A year earlier I had felt in control; it didn't matter what happened with the show, with the law, as long as I had Naomie. But without her, I felt like I was losing everything. My emotions were shot, my patience was gone, and I couldn't see a way out of it.

And it was while I was in this headspace that Graham and Anna Heyward let me know they would be back in a couple weeks. Typically, I procrastinated on cleaning the house for their return. Naomie knew I was procrastinating and finally decided to come over to help, over my protestations. It was such a stupid thing to get angry about, but once again, I thought, *She thinks I can't do something; she thinks I'm not good enough.*

Hopped up on Adderall, I told her I would do it, that she didn't need to be there. But she ignored my protests and started cleaning, and she cleaned in a way that made me even angrier. It wasn't how I would clean. She wasn't doing it right. I was going to do it right. I could do it. Let me do it!

"No, you won't," she shouted. And that's when I snapped.

"Get the fuck out!" I heard myself shout.

She paused. Only for a moment, before she grabbed her stuff, picked up Zee, whose home was always the house where Naomie and I lived, and walked to her car. I watched her from the kitchen window. She sat in the driver's seat, her head down. She started to cry. Then she picked her head up, wiped away her tears, and backed out of the driveway.

I could've run after her, but I didn't.

6

SEARCHING FOR SOMETHING

*W*hen I was a child, I used to pray at night for homeless people to have something soft to sleep on to find some moment of comfort. Maybe that's a strange thing for a child to pray for, but I just thought how terrible it was for them to have to sleep on the ground. For some reason, this memory came back to me when I was living at Anna Heyward and Graham's house. Because my machine was packed away in a U-Haul, I was sitting at Anna Heyward's sewing station trying to come up with an idea of what to create. My attempts at starting a clothing line, Flawed, had fizzled, mostly because I eventually realized how difficult it was to sew clothes. But I had settled firmly on the notion that I should create *something* that would lead to a commercial endeavor—or perhaps just a side hustle.

My law career was in limbo (again) at that point, for reasons I'll address later. But honestly, I wasn't ready to start practicing.

In the years since I had left law school, and having filmed four seasons of *Southern Charm*, I saw my law career as something I would fall back on later. Yes, I was determined to get sworn in as a lawyer in the state of South Carolina, I just wasn't ready to settle into *being* a lawyer. I had never forgotten Akim's advice to me four years earlier, which boiled down to: Enjoy being on television now; you can always be a lawyer later. Indeed, it seemed wasteful to me to not use the platform I had developed since being on the show. My law degree was an insurance policy; it would be there when I needed it. But my status and my platform were likely more fleeting. They wouldn't be around forever, so why shouldn't I take advantage of them now?

Except I didn't know how to take advantage of them. Which was why I was sitting at Anna Heyward's sewing station, wracking my brain for a viable idea. The one that popped in there was to start sewing portable sleeping mats for homeless people and develop some kind of charity around giving them out. It wasn't much, but it was enough to send me to the store that day to look for materials. I bought faux leather, vinyl, thread, and whatever else I thought would be useful for a sleep mat. Back at the house, I started to experiment with some designs, but I couldn't make any work. Maybe I wasn't good enough . . . or maybe it was just a bad idea.

I grew frustrated. I needed to complete something, but what? Then I thought, *How about a pillow?* I knew how to make those from my home economics class way back in seventh grade. I went out to the U-Haul, where I was keeping most of my stuff, and grabbed some shirts I didn't wear and used them for fabric, cutting them into squares. I sat down at the machine and went to work. When I finished, I turned the cover right side out to inspect the stitching. All hidden. Not bad. I then put in some cheap polyester stuffing and closed it up. And there it was: my first pillow. And damn, did it feel great. I immediately wanted to make more. So I dashed over to Hobby Lobby for some more fabric and materials, then went back to the house and started on the next one. Then made one more after that. When I finally stepped away from the machine, I had three pretty good-looking pillows. I set them up nicely and snapped a picture, which I posted to Instagram.

Maybe it's not quite as inspiring as building a computer in your garage, but it was a start. And that was all I needed: a start.

DESPERATION AND RIDICULE

It's a mistake to think that my first pillows provided me with immediate happiness. When I sat down to make them, Naomie and I were still together, even if I had already moved out. But the end was approaching, in that terrible, agonizing way that most relationships end. I could see it even if I couldn't believe it. It's like events had outrun my ability to process them. Making pillows helped me take my mind off some of it. I don't just mean the relationship. I mean all those emotions that wrapped themselves into this ball of anger, confusion, and regret. It would take time to unwrap that ball, but it wasn't going anywhere for the moment. I had to sit with it. And as long as I was sitting, I might as well be sewing.

The point is that those first pillows didn't suddenly erase or alleviate all those feelings. They didn't suddenly eradicate my Adderall addiction or make me more disciplined. There was no lightning bolt from the sky that suddenly made me look up and say, "I have found my passion!" while a choir of angels sang. In fact, I don't recall a moment like that, ever. I feel like we wait for that magical moment because we think things will get easier afterward. Things might get clearer, but they don't get easier. I had a long, dark valley to walk before I would end up on the other side with something resembling a pillow business. At that point, with filming for season 5 just around the corner, I was on the precipice of depression and about to dive right in.

It would take more than a year for me to realize that I was depressed. When you're in the middle of it, it's very difficult to look at yourself critically, unless you've experienced it before and can recognize the signs. I reverted to my old habits after the breakup, going out all night, sleeping all day. I would find the time to make a pillow here or there, but those moments were few and far between. I had nothing that one would consider a "business plan" or even the beginnings of a business. I fell back into the Neverland world of Charleston and got lost in it once more. My housing situation wasn't helping things. With the money I made from the show, I managed to buy my own house, but because of some water damage, it needed a lot of repairs. So, I lived like a vagabond for a bit, shuffling from one rental or friend's place to the next, waiting for my house to be ready. This constant moving leads to a certain kind of lifestyle: messy, aimless, undisciplined. I had no sanctuary, no place to call my own, and I indulged in the

Learning to play the drums on pots and pans

Halloween 1990 (two years old)

Learning to surf at five years old on Fenwick Island, in front of my grandparents' house (Stormbait)

My first karate tournament, on my way to black belt

Looking dapper with Christopher for Easter Sunday

On my way to little league baseball in what would become my first car

My best friend Champ

Winning my first art contest with pastels

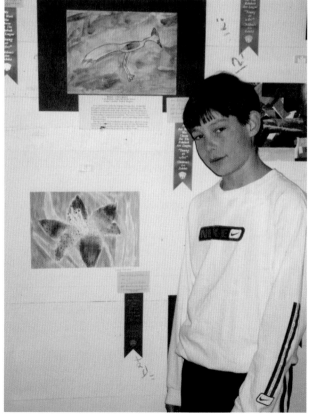

Beach day with my brother, Christopher

Celebrating my favorite holiday with my family

Christmas with my mom's parents, Granny and Pop Pop (at seventeen years old)

Celebrating my eighteenth birthday with my parents

High school graduation with Mom-Mom and Grandad (my dad's parents)

One of my proudest moments, being sworn in after passing the bar, with my mom and dad

Some of my fondest memories from my time in Haiti are of spending time with Tin Tin

One of the hardest moments in Haiti was visiting these young children with cerebral palsy amid dire circumstances

Spending time with the local boys down in Haiti, trying to become a better version of myself. This was an important moment for me because I realized how the platform I have can truly help those in need.

The pure brightness in their smiles and the positivity these kids put out into the universe left a profound mark on my soul. It allowed me to realize that even in the worst of times, a smile can go a long way.

Sean, Jerry, and me cooking Valentine's Day dinner for friends in 2007. Thankfully our fashion has evolved.

Kicking it back to the college days, rocking my bow tie with Matt

With my Kappa Sig brothers in 2009

Night out in Charleston with two of my best friends, Sean and Kory

Cougars for life!!

Gone huntin'

I bleed purple.
Go Ravens!!!

Some of us could handle the smell; some of us couldn't. Also covering our mouths to keep the black water out.

Taking in the destruction caused by hurricane flooding and trying to keep it together while lending a hand to those in need

When I knew my sewing wasn't pretend: signing our deal with Thomasville and Nick Woodhouse, president of Authentic Brands Group

The start of my pillow empire—doing a little sewing down at the factory

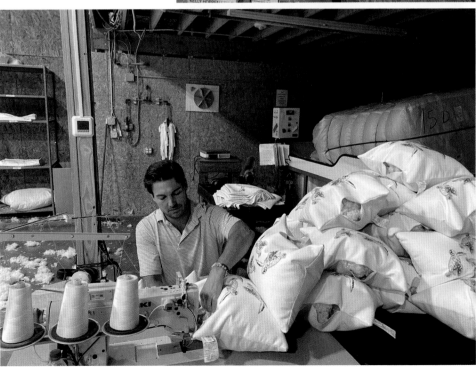

BTS of my HSN debut from my Charleston home during Covid (April 2020)

Pilllows on pillows on pillows, part of the ten thousand units HSN ordered

Austen and me with a little Pillow Talk on *Watch What Happens Live*

Jerry and me enjoying Halls Chophouse and celebrating signing this book deal

Team spirit after our grand opening of the flagship Sewing Down South store

Baby Marlowe, Jerry, Alexis, me, Amanda, and Ben at the friends and family opening of the Sewing Down South flagship

Just a little Pillow Talk!

worst kind of behaviors. And those behaviors pushed me deeper into a nihilistic misery.

There's an obvious question in there, which is: Why wasn't I practicing the law? I might have wanted to save the law for my post-TV career, but at this point, all I had was my television career. At least I could get sworn in as a lawyer and have that route open to me. The answer is that I couldn't get sworn in. I was notified by the Supreme Court of South Carolina that my application to be sworn in had been put on hold, and that I was called to appear at a character and fitness hearing. I would come to learn that the court had received an anonymous tip that I was ethically unfit to perform the responsibilities of a lawyer. There was nothing I could do about it until my hearing date, which was scheduled for the winter.

Once more, the closer I got to becoming a lawyer, the further away I felt. My own mistakes aside, I felt at this point that my long run of bad luck was simply ridiculous. First, my thesis, then my law school closed, now this. I don't know if I was necessarily feeling sorry for myself, but my attitude started to affect other areas of my life. In season 5, there are several shots inside the house, which my friend, Sean, shared with me as a renter, and dear Lord, it's a damn mess. Sure, two bachelors living together aren't going to maintain the same level of cleanliness as Naomie and I did, but I'm embarrassed by how I lived—and it definitely wasn't Sean's fault! Of course, I wasn't entirely blind to what was going on. I knew something was wrong, and this was the reason I saw a "life coach" during this period. Well, I saw her twice. She would give me "homework," to work on building discipline and overcoming my procrastination. I didn't do the homework because it was just another source of anxiety for me. I stopped calling her back because I was ashamed of my own inability to finish anything. Which is crazy: I stopped seeing my life coach for the very reason I started seeing her. Fuck it, whatever.

Perhaps the only good part of my "fuck it" approach at this point was that I didn't much care what others thought about my sewing. The jokes had started the previous season and only picked up pace during season 5. I've never been blind to the optics of a straight man enjoying a more "feminine" hobby. But the optics never bothered me, nor did the occasional jabs. I had never felt self-conscious about it, and I certainly wasn't going to let my friends make me feel bad either. I don't know what would have happened had I let their ridicule get to me. Maybe I would have quit. Maybe I would have put all my energies toward the law. Regardless, I wouldn't be where I am today. I suppose that out of all the darkness going on in my life at that time, my ability to rise above the haters stands out as the one bright spot.

I also had some supporters in my corner, even in those early days of pillow-making. For starters, there was Kathryn, who offered some much-needed validation of my newfound pillow passion. She also said something to me in episode 5, when she came with me to that fabric store, that has stuck with me. "Prove your worth to yourself, not to someone else." More on that later. Kathryn was one of my earliest and staunchest cheerleaders. I think she had a degree of sympathy for me during this period. She saw I was often the butt of jokes, same as she had been. Our lives—from both the inside and outside—looked like wrecks. She, too, had to struggle with her perception on the show just as I did. It is very difficult to break free of those impressions, especially when that's what a lot of viewers *want* to see. Of course, there was truth to my lack of direction and focus. But when that's all that viewers see, then of course they see a loser. It was the charge of being a loser that *did* get to me, not jokes about my sewing.

The other source of encouragement I received was from the fans themselves. I got my first sense of their support when I posted that IG photo of those first three pillows. The outpouring of appreciation was . . . well, incredible. I knew I had my online supporters, those who were pulling for me to "make something" of myself. (I also had plenty of detractors.) But this was the first time I had seen such a display of respect and appreciation. What I had been able to stitch together in a rare moment of manic inspiration had somehow found an audience, and for the first time I read a comment that I would read again and again, thousands of times over the next two years: "Where can I buy one?"

Well, nowhere. I wasn't selling them yet. I had thought about it, but that's where my progress ended—in my thoughts. But it was the encouragement I needed to make more, and post more on IG. More encouragement, more questions about buying my pillows, and then more pillows. And during this erratic process I discovered something that I hadn't considered before. I had the power to address my supporters directly. With my IG account, I could go around the cameras. I could use my voice and my platform to share a side of me that few saw. And I learned something else: Those who were pulling for me to "make it," didn't do so because they really wanted some kid from Delaware who already made plenty of money being on a television show to make more money. They were pulling for me because they saw a part of themselves in me. If I could overcome my demons and failings, then they could too.

I can't explain it any better than that, and I don't mean to sound conceited on this point. Sewing Down South simply wouldn't exist if it wasn't for my supporters who stood by me during this rough patch of my life. Initially, I might have turned to sewing pillows to help alleviate the pain and confusion I was feeling because of my breakup. That much is true. But I continued to sew pillows because of those who saw value not just in what I was making but also in what I was doing. I was carrying on. I was trying.

Then of course I almost screwed it all up again. In episode 6 of season 5, I met with Patricia Altschul, who wanted me to design a couple of pillows for her home décor brand. The background to this on-camera meeting is that Patricia's business partners had approached me to do a line of pillows for her company. They, too, had seen what I had seen from my IG posts: There was demand for Craig Conover pillows. But demand without a company or a sales channel doesn't amount to much. That's where they saw their opportunity. The idea was that I would design a few pillows, which they would slap my name on and sell under their own company. Not having any other opportunities, I accepted their offer. Why not? I was no closer to starting my own company than I had been when I sewed my first pillows.

The partnership with Patricia was a legitimate opportunity, one through which I would finally have a channel to sell my pillows. But I think it's important to remember that Patricia and her business partners didn't approach me because of my design capabilities. At this stage, my design "style" amounted to what kinds of patterns and fabrics appealed to me at the store. Rather, my value to Patricia was the demand I brought. She would get to sell pillows with my name on it. In that way, it was a very transactional deal, and wasn't really a validation of my artistic abilities. Nevertheless, I was on the hook for designing two prototype pillows. My deadline was two weeks.

Almost two months later, I still hadn't delivered anything. That was on me. The explanation for why I had failed to deliver was a combination of my age-old procrastination matched with my ongoing depression. In this case, my procrastination manifested as an inability to make a decision unless everything was perfect. This would be a recurrent problem for me as I set out to build my own company. Hopped up on Adderall, I would stay up all night working on designs but unable to decide on any of them. They weren't perfect, and if they weren't perfect, then I was paralyzed. So I had nothing to show for all those hours I spent "working." The other part, of course, was that I simply didn't have the discipline to stick with it. My partying, my addiction, my ongoing anxiety over Naomie were all factors that led me to just stop trying. I couldn't find it within me to finish something I had started. It's like my passion would simply die, and once dead, there was almost no power in existence that could reignite it.

Oh, and I injured my hand, almost permanently. That, too, is entirely on me. Sean and I had moved into our new house, and I spent a lot of time staying up drinking and watching movies with friends. If I'm being honest, I chose partying over sewing as my main coping mechanism for getting over Naomie. In any case, there was a wall in our new house that I wanted to take down. I had made some progress, but mostly my attempts amounted to shedding drywall dust all over the living room. Then one night, while I was drunk, Sean told me to stop making a mess, and for some reason I grabbed a butter knife and tried to stab through the drywall. I thought it was hollow on the inside. It wasn't. The knife hit wood, slid out of my grip, and ended up slicing my hand, severing two tendons and almost my entire pinky finger. I had never bled so much in my life. Hell, I had never seen so much blood in my life. Sean and I wrapped it, and I prayed for the best. I would eventually get it all fixed with surgery, but the most immediate consequence of my drunkenness was that I couldn't sew for a while with my hand wrapped up and in a brace after the surgery. The knowledge of how it happened—because of my own idiocy—matched with the loss of the one passion that had taken my mind off Naomie (in a healthy way) worked to deepen my depression.

So when Patricia called me out of the blue to ask about the pillows, I had nothing to show her. I was stuck. I had to come up with something in an hour on my laptop. The result was predictably terrible, just some clip art I slapped on a pillow image. Patricia was unimpressed and more or less canceled our deal with the cameras rolling. I was humiliated and angry. "Deadlines are arbitrary," I muttered as I left the house. I don't really believe that. As usual, I was trying to find some justification to show that I hadn't been in the wrong. Humiliated, I wouldn't talk to her for several months afterward. But I also accepted that I had failed.

Even if the opportunity wasn't what I truly wanted, it was *an* opportunity. Patricia and her partners were offering more than I had at that moment, and I didn't deliver. I wish I could say that I'd failed because I wanted to fail; that I realized that selling my name was not how I envisioned my pillow career to take off. But the sad reality was that I just didn't get it done. It didn't matter if the opportunity, in the end, wasn't right for me. Someone had taken a chance on me, and I had failed to meet their expectations.

Of course I can't finish off talking about season 5 without mentioning the source for the subtitle of this book. Even though Naomie and I had broken up, she was a full-time cast member on the show, and I saw her often. We also saw each other away from the cameras as well, as we both tested whether the relationship was truly over. In this case, we were both at a baby shower thrown for Cam by Patricia, for which I had a half-made teddy bear for the newborn. During the gift-giving, while the rest of the cast cooed over my stitchwork, Naomie and I were in another room talking. As usual, the topic was Kathryn, whom Patricia hadn't invited to the party. Naomie's attempts to stick up for Kathryn with Patricia had been met with a very cold shoulder, and she sought me out to commiserate. I attempted to make her feel better about it by telling her not to take Patricia's cold shoulder personally.

But in what is probably normal for a couple who had never resolved their issues, our conversation quickly devolved into an argument. Naomie made a comment about my lack of action in the three years we had been dating, as a backhanded way to applaud what I was then trying to do in the two months since we had broken up. What I heard was that she was comparing this new Craig to the loser she had dated, and I lost my patience. Then Naomie lost hers.

"You sit home and you sew and you pretend to do things," she said.

It wasn't so much what she said, it was how she'd said it. With her hand gestures and tone of voice, she was incredibly dismissive. This thing—this hobby, this passion, this pursuit—was just waved away as if it meant nothing. I was hurt and humiliated. It was perhaps the only time that someone's mockery of my sewing truly got to me—and it's no accident that it was Naomie who said it. I paused. And for a brief moment I lowered my voice, in pain as much as anger.

"What's wrong with my sewing?" I responded quietly.

Of course, it wasn't my sewing she was mocking. The sewing was just a symbol of everything that I had failed to be in her eyes. It was the late nights. It was the sleeping all day. It was the thesis, then the bar. It was my procrastination. It was the man I hadn't become for her.

If sewing was a symbol of my pursuit of passion and purpose, it was for her just another sign that I would never change.

TRAVELING TO ESCAPE

After season 5 wrapped, I escaped. Or tried to. Several factors made me want to leave Charleston, and yes, most involved Naomie. I was still in love with her *and* I knew that our relationship was broken. That's a bit of a no-win situation. I traveled to Los Angeles with my friend Austen for a press tour, and while there I sort of realized that an entire world existed beyond the suffocating confines of Charleston. I wanted to keep traveling, much as one does when they attempt to "find themselves." It was the right decision, but not in the way I expected.

In between my travels, I had to confront my status with the South Carolina Supreme Court. Rather than try to fit this story in a chronological framework, I'll simply tell it now. As I said, the court had notified me that my application to be sworn in was on hold pending a hearing. I wasn't informed about the reasons for the investigation, although I suspected that it involved my arrest in college. Little did I know . . .

On my way to the hearing, the father of a friend of mine, also a lawyer, had called me to wish me luck. He also asked if he could pray for me. I felt it was a bit overly dramatic, but I appreciated the gesture and joined him in prayer. When the hearing started, I faced all five justices of the South Carolina Supreme Court. As they began to talk, I suddenly realized that this had nothing to do with my arrest in college. This was about my association with the show, as well as my connection with a convicted felon, Thomas Ravenel. There also was reference to a "tip" the court had received, which accused me of substance abuse on the show. The justices had zeroed in on specific moments in the show when my friends had indicated I could have a drinking problem. Per the court's request, Cam and Shep had even provided affidavits to explain some of their comments about me from the show, in order to speak to my character.

As the justices went down their list, my mind reeled. I was wholly unprepared to defend myself in this manner. I was fortunate in that both Cam and Shep had extolled me as a person, but I had to answer for some of my antics. I had to take them through every moment that had caused them concern from the show. I had to convince them that my connection to Thomas began and ended with my time on the show. And after about an hour and a half of this grilling, the hearing ended. Sweating and exhausted, I felt I had defended myself well, but there was really no way to tell. I left the courthouse dejected and afraid—afraid for perhaps the first time in my life that this was something I couldn't escape. The justices held my future law career in their hands. It didn't matter how much work I had put in; how many hours I had agonized over first getting my degree, then passing the bar; or that in my private life I was a genuinely decent person with nothing shady or criminal in my background. I would make an excellent lawyer, if given the chance. I knew I would. That prayer I had said earlier suddenly felt very much needed. Now I just had to wait.

But at least I didn't have to wait long. On my way home, the court clerk called me.

"I just wanted to let you know that the justices are going to give you the all clear," she said.

I nearly cried in relief. My swearing-in ceremony happened a few weeks later, with my parents in attendance to witness the culmination of a journey that had begun nearly a decade earlier. During a very dark chapter of my life, I had reached a goal that had been so tantalizingly close for so long that at times I had taken it for granted. Close enough was good enough, right? Not at all. I think what scared me most was that I realized how much I had lost control in the direction of my own life. Partly through my own mistakes, and partly through just bad luck, the court had the power to decide whether I would be a lawyer or not. This terrified me. For over a year, ever since I felt my relationship with Naomie slipping away, I had felt increasingly subject to the decisions of others. The show could drop me the next day and where would I be? *Who* would I be? Just a washed-up former reality star? That wasn't a life I wanted; it wasn't the life I had accepted when I first decided to go on television. Or . . . was it? Had I willingly handed the control of my life over to others?

My court debacle made me ask these questions. It made me start to fear whether I was choosing the direction of my life or whether I was simply following the path others had chosen for me. I had accepted this bargain with the show as the opportunity of a lifetime. I had accepted that I couldn't have a law career *and* a television career at that time. It was one or the other, and I chose television. I couldn't have both. Now I started to understand that my choice was somewhat different. I could have the television career as my sole means of employment, which also meant I gave up a lot of control over my life. Or, I could have the television career *with* control. But what would give me that control?

Trying to answer this question is what sent me traveling during the winter of 2017 through the spring of 2018. With my life in Charleston once again in shambles, I set off in search of . . . something. I had fallen into the destructive mindset that living the life of a celebrity would bring me the happiness and comfort I couldn't find elsewhere. I visited friends in Los Angeles, New York City, and Miami. I stayed at the best hotels and partied with other celebrities. I went to swanky clubs and attended movie premieres. I socialized with others in my strange circle of celebrities and those who cling to them. I'd stay up late, sleep late, order room service, and repeat it all again. In L.A., I hung out with the cast from *Vanderpump Rules*. I saw Whitney several times and tagged along with him to parties where people would shower me with attention.

I wanted to believe that I was expanding my horizons beyond my insular world of Charleston. I wanted to believe that by hanging out with other celebrities, it showed I, too, belonged in this elite world of money and fame. I wanted to believe that the selfies and shots I took with fans meant I had made it. I didn't need Naomie. Look at everyone who wanted to hang out with me! How could I ever have thought that I had failed in my own aspirations when I was let into exclusive events and hobnobbed with the rich and famous? Didn't this mean I had made it? Didn't this mean I was someone? Didn't this mean I had control?

While in L.A., I brought a girl to one of Whitney's parties. It happened that another girl at the party caught my eye, which was fine because the girl I had brought caught Whitney's. I ended up talking with the new girl, whom I'll call Sophie, a model by profession, all night. Just like that, I felt happy again. The dragon I had been chasing but never caught turned out to be a connection with another human being. We spent the next couple days together, just hanging out and enjoying each other's company. One night we went out to a club together. While there, some monied older guys showed up, and one of them started talking to Sophie. He then looked over at me, before motioning to one of the bouncers. Before I realized what was happening, the bouncer was escorting me out of the club. I called to Sophie, asking her to vouch for me. She looked at the older man, then at me.

"I don't know you." I was crushed. How could she say that to me after the time we had spent together? The bouncer then kicked me out.

I flew out to Miami the next day. I knew what I had just witnessed. I knew I had just looked into a mirror that revealed the emptiness of my own "celebrity status." But I wasn't prepared to admit what I knew to be true. It would have exposed the lie of my travels. This wasn't about me "finding myself"; it was about me seeking validation from absolute strangers. The moment I felt a real connection with another person, I experienced immediate joy. I had latched on to it like a drowning man to a life raft. Did it matter that the person who let me *feel* again was herself trapped in this game of empty validation? I could not allow myself to admit these things. Not yet. The pain I felt was like a time machine, hurtling me back to my high school days when I had felt different and alone. I hated that feeling. And damn this woman for making me feel it again. So I left, flying to yet another city where I could lose myself and fill the bottomless void with attention, fame, and substances.

A few years later I would receive a message from Sophie. She wanted to apologize. More, she wanted to let me know that she was sober and going through the recovery process. Having known others who had gone through recovery, I could only imagine the courage it took her to reach out to me like she did. She had never been able to forget what she had done or said that night. What made it worse was that she had felt the connection that I had felt. She knew it was there. She had enjoyed our time together. And she had thrown it all away for a brief moment of validation from a rich, older guy. Just by her words to me I could tell she was hurting. Whatever satisfaction I might have received at her apology was overshadowed by my sympathy for her plight. We had been on the same journey. We had both been caught up in the empty promises of outside validation. And we had found each other in the maelstrom of celebrity culture. Neither of us had been ready then to admit that what we were doing was only prolonging our misery. And, strangely or not, we likely both realized the shallowness of what we had been trying to do.

My escape to Miami was no different than my escapes to New York or L.A. had been. More expensive hotels. More partying. More empty validation from strangers. Had I at least gotten over Naomie? In a way, I guess. My travels weren't entirely without benefit. I was able to meet new people and explore new places. I was able to stop thinking about Naomie all the time. What I wasn't able to do was replace the purpose she had given me with something else. I crossed the country in search of something I never found. And as summer approached, I found myself back in Charleston, but with no real plan on what to do next. I flew out to L.A. for a press tour, and that's when I got a call from Whitney. He was casting for a new production and wanted my help. The hook was that he would fly me down to Bimini in the Bahamas. I was on a plane the next day.

FINALLY, CALM

I joke that I got my groove back, like Stella, in the Bahamas. I
didn't travel there for that reason. My trip down there was simply
another location on my seemingly endless jet-setting lifestyle that
had brought much in the way of fun, but little in the way of progress. *What's one more place?* I thought.

When Americans think about the Bahamas, most think of
Bimini or Grand Bahama. They attract tourists who want to fish
the same waters as Ernest Hemingway or take advantage of the
great scuba diving and snorkeling. Or simply to party. That, in
any case, was my first experience with the Bahamas. A tropical
paradise that functioned primarily as a tourist hotspot. I stayed
there with Whitney for a few days and was scheduled to fly out
when I got in touch with my friends, Anna Heyward and Graham
Hegamyer, recently married. I had met both a year earlier through
Naomie, who was friends with them. They were engaged then and
planning a wedding in the Bahamas, which Naomie had been
invited to. I, however, was *not* invited, mostly because the bride
and groom had wanted a very small, intimate gathering of only
close friends. Which was why Naomie suggested a double date
in advance, where Anna Heyward and Graham could learn what
a fabulous guy I was. And for the most part, the trick worked,
although perhaps not as Naomie had expected. While we were
at the bar, and as Graham and I bonded over our mutual hatred
for some guy we both knew from our College of Charleston days,
someone had bought a shot for Naomie. She declined, instead
insisting on heading home. So the shot passed to Graham, who

happily downed it. About fifteen minutes later, I started to notice that Graham was slurring his words and wobbly. I helped steer him home. We both realized the next day that the shot intended for Naomie had been spiked. Unfortunately, we never knew who sent it. It might have led to a terrible hangover the next day, but at least it had forged a friendship between Graham and me. Point is, I got the invite to the wedding.

So when I was hanging in Bimini, I called Anna Heyward and Graham and kind of invited myself to visit them at their place in Marsh Harbour in the Abacos island chain. Fuck it, why not? A couple of days later I found myself sitting in a rickety seaplane that was probably older than I was. I was staring out the window as this thing lurched off the surf, the azure waters of the Bahamas expanding in every direction. The trip was so short that we didn't even pressurize; instead we descended into a steep dive that brought the plane, somehow intact, to the water. Somewhat shakily, I emerged from this tin can of an airplane and looked around at the divine beauty of the Abacos. Anna Heyward and Graham picked me up and we drove to their house in Marsh Harbour, which sits nestled on the northeastern edge of Great Abaco—as opposed to Little Abaco that juts out like a finger from the northwestern side.

The history of Abaco is fascinating in its own right, but is also relevant to my experience living there. The Marsh Harbour community is made up of the descendants of American colonists who had remained loyal to Great Britain during the Revolution and fled when their side lost. (Go, America!) It is an isolated community, even from the rest of the Bahamas, and also fiercely protective of its little slice of the world. Marsh Harbour is something of an anomaly in the interconnected world of the twenty-first century—not that it doesn't have all the technological benefits Americans are used to. Rather, it's a place where everyone knows everyone else and is leery of outsiders. And when I say "leery," I mean that they will welcome you as a tourist, but there's a definite separation between you and them. Which isn't to say they aren't friendly; they're extremely friendly. Tourists can fish and snorkel and enjoy the natural surroundings of this gorgeous island paradise, but to become part of the community first requires their explicit acceptance. Anna Heyward and Graham had worked hard to achieve this rare status inside Marsh Harbour, and I knew enough of the community's strict standards to understand that to be invited there was a sign that I was part of their inner circle. As long as they "vouched" for me, I was welcomed by the natives.

I ended up staying two weeks at the Hegamyers'. I spent the first week doing most of the typical touristy things one does: fishing, diving, going out on the boat, and spending quiet evenings on the dock with a cool drink listening to the sounds of the ocean. The change happened so suddenly that at first I didn't realize what was going on. But by the second week, I started to feel *home*, in a way that only Ocean View felt like home, and very different from the way I had felt staying in fancy hotels in L.A. or New York. There is a lot of similarity between where I grew up and Marsh Harbour, and if there's one place on this planet that gives me the same sense of comfort and protection, it's this tiny place in the Bahamas. I was living on the water again, as I had done as a kid. A calm had settled over me, which was a feeling I hadn't felt since the good days with Naomie. It's like I had found a place that stood outside the world that had battered me down. The anxieties, the fears, the constant need for validation—none of those things could touch me here. And for the first time in a long time, I wanted to stay in the same place. I was home.

During my second week, Graham returned to the States for some business, so, with our boat captain gone, Anna Heyward and I were able to explore the island and community in a different way. I met her friends, ate at her favorite restaurants, drank rosé on the dock, and was finally accepted by the couple's German shepherd, Deuce, as part of the pack. When Graham returned at the end of the week, he saw how I had made myself at home.

"So . . . ," he began, "should we find you a place down here?" It was the nicest way I've ever been kicked out of someone's house before. It was also one of the greatest compliments I've ever received. Basically, Graham, himself considered a Marsh Harbor local, was inviting me to a be a local as well. I was no longer a tourist.

"Absolutely," I replied. I boarded a plane for Charleston the next day to get more stuff. I realized then that I didn't even have suitcases large enough to meet the needs of an extended stay. I hit up Walmart where I bought two oversized suitcases, packed as much as I could, and was back on a plane a day later, headed to Marsh Harbour. When I returned, Graham picked me up and told me he had found a place for me. So we drove a little ways outside town and up a steep hill. There, beside a cliff that overlooked the turquoise waters, was what would become my home for the next year, nestled in a grove of citrus, mango, and coconut trees. There was a main house, and a guest house, where I would stay. Graham gave me a tour, explaining that the owner, a friend of his and a ninth-generation Bahamian, usually rented the place out on Airbnb, but that he would allow me to stay there for the summer if I wanted—or as long as I wanted. We entered the main bedroom, and as I stood there, the entirety of the ocean spread out before me, I simply asked: "How much?"

"Rent would be two thousand dollars," said Graham.

"A month?" I asked, pretty sure I had misheard him.

"A month," Graham confirmed.

I would be saving money staying here, even with the mortgage on my two properties in Charleston (my house and an income rental). I'm not sure what I would have ended up paying to stay in this place as an Airbnb, but it would have been a lot more than two thousand dollars a month. And that was that. I was now a part-time resident of Marsh Harbour.

I settled into the rhythms of island life as if I were a native. Every day found me in the water, harkening back to my child-hood during our summers in Fenwick Beach, Delaware. I usually spent my evenings with the Hegamyers or, if they were busy, by myself. In time I found my own friends and was greeted by the locals whenever I was in town. I still drank, and I was still on Adderall, but my typical late-night revelries quickly gave way to quieter evenings sipping a glass of wine by the water. The excitement that I thought I craved in the big cities of L.A., New York, or Miami transformed into a need for peace and calm. I drunk-texted Naomie once during my first few weeks on the island, but that was it. I didn't need to drink to forget her anymore; I simply started to move on. I had learned acceptance.

During this time I started to pick up free diving and spearfishing. On one of our excursions on the water, while Anna Heyward steered the boat and Graham descended under the water with a spear, I was on "shark patrol." What this means is that if the person in the boat saw a shark (usually a dark shadow in the water), they would alert the person on shark patrol, who would then descend underwater to warn the diver and use a spear to guide the shark away. It was my first day doing this, and sure enough, Anna Heyward spotted a shadow.

"Shark!" she screamed.

Seriously? I thought as I bobbed in the water. Heart racing, I tried to dive under to alert Graham, but I found that I couldn't hold my breath for more than a few seconds. I came up struggling for air.

What the hell? I thought. I tried again—and again. But each attempt ended the same way. I just couldn't hold my breath long enough to get to Graham. By that point, I was in a panic. Somewhere near me was a freaking shark, and all I had to do was get my friend out of the water. And it was the one thing I couldn't do.

Finally, I took one last deep breath and plunged under the waves. This time, probably because of sheer willpower, I was able to alert Graham, and we both scrambled out of the water and to safety. I should have been relieved, but all I felt was shame. It was such a simple thing and I—a healthy man—couldn't do it. I had put my friend in danger because the Adderall I had taken that morning had sent my heart rate soaring. *That* was the reason I couldn't hold my breath for more than a few seconds. I realized I needed to stop taking that poison.

Now, I didn't consciously quit Adderall in the same way an addict goes cold turkey from his drug of choice. I had brought enough pills down with me to last for most of the summer, and I don't recall when exactly I stopped taking them. But I did, and part of the reason was so that I could get better at diving. That, at least, is the one reason I remember for slowing down. But the larger, less deliberate reason is that I started to forget to take it. I would sometimes rifle through my backpack and come upon a tissue that I used to protect the pills from the moisture. I'd open it up and there would be pink dust everywhere, the remnants of what had once been an Adderall pill.

"Oh yeah," I would think, "that was where I put my Adderall."

The casual way that this thought popped into my head was a revelation to me. Could it be that I didn't *need* my Adderall in the way I thought I did? Back in my former life, I obsessed about it constantly. It was more than a habit; it was a ritual. I always popped a pill before filming; before I went out; after dinner; before a long drive. Two out of every three thoughts I had was about my Adderall. It was the one thing that my procrastination couldn't touch. I might hold off one task for weeks, even months; but I made damn sure my Adderall prescription was always up-to-date and my bottle was full.

And now . . . I had *forgotten* about it? What the hell was happening?

But I didn't dwell on it. I just stopped taking it, and not only did my diving improve, but my general health and anxiety did as well. I simply stopped worrying. My obsession with it was gone. Looking back on this now, I probably should have been more deliberate in my determination to actually quit Adderall, not simply forget about it. In Marsh Harbour, my worries and concerns were few. The triggers that would normally send me straight to the pill bottle were gone. I assumed that meant they were gone forever, but that's not how addiction works. Those triggers would return, and my ability to overcome them would prove to be wholly inadequate. But for the moment, I was free of this horrible addiction. My mind had finally settled and I could see clearly with new eyes.

In my little rental house, I had set up a sewing station and I sat down one day to work on a design that my new surroundings had inspired. It was a pillow with a flamingo. Nothing too special, but it meant something powerful to me. I stared at it once it was done and the thought came to me, in a moment of intense clarity: This *is what I want to do*. This thing that I had just made—that I had *created*—not for anyone, but for me. It wasn't anything I had to chase. It wasn't a feeling I was craving or a responsibility I was running from. It was just me, at my sewing machine, doing something that brought me so much damn joy. I used to think that happiness came from the high, the almost unnatural euphoria that would sometimes wash over me while I sank drinks and partied. *That*, I had thought, was the only feeling that gave me true happiness. But there was always a cost to those highs; the lost hours the next day, the fogginess of mind, the emptiness of my soul as my eyes opened to the late-afternoon sun. I had created nothing. I had inspired no one. I had sucked the life out of a moment, and it had left *me* drained. Instead of finding calm and happiness, my life had been an endless parade of searching for that next high; that next jolt of what I thought was real life. But it had been an illusion; a trick that my money and fame had played on me.

The journey I had started months earlier, in a moment of depression and loneliness, had brought me to so many dead ends, so many empty moments. But that road that had led nowhere had finally brought me here, with the ocean outside my window, and a pillow in my hands.

I had found my purpose. I had found my validation.

"Prove your worth to yourself, not to someone else."

That's what Kathryn had said to me nearly a year earlier. I thought I understood at the time, but it was only now, with a quiet mind and a peaceful heart, that I finally heard those words. I still didn't know how I would do it, but somehow the pillow I held in my hand would be a pillow that anyone could hold in their hand. I knew what I wanted to do, and I knew I could do it well.

7

THE TURNING POINT

*A*fter spending several months in Marsh Harbour, I returned to Charleston at the end of August 2018. I couldn't remember being so . . . ready. I was happy, yes, even if I didn't want to leave paradise, but I was excited to finally start *something*. I had also come to grips with my breakup with Naomie. It had been a year since our relationship had officially ended, and I could finally say that I had moved on. I was no longer caught in that destructive cycle of validation-seeking that always left me feeling emptier and sadder the next day. I had worked through my depression by removing myself from the pressures that had caused it. I was at peace with what had happened, and I was determined to keep moving forward. It helped that I had had a little love tryst during my final weeks in the Bahamas, one in which I could focus on the girl in front of me and not the one thousands of miles away.

It all started when Shep came down to visit me toward the end of the summer. Graham and I took him to Baker's Bay, a resort on the island of Great Guana Cay. We were having drinks at a bar called Grabbers on the other side of the island when I set my phone down on a table. There isn't much crime in the Bahamas, at least against tourists. It's sort of a rule among the "criminal" elements that do exist in the islands to stay away from tourists, so as not to harm the country's main source of income. But someone didn't get the message. When I looked down to grab my phone, it was gone. I knew immediately what had happened. Fortunately, one of Graham's friends was hanging with us, a local who was widely respected by all levels of Bahamian society. He took the loss of my phone personally. He immediately snapped his fingers, and a bunch of kids came running up. He questioned them all, trying to get to the bottom of the crime. The kids, however, knew nothing, and judging by the fear in their eyes at being questioned by Graham's friend, I didn't think they were lying.

Then the man said: "One hundred dollars to anyone who brings me this phone." The kids' eyes grew wide, and they scattered. I looked to Graham with an expression on my face that said: "Who *is* this guy?" Graham just smiled and shrugged.

I tried to intervene, telling Graham's friend that I didn't really care.

He stopped me. "I fucking care."

Graham brought out his phone then and used the "find my iPhone" feature. We got a ping near the docks, moving toward the water. Graham, his friend, and I took off in a dead sprint, Shep taking up the rear and none too happy about this sudden turn of events. As we got near the docks, we saw that my phone was now out on the water. And sure enough, there was a two-story ferry boat pulling away, headed back to the mainland. All of us, including Shep, who by this point was seriously questioning our sanity, jumped in Graham's motorboat and gunned it toward the departing ferry. With the ocean spray soaking our faces, and Graham's friend hanging off the bowline like a damn pirate, we easily caught the ferry. Graham then steered the boat in front of the ferry, back and forth, back and forth—three times, which in the Caribbean is the universal signal that you are about to be boarded. The ferry captain looked down on this little boat that dared get in his way . . . and then saw Graham's friend. He immediately stopped the engines, as Graham maneuvered the boat alongside the ferry. Graham's friend started to climb the ladder, and that's when the phone signal went dead. Likely tossed over the side.

"Get me off this boat!" I heard Shep shout.

The result of this little adventure was that I needed a new phone. But we learned that it would take two weeks for the phone to get to me. Graham provided a solution. He had a friend from Charleston—Stella—who had been wanting to come to the Bahamas for a few weeks (and who had visited several times before). She could pick up a new phone for me and bring it down. It wasn't long after she arrived that we hit it off. I guess you could say we started "vacation" dating, but I'd stop short of saying she was my girlfriend. Like Graham and Anna Heyward, she sort of came from the "society" portion of Charleston and didn't expect to like this *Southern Charm* boy. But she had also been through a bad breakup recently, and perhaps that's why we bonded so quickly. I think it also helped that I wasn't out of my mind all the time on

Adderall; I was the closest version of my true self that I had been in years. And, to my joy, I learned that this version of me was still fun, charming, and outgoing. It felt so good to just find a real connection with another person again. Stella was there during my going-away party, which a lot of the town came out for. We had it at one of my favorite spots in town, the Jib Room, where I would walk to every morning on my way to the docks where Graham kept his boat. Anna Heyward and Graham surprised me with a huge board that all the guests had signed. Stella and I flew out a day or two later. I had to go straight to New York, while she went to North Carolina to visit family. We made plans to see each other, but she had no interest in filming or even being around the show. I knew enough by now to respect those wishes and not force my lifestyle on anyone. And so we parted ways, amicably.

I came back to Charleston to a nearly brand-new house, since my friend Cintra had renovated and redecorated it in my absence. I set up my sewing room and started knocking out pillows, full of the energy and motivation I had gained while down in the Bahamas. My mind was clear for once, and my determination to do something with this little hobby I had started was stronger than ever. I visited the fabric store nearly every day, working with the owner, Kathy, to improve my designs and the quality of my pillows. I picked up materials so that I could photograph my finished products in a more professional way. I started listening to podcasts about creating an e-commerce business and researched building my own website. I felt this urgency that I hadn't felt before. Every time I posted a picture of my pillows on Instagram, I would get flooded with responses about buying them. I still didn't have an answer to that yet, but I had this sense that the demand I saw out there wouldn't last forever. The moment was now, and I had to figure my shit out. Another source of urgency came from Shep, who had launched his own clothing line a year earlier called Shep Gear. While I was happy for him, I was also jealous. He was doing what I was *trying* to do.

I quickly realized that my problem was scale. I simply didn't have the resources to fulfill orders if and when I set up a sales channel. I could make one, maybe two pillows a day. And that would be *all* I could do. But a business, even a side hustle, needs more than the manufacturing. It needs to jump through the regulatory and tax loops; it needs administrative work; it needs website design and upkeep; it needs marketing and promotion; and, particularly important to my business, it needs a way to get the damn pillows to the customers. It was like the more I worked toward solving these various problems, the longer the list got. I was in over my head and that realization started to greatly distress me—and slow me down. One of my solutions to keep demand up was to simply give the pillows away. Since I couldn't do this for everyone who asked, I ended up gifting pillows to those who made a particularly strong case. I remember one woman asked for a pillow for her daughter who had cancer. I gladly obliged. This kept me busy—and forced me to keep sewing pillows—but it was hardly sustainable; and it certainly wasn't a business.

And this was where my motivation ran up against a brick wall. It wasn't that the solution to this problem was particularly hard—I wasn't the first person who was trying to turn a passion project into a moneymaking side hustle; it was that I couldn't bring myself to make a decision about what to do. I had been talking with the guy who had helped Shep start his company, Jason Benjamin, who offered to set up a website and connect me with a manufacturer. It sounded reasonable, but I sat on it for a while. The focus and clarity that I had left the Bahamas with was slowly giving way to my age-old anxieties and procrastination.

And there was a good reason for this: I was back on Adderall.

When I had stopped using Adderall in the Bahamas, I didn't make a conscious decision to quit, in the sense that I had devoted myself to never taking it again. I just stopped taking it. The triggers that would normally make me pop a pill just didn't exist for me in the Bahamas. And while I saw and lived the benefits of being off Adderall, I never got to the bottom of *why* I had been on it in the first place. Nor did I prepare myself for facing those triggers once I returned to Charleston and my everyday life. In fact, I failed the very first test. The first day of filming for season 6, I felt those old anxieties surge forth in a way that I hadn't felt in a long time. I wasn't ready for them. I simply didn't know how to film without being on Adderall, and in that split second, I took a pill. Then I took another one. Then another. And before I even realized what had happened or why, I was hooked again.

Which is why there are several moments in season 6 when I look like I had looked in earlier seasons: tired, stressed, and hardly a man on top of his game. Certainly not the man who claimed he had found himself in the Bahamas. That man disappeared the moment I took that first pill, and he wouldn't come back until I was off the damn stuff for good. By this point, I had hired Anna

Heyward as my executive coordinator. Even the best version of me from the Bahamas struggled with the minutiae of daily life—bills, taxes, calendars, meetings. I've never been particularly good at juggling this stuff, and so Anna Heyward, a trauma nurse by training, stepped in and helped me out. Her appearance in my life was played for laughs on the show—"Why does Craig need an assistant?"—but the reality is that she helped me organize my life in a way that I never could. I am eternally grateful for her support during this period, and since then.

In a matter of a few weeks, even with Anna Heyward's help, the sense of purpose and discipline I thought I had found in the Bahamas had disappeared. I was back to where I had been before. An addict with a lot of pillows but without a business.

HURRICANE FLORENCE

Season 6 was filmed erratically. There were several starts and stops that carried filming into 2019. It's difficult to piece together a chronological telling of that season just using the episodes, so I won't even try. And no one, except my Instagram followers, knew that I had spent a week helping with relief efforts after a hurricane ravaged the Carolinas.

Before we get to that, I'll preface the story with something that viewers definitely did see: my fingernail painted blue. While I was in the Bahamas, I had seen posts with men sporting blue nail polish on one finger. I was intrigued, and not only because I kind of sought out excuses to put on makeup from time to time.

A little eyeliner is a fun way to spice up one's look. In any event, the nail polish was part of a social media awareness push known as the Polished Man Campaign, an organization that seeks to bring attention to child abuse. The single painted nail is meant to symbolize that one out of five instances of child abuse goes unreported. By painting your nail, you are inviting a conversation, which can bring awareness, then action.

I was immediately sold on both the mission and the tactics of the Polished Man Campaign. Ever since I joined the show, I had wanted to get back into helping children. During the summer after my first year of law school, I had become a Guardian Ad Litem, which is essentially someone who represents in court a child who is under the care of the state. Guardians Ad Litem stand in as the child's counselor, representing their best interests, advising the court, and suggesting proper courses of action to the judge. Since many of these children come from abusive homes, my experience was both harrowing and rewarding. I learned from my colleagues that the best way to get a child to open up to you is to give them a crayon. Once a kid starts coloring, they will start answering your questions.

But once the show started, I had to give up on this work. I missed it terribly. The Polished Man Campaign gave me a chance to get back into helping the most vulnerable in our world. I jumped at it, and I knew that every viewer would wonder why the hell Craig had a painted nail. Well, now they know. I also saw the campaign as a way to start being myself again on television. If the Bahamas had taught me anything, it was that I had to start taking control of my life where and when I could. I didn't have a say in how I was presented on the show; but I did have a say in how I behaved. And after years of filming, and having learned hard lessons about trying to protect myself and others from the cameras, I knew I just had to be me. And this was me: a man who painted one nail to bring awareness to child abuse. And, well, because I liked having a painted nail.

So as I entered season 6, my mind was on philanthropy. And then just as the filming started, we had one of our stops, when Hurricane Florence threatened the Carolina coast in early September. We shut down production to ride out the storm, which missed Charleston but slammed into North Carolina on September 14. Sean, my roommate, had taken off for a while, so I sat in my house by myself, staying up all night sewing, listening to Taylor Swift and Eminem, and watching the news as Florence ravaged the coast. After a couple days, the storm moved inland toward West Virginia, where it eventually dissipated. After the storm passed, the news was able to capture footage of the devastation left in its wake. These images appalled me, and also brought up memories of my trip to Haiti. I was gripped with the sudden urge to do something to help. I kept talking about my philanthropic ambitions; well, here was my chance.

But what could I do?

I had seen on the news that one of the most critical problems facing relief efforts was getting supplies to people stranded because of the flooding. I started putting up IG stories asking people for what was needed. Answers came pouring in. I then called Anna Heyward.

"We need to go to Costco," I said.

"Why?"

I explained my half-baked plan to fill my Jeep Grand Cherokee with as many supplies as I could and just drive to the center of the destruction. She didn't argue with me, and we met at the megastore an hour later. I spent almost two thousand dollars on supplies, mostly food and water, but also dog and cat food, bug spray, and bleach. As I was packing up my car in the parking lot, a woman approached me, saying that she knew who I was from the show and had seen my Instagram stories about the hurricane. We got to chatting and I told her what I was doing. She mentioned she knew of a relief group that was headed to North Carolina as well.

"I'm sure they could use all the help they can get," she said. "I could put you in touch with them, if you want."

So I gave her my contact information, then hit the road. I didn't have any idea what I was doing. I just assumed that I would drive to the most heavily damaged communities and start handing out supplies. As I continued north on I-95, getting closer to the hurricane's trail of destruction, I started to see signs of the storm's wrath along the roadside. Abandoned cars; destroyed homes; personal items like clothes and toys strewn about. I was also listening to the news and heard terrible reports of supplies being stolen, and stories of dehydration. When I crossed the state line, I got a call from a man who said his name was Jaime.

"My sister said you had some supplies," he said gruffly. I confirmed that this was the contact of the woman I had met in the Costco parking lot.

"Where are you headed with these supplies?" he then asked.

I couldn't give him a good answer to that question. I just said I was driving north and the first place I found that needed help, I would stop.

"Well, why don't you bring the supplies to us?" he offered. "I run a group called Triton Hurricane Relief. We go in when the emergency crews can't. We could use your supplies."

Lacking any other plan, I agreed to meet him. He directed me to the aptly named town of Florence, where his group had set up headquarters beside a church, and where the pastor was directing supply drop-offs. When I got there, dozens of people were milling about amid the debris from the storm and downed power lines. Emergency crews mingled with regular people, all trying to help. The problem was that the emergency personnel had to obey orders, and at that point, they were prohibited from entering the most dangerous areas. The regular folks, guys like Jaime and his friends—Kyle, Dan, Paul, and Rob—weren't officially allowed to go in either, but this was one time where the law on the ground looked the other way. The emergency crews knew that if supplies weren't delivered to those stranded by the storm, they would die.

I had started to unload the supplies from my Jeep when a distress call came in. Jaime and the guys organized a group to go help. He looked at me.

"We got a spot on the boat if you want to come," he said.

Hell yes.

It was Rob, a bear of a man, who looked down at my tennis shoes before I jumped in the truck.

"You're going out in those?" he asked.

Of course. I didn't have anything else.

"Here," he said, and handed me a pair of snake boots. And thank God he did, because my shoes wouldn't have lasted the night.

Fan boats were needed because the flooding meant most other vehicles couldn't get to the worst-hit areas. We drove a ways to a landing and boarded the boat at around three in the morning. As we passed homes half-sunk in the water, we'd see survivors sitting on their rooftops. Slowly, our boat filled with these stranded people, a lot of them grateful, but not all of them. Some of the survivors refused to leave, even though the governor had issued a mandatory evacuation. But there was little we could do for such people.

After one man refused to get in the boat, Jaime handed him a Sharpie pen.

"What's this?" the man asked.

"Write your social security number on your arm," Jaime said. "That way it'll be easier to identify your body later."

Sometimes this was enough to scare the survivors into the boat. Sometimes it wasn't. I saw my first dead body the next morning at sunrise, floating inside a house. But it wouldn't be my last.

We spent three days in and around Florence rescuing people in this manner. When I had first arrived, I was concerned that the other guys wouldn't accept me. They'd see me as just another celebrity trying to exploit a tragedy. But the reality was that they didn't care. No one cared about who I was, much less *Southern Charm*. They were there to save lives, and they accepted any and all help. After our first night on the water, I learned that the Triton guys had spent the previous night sleeping on hay in a barn. The next two nights we slept at a home whose owners had evacuated. I wanted to give back, so I called Anna Heyward and had her rent a house in Myrtle Beach. The guys wanted to pay me back, but I said the homeowner, a fan, had donated the house. That probably went a long way toward them accepting me as one of their own. They even gave me the call sign "Hollywood," for obvious reasons.

We then moved our operations to Myrtle Beach because the flow of the floodwater was moving southward, catching more people unaware. I also realized the guys were carrying guns with them on the boat for protection. As you might imagine, a natural disaster of this scale brings out the worst in some people, and looting was a serious problem in and around the supply depots. More than once, looters had tried to steal food, water, and sand bags from our site. One time when we were on the water, we got shot at, not by looters, but by people who thought *we* were the looters. It was the first and I hope the last time I was ever fired upon.

It wasn't just people we saved, either. This part of the state was mostly rural farmland, and when some people flee for their lives, they aren't thinking about their animals, which infuriated those of us who found the bodies later. In addition to human remains floating in the floodwaters, we also saw dozens of horses and goats. We came upon a farm where we heard hysterical neighing from the barn. In their panicked flight, the owners had forgotten to unlock the fence around the barn, trapping a dozen or so horses inside. We got the doors open and found the horses standing in knee-high water. All we could do was release them, hoping they'd find dry ground. But it was better than being locked in a barn. We did field calls from remorseful owners who asked us to save their animals, but unfortunately it was usually too late by the time we got there.

Toward the end of my five days with the group, we came upon a house in the path of the flood where we found a little girl sitting on her front porch. She was crying because she didn't know how she was going to get to school the next day. We asked where her parents were, and she called to her father.

"I'll be down in a fucking minute," we heard a voice scream from inside. A man then appeared at the door, swaying and slurring his words. He carried a holstered pistol on his hip. We urged him to get in the boat with his daughter, but he said that the water wasn't even in the house yet. Paul explained that the water was only going to get higher in this part of the country because the flood was receding back to the ocean. Still, in his drunken state, he resisted getting in the boat. Finally, and with an eye on his gun, we convinced him to come aboard. When we got to dry land, the girl's mother came and picked her up. The whole episode was a reminder that human cruelty can happen anywhere, even in the United States.

Throughout my time in North Carolina, I was documenting my exploits on Instagram. Followers, friends, and other celebrities started asking me how they could help. They wanted to donate money, and I could have collected thousands upon thousands of dollars. But I held off. I didn't know how to process that money, and I was concerned that even collecting it would be illegal. But it emphasized to me that I had a platform that could do a lot of good. I wouldn't always be able to be on hand to help relief efforts, but there was still a lot of help I could provide.

After almost a week of rescue and relief efforts, I returned to Charleston, once more humbled by the heroics of everyday people and the true nature of human suffering. I watched the news with a different set of eyes. Because the camera crews couldn't reach the most devastated communities, they couldn't tell the whole story. The full scale of the disaster that I witnessed was lost on most of the country. As far as terrible hurricanes go, Florence barely registers on the charts. It made landfall as a category 1 storm, hardly the stuff of major headlines. But I was able to see the true toll that even a category 1 hurricane could inflict, especially on poorer communities.

When I left Haiti, I had decided that I would make philanthropy a part of my life. Then life got in the way. Hurricane Florence and my experience in North Carolina shamed me into a new sense of urgency and resolve. For as many as we had saved, there were so many more that we couldn't.

A CALL FROM JERRY

As winter approached, I was still without much of a business plan for my pillows. The furthest I'd gotten was having conversations with Shep's guy, Jason, about setting up a website to sell my products. Jason wasn't going to take any ownership in my company; he would do it for a flat fee. I was interested, but I wasn't ready to pull the trigger on it. If all I wanted was to have a little online pillow business, then I likely would have gone with Jason. But I wanted more than that. I wanted a brand. I wanted a whole line of home décor products; I wanted cookbooks and candles; most of all, I wanted a store. In other words, my heart was set on building a company that could grow beyond pillows. My pillows were just the way to start, but they wouldn't be all I offered. Jason was very good at what he did—Shep's success was a testament to that—but he wasn't the right fit for what I *really* wanted to do.

Or maybe I just couldn't make a decision. The truth is probably somewhere in between. By Thanksgiving I was still on my own, with no company, and no real path forward. And that's when I got a call from my old college friend, Jerry Casselano. It was the phone call that changed my life.

I had known Jerry ever since he bounced for one of the college bars I used to frequent as an underage undergraduate (Jerry always let me in). We had stayed in touch over the years, but not regularly. Jerry had relocated to Washington, DC, where he helped start a very successful sports marketing agency, ProVentures. We would run into each other at golfing events every once in a while, since a lot of Jerry's athletes played in them. I also had done a little bit of Instagram promotion for him over the years. Still, despite this history, we hadn't kept in close contact. I do remember admiring his success from afar. He was someone who, at thirty-one, was where I wanted to be.

That said, his call to me came out of the blue. After a bit of small talk, Jerry got right to the point.

"I was wondering if you were working with anyone on your pillows," he said.

I told him I had spoken with Jason but hadn't formed an official partnership with him yet. I had very little guidance or help from anyone. I said that I had an inbox full of hundreds of people who were interesting in buying my pillows, but that I was stuck on how to proceed.

"Well, I think I might be able to help," he said.

Now for the background to this call. During Thanksgiving dinner, Jerry was with his then-girlfriend (now wife), Alexis Latifi, and her sister, Amanda, a brand marketing expert with several businesses already under her belt, including the retail-development app, Hafta Have. Amanda had been watching *Southern Charm*; in particular, she had been watching me struggle with doing something with my pillows.

"Jerry, you're from Charleston," said Amanda over some turkey and stuffing. "Do you know this guy?"

"We were friends in college," Jerry said. "But we're not close buddies or anything."

"Do you think there's an opportunity with those pillows he's making?" asked Amanda.

Honestly, Jerry hadn't thought about my pillows one way or the other. But being an entrepreneur at heart, he immediately gave it real consideration. And that's how it happened. Right there at Thanksgiving dinner, Jerry and Amanda put their heads together and came up with a business plan that they could pitch to me. Jerry called me a few days after that. His purpose was to find out if I had partnered with anyone. He gave me a very short rundown of what he and Amanda had in mind, but said that all three of us should get on a Zoom call to discuss. I happily agreed. I was playing it cool, but in fact, I was overjoyed. This was the phone call I had been waiting for. Stuck, full of indecision, I was lost about how to move forward. Some might think that a celebrity with a product would need to be fending off potential business partners, but that wasn't my experience. Other than Jason, no one had approached me about it at all. Perhaps they stayed away because of the reputation I had from the show. Or perhaps it's simply not that easy to start a business whether you're a celebrity or not. All I knew was that Jerry and Amanda came along at the exact moment I needed them. But I was smart enough not to let *them* know that. Unlike Jason, Jerry and Amanda, two pros, weren't going to settle for a flat fee. They would ask for equity.

During our next call together, where I met Amanda for the first time, they walked me through their business plan. I couldn't have been happier with their vision. They saw my pillows as the start of a brand, not a little online shop that was simply cashing in on a popular television show. If anything, they were pushing me away from the show, hoping that the brand could grow and sustain itself on its own.

"We're not creating a kitschy little boardwalk company," said Jerry. "We're creating a real brand, something that will outlive Craig Conover and *Southern Charm*. Success is when people buy our products when they don't know who you are, but because they love the brand."

This was exactly what I had been hoping to achieve. Bethenny Frankel, Kristin Cavallari—these were reality stars who nevertheless broke free from their shows to become wildly successful business owners. They are just as known for their businesses today as they are for the shows they starred in. And their companies will long outlive the shows. That's the type of company I wanted to have. And that's the vision I heard from Amanda and Jerry that day.

Then they hit me with it.

Jerry put it like this: "We think the only way this will work is if we're all equal partners."

He paused, waiting for my reply. I was a bit stunned. *Equal?* They were asking me to give up 66 percent of my company. I had never owned a company before, but I knew enough about math to know that I wouldn't be the primary owner. While in the Bahamas, I had talked to Graham a bunch about starting a company, since he was then in the middle of launching his rum company, Frigate Reserve. The one thing he always said to me: "Never give up more than 50 percent." If I had any firm opinions on what would happen when I partnered with someone, it was Graham's dictum. It wasn't the money; it was the control.

So I pushed back. I wanted to maintain ownership, I said. And so began a back and forth that dominated the rest of the conversation.

Finally, Jerry said, "Look, Craig, you can have a large piece of something small; or you can have a small piece of something large."

That shut me up. The conversation wasn't over, but I had to admit that Jerry's point was a strong one. They were offering me something. If their plan worked, then it could be something very big. None of us realized how big it would be, but I really didn't have much to bargain with at the time. It's not like I had a proven concept or anything. I hadn't sold a single pillow yet. If this was *Shark Tank*, I would be laughed out of the room for wanting to hang on to 51 percent. Without them I had nothing; with them, something—maybe. But I wasn't ready to accept their offer just yet.

"Okay," said Jerry as the call concluded. "Just let us know."

Over the next few days, I mulled over what Jerry and Amanda had offered me—and what they wanted from me. I oscillated between being wildly excited and wildly offended. I had spoken to my parents, and they asked me one question: "Can they help you?" I said yes. "Well, there's your answer," my dad said. While I continued to believe in what Graham had told me, I couldn't deny the wisdom of what Jerry had said. I did, however, try to push back. I talked to Jerry during this decision-making moment and said I wanted to keep at least half of the company.

"I'm sorry, Craig," he replied. "This is the only way we're going to do it."

Ugh. I was stuck.

I procrastinated a couple more weeks. Fuck it. I was back to doing what I had been doing before they called me: nothing. If I wanted to hang on to ownership of my company, then this should have been the whack that spurred me to action. Instead, I did shit. So I called him back.

"We have a deal," I said.

ON THE TARMAC

Throughout the winter of 2018–19 and into the spring, while filming continued off and on, I visited my rental house and Anna Heyward and Graham in the Bahamas often. Part of my hesitation in accepting Jerry and Amanda's offer was that I was spending a lot of time with Graham, who was insisting that I hold on to 51 percent. There were embarrassing moments when I, drunk and fired up, would call up Jerry from Marsh Harbour, telling him how screwed I was getting in this deal. To Jerry's everlasting credit, he listened to my ramblings with patience, but stuck to his guns. He wasn't going to let me bully him into going against what he thought was right.

But as you can probably guess, I wasn't at my best during these trips back to the place where I had rediscovered myself. The Adderall was kicking my ass; on top of it, I was piling on the booze and losing control. During New Year's, which I spent in the Bahamas with Austen, Graham got so fed up with me that he threatened to lock me in the basement if I didn't calm down. Yes, I was a mess. Again.

Throughout this period, talks with Jerry and Amanda had proceeded, and our verbal agreement had started the wheels in motion. I helped where I could, but I was dropping the ball a lot. I would simply disappear for a week or two, letting them get the foundation of the company in place. Then I'd pop back up and do some actual work, before disappearing again. I don't know why Jerry and Amanda put up with it, except that they truly did believe that they could build a brand off my pillows, whether I was involved or not.

In March, I was back in Marsh Harbour, and this time I had brought a girl with me. Already, Graham was upset with me. For months now, he had patiently put up with my increasingly annoying antics, but one night at dinner he'd had enough. Graham let me know that he was going to "disown" me, meaning he would cease to vouch for me with the other locals. That woke me up, so I promised to meet him for breakfast the next day. Only I slept right through it. I was scheduled to fly out to Florida in the afternoon to attend the Players Championship Golf Tournament at TPC Sawgrass in Ponte Vedra Beach with Shep and Austen. While on the tarmac, I called Graham to apologize, and that's when he told me I had turned into this person that he didn't like.

"Craig, if you come back, you must understand that things will be different," he said.

I knew what he meant. Marsh Harbour is tight-knit community, where standards of behavior are expected from all who visit. Over the summer I had been accepted by the community as one of them, but it was a distinction I had lost. It was my fault. The revelation rocked me. I was humiliated by my actions, and ashamed that I had allowed my darkness to take over the man I was meant to be.

And while you would think that would be enough to make me change my ways, you don't understand the mind of an addict. When I went to Ponte Vedra, I drank away that humiliation, that pain, that regret. I drank and partied and lost myself in a world of strangers and oblivion. I didn't know how else to act. I didn't know how else to relieve the pain.

Which was how I found myself slumped next to a dumpster in the pouring rain, hoping, praying, that someone would come pick me up. They say addicts must find their bottom before they can begin to rise. I hope I don't ever experience a bottom like that again, although I must also remember that the possibility exists for me. It can always get worse for an addict.

I returned to Charleston humbled. Filming was wrapping up, and I decided that I would try not taking an Adderall for once. Then, I decided I wouldn't refill my prescription. I made a conscious decision to quit the stuff for good. It was a decision I should have made in the Bahamas the previous summer; perhaps if I had, then I would have been able to resist the triggers when they came. But I was unable to resist them, and all the positive things that had happened in my life since then were in danger of disappearing. I had to rise up and admit to myself that I was an addict and that I had to go clean from Adderall forever.

And this is where Sewing Down South saved me. I don't know if I could have succeeded if I didn't have this passion pushing me forward. If I had gone back to Charleston with nothing except my social life, then I would surely have fallen right back into my destructive ways. But I had something to be clean for; I had partners who depended on me; I had a company to create and a brand to build. I had supporters who *wanted* me to achieve my dreams, because if this boy from Delaware could overcome his darkness and follow his passion, then perhaps they could too.

For them, for Jerry and Amanda, and for Sewing Down South, I had a life that was ready to be lived.

A REAL COMPANY, FINALLY

It was now March 2019, and much had happened since Jerry and I first started talking. Even though we hadn't made our agreement official, we were moving full-steam ahead on getting the business off the ground. A lot of this was on Jerry's and Amanda's plates, and I'm still quite astonished and impressed by what they were able to do in such a short time. In no particular order, they had to find a factory that could hand-stitch the pillows themselves. I was adamant about the handmade part, since I felt it added a level of authenticity to my pillows and helped us stand out in a market that is saturated with machine-made stuff. Knowing next to nothing about the pillow-making business, Jerry ended up asking a friend of his who made her own pillows how she was able to scale her business. She provided a few contacts, which was how Jerry found a factory in North Carolina that could make the pillows on demand. But we also wanted to launch with hats and shirts, which required a totally separate factory to produce. Again, Amanda found one in Alabama that met our on-demand needs. Both factories satisfied my wish to keep the manufacturing in America. While some of the materials we use come from abroad, everything is in fact made right here at home. It's also quite extraordinary that for someone who didn't even know what the word "textile" meant when he first called me (seriously, ask him if you want), Jerry was able to get a company based on tex-tiles off the ground.

We also had to come up with a name for the company and a logo. These were big decisions, but they both came together quite easily in the end. Everyone involved wanted to bring the Charleston angle into the name and logo. Although the com-pany would exist entirely online at first, we wanted a name that reflected an actual place, a feeling of comfort and home. The very things I loved most about my home I wanted to be reflected in the brand. But "Delaware" doesn't exactly convey much of any-thing to most people. I love my home state, but it wasn't right for the company name. That left Charleston, but here again we ran into issues. Clearly the only reason anyone knew who I was, was because of my association with the city and the show. But bring-ing Charleston into the name of the company would be piggy-backing off the show too much. How could we give a nod toward my beginnings—and those who had supported me because of the show—without directly tying the brand to the show? Well, where is Charleston? It's in the South. It's a southern city. And the south-ern lifestyle has come to convey a certain bit of old-fashioned homeyness, a sense that things are done with care and with your hands. The North has its cities and its automated ways, but things are done differently in the South, which is why it is a place utterly unique in the country. Quieter, slower, more deliberate, people take their time in the South, to make sure what is made is made to last.

As we batted around using "South" or "Southern" in the name, Jerry suddenly recalled a slogan he knew from his love of college football. Saturday Down South is a website devoted to covering football in the Southeastern Conference. I don't remember who first said it; maybe all three of us just suddenly blurted out "sewing down South." But there it was. Perfect. We then connected with a local designer who put together the old-fashioned sewing machine logo. After a few iterations, we had it. Of all the decisions and headaches we had in those early days, the name and logo were perhaps the easiest. They just came together. But I also don't want to underplay their importance to the whole idea. Thank God we didn't go with something that had my name in it. Thank God we stayed away from tying the brand too closely to the show. Yes, I would be the face of the brand, but the brand itself had to be larger than all that. It had to be able to stand on its own. These were the lessons Amanda brought with her, given her vast success at brand marketing. She understood that its brand is perhaps the most valuable thing a company owns, and it all starts with the name and the logo. They both must work together to tell consumers exactly who you are and what you stand for. And I'm quite proud of what we chose.

All that said, in one instance, the show itself proved quite useful. While I remained in Charleston during this time, and Amanda was in Los Angeles, Jerry went to open a company bank account in Washington, D.C. His first attempt at Chase failed, since the manager told Jerry he needed to have all three of us there to sign the papers. Jerry was livid. He had all the paperwork ready to go, but the manager wouldn't budge. So Jerry walked to Wells Fargo. Same issue. He was told he needed all three of us there. Dejected, Jerry walked down the street and passed a Bank of America. He popped in to try his luck there. As he sat down with that manager, explaining the business, the man stopped him.

"Wait, this is Craig Conover's company?" he asked.

Jerry nodded.

"From *Southern Charm*?"

Jerry nodded again.

"Is he finally selling his pillows?" The manager was almost giddy with excitement.

Jerry laughed. "So, can we get this done?"

"Absolutely," said the manager. "You don't need everyone here."

Bank account made.

There were other decisions to make, of course. We needed to find a designer who could work with me on the pillow patterns. Our initial run would be patterns that reflected the brand: whimsical, homey, with nautical notes, not just to represent Charleston, but to bring in Delaware's eastern shore. I'd sketch and relay what I wanted to the designer; she'd mock up a few options, and we'd go back and forth. We'd work out colors, welting, and shades. It's a process that we continue to this day.

All of this work was going on before we signed our operating agreement. But then Jerry and Amanda came to my house soon after I returned from the golf tournament, agreement in hand. I was finally ready. I trusted Jerry and Amanda could do what they said they could do. The rest would take care of itself. It was time to do this. We signed, then toasted one another with champagne. The toast wasn't just for Sewing Down South, either. Jerry and Alexis had just gotten engaged the night before.

All that was left was to launch the company.

THE LAUNCH

Sewing Down South opened for business on April 1, 2019. It was a humble beginning. The entire company consisted of three people: Jerry, Amanda, and me. We had a factory in North Carolina that produced our pillows and one in Alabama that produced the hats and shirts that would go on sale with the pillows, but everything was made-to-order. No inventory. I never liked this aspect of Jerry and Amanda's business strategy, but I accepted their view that it was better to keep costs low. My problem was that in an age of Amazon Prime, when consumers expect swift delivery, waiting three to four weeks for a pillow wasn't going to go over well. I also worried that the delay would sink my brand before it had a chance to grow. After all, I was the "loser," the guy who couldn't ever finish anything, who procrastinated, who got distracted by other hobbies and interests. So even though we made the delivery time abundantly clear on our website, my fear was that customers would get frustrated: "It's Craig! Of course it's late."

Another business element we skimped on was marketing. To be blunt, we had spent *nothing* on it. Our entire promotion strategy consisted of using my social media channels and those of the company to advertise the launch and range of products. The response had been pretty great, but liking or commenting on a post is not the same thing as handing over money. Not that I was too worried about this. Since I had first started talking to Jerry and Amanda five months earlier, I had tried to convince them that the demand was there. They accepted that it was—after all, we were partners—but they still weren't about to dump a lot of money into the business just yet. We had managed to get a few articles written in Bravo-focused blogs, but it's not like I was on the cover of *Southern Living*.

This tug-of-war between my partners and me was a continual struggle in those early days of the company—and still is today. It's not a bad thing, necessarily, if you can continue working together. I deferred to Jerry and Amanda on a lot of business-related matters. They were the ones who had started companies and built brands before. And I think their "slow and steady" attitude matched well with my "hell for leather" outlook; we often found a middle course. Still, all three of us had high hopes for launch day. For almost two years I had received a constant barrage of IG messages asking when and where one could buy my pillows. That day, I could finally give an answer.

On launch day itself I was in Miami with an old friend, Kory Keefer. Since he now reenters the story, it would be helpful to explain how we reconciled. Three years after Kory left Charleston to spend several months traveling around Europe before settling back in Greenville, South Carolina, season 2 of *Southern Charm* was airing. The show was a hit and I had been offered several promotional gigs. For one, Lola's Chic Boutique, down in Palm Beach, Florida, offered to fly my manager and me down there to make an appearance. I had a manager, Dan in New York City, whom I had never met in person. But I didn't want to bring a business associate. I wanted to bring a friend, and the first person I thought to ask was Kory. So just like that, I shot him a text, asking if he wanted to come with me to Palm Beach. He happily accepted, and thus our friendship was renewed. We didn't much discuss the issues that had split us apart three years earlier, but I don't think we needed to. We both recognized our blame in what had happened and exposing those old scars wouldn't have been beneficial to anyone. Instead, we thoroughly enjoyed ourselves in the Florida waters and attending the U.S. Polo Open. I will say that the show's success seemed to help mend the rift between us. Had the show bombed, then what would it have all been for? But Kory was on his way toward a successful entrepreneurial career, while I had a burgeoning television career. We were both where we were supposed to be, and if we had reached these separate destinations by going over rocky terrain, well, that's the journey of friendship.

When Sewing Down South was about to launch, Kory and I were back in Florida spending the day together celebrating. There wasn't much for me to do. The website that Amanda had put together was just going to go live, and then that was that. But the anticlimactic nature of the launch didn't stop us from enjoying the moment. Kory understood what this day meant for me, and not only because he too had joined the entrepreneurial world. For both of us, it was the realization of something that we had wanted for each other going all the way back to our college days. Now, friends again, that day was here, and I wouldn't have wanted to celebrate with anyone else.

In fact, none of the Sewing Down South employees were in Charleston that day. Jerry was in Washington, DC, where he lived, while Amanda was in Los Angeles. I didn't speak much with them, except to check in to make sure the site was working well and wasn't crashing. I knew Jerry would be laser-focused on sales while Amanda kept an eye on the site, but I wasn't going to worry myself. Everything had come together, and now we could relax for a brief moment to enjoy what we had created. I'm kind of glad I didn't bother myself with worrying, because the next day Jerry told me what we had done.

"Hey, man," he said on the phone, "so sales weren't what we had hoped for."

I knew Jerry to be somewhat of a worrier, so even his tone didn't scare me.

"What did we do?" I asked.

"We got twenty-three orders," he said somewhat dejectedly.

That was a bit low. Jerry's sights had been set on forty to fifty orders a day during launch week. But still, it was just Day 1. Things would improve. I said as much to him, urging him not to stress. The orders would come.

Day 2 happened. Thirty orders. See? Picking up.

Day 3: Six orders. Hm.

Day 4: Four orders. Oh.

Day 5: Two orders. Shit.

IT HAD ALL BEEN WORTH IT

The first week of Sewing Down South made all of us question our prior assumptions. We had assumed that the demand that had been building since season 5 of the show was still there. Everything I knew—my inbox, my social media accounts, word on the street—said it was. We had assumed that we could put very little initial investment into the business, just a few thousand dollars to build a website and start production. The danger of having no inventory was real, but Jerry was convinced that it was the smart way to start off. We also assumed that we didn't need to do much up-front marketing to announce our launch day, aside from pushing the news through the social media channels.

And then in our first month of operation, we got ninety-nine orders, and all our assumptions suddenly looked wrong. As I said earlier, Jerry's sights had been set on forty to fifty *a day*. Jerry was disappointed, and he started to grumble that maybe this wasn't going to be the big hit that we all had hoped for. I remained confident that we were sitting on a winner, but that our decision to skimp on putting money in was now hurting our sales. In truth, I felt a little misled. I had trusted Jerry and Amanda's business acumen over my instincts. Now, I started to think that my instincts hadn't been that wrong. I badgered my colleagues constantly about building up inventory, but Jerry continued to resist. We stayed the course, even though I felt that the decision would come to haunt us.

Things did pick up in May, when we received 273 orders and made around $20,000 in sales. These were numbers we had been expecting from the start, although they proved quite overwhelming for a three-person team. Jerry bore the brunt of most of it. Once a week, we'd send the orders to the factory in North Carolina, which would then make the pillows and send them back to Jerry at his condo in Washington three weeks later. Jerry was our "logistics operation." He would get a full shipment of dozens of pillows, check them against his order sheet, and then spend all night packaging them to ship them out the next day. Remember, Jerry was still working full-time for his sports management agency; Sewing Down South was a side gig. Of course, the pillows that we shipped were without inserts. This was another decision that I had at first been adamant about. I wanted the pillows to ship with inserts, but Jerry and Amanda disagreed. To keep shipping costs low—the inserts would have ballooned the price—they wanted to continue selling just the covers. But I wouldn't back down, so we took a vote. I lost, two to one.

In June, sales dipped to only $12,000, but jumped back up to $27,000 in July. It was a bit of a roller coaster. There were days when we thought the whole thing was going to fall apart, only to think, come the next day, that we were sitting on a gold mine. And it went on like this most of that first summer. Then August rolled around. As a company, we agreed that we needed something big to boost sales. So I reached out to Cam, who had a million followers, and asked if she would do some IG pictures with our pillows and help drive traffic to the store. Well, the gambit worked, and sales exploded to $42,000. Thank you, Cam. That wasn't our total sales for the month, however. August was also when we held our first pillow party, but more on that in the next chapter.

On September 1, Hurricane Dorian, a category 5 storm, made landfall just east of the Abaco Islands in the Bahamas. It remained over the islands for two days, blasting it with winds of 185 mph. When it finally moved off, most of the Bahamas were devastated, especially Marsh Harbour. I was on the phone with Graham and Anna Heyward, who fortunately weren't down there at the time, but they had heard that everything was gone, their home included. My rental house was gone as well, including all the stuff I had kept there. I felt like I had lost a piece of me. The place that had sustained me during some of my darkest moments, and which had helped me to rediscover my true self, had been nearly wiped off the map. I had to do something.

On September 2, I posted an IG story announcing that all proceeds from sales of our Spiny Lobster Pillow—a pillow I had designed to commemorate my time in the islands where the lobster was my main food choice, from diving—would go toward relief efforts in the Bahamas. We had managed to set up a fundraising arm—another one of my goals—and were prepared to donate however much money we received to the crews that were headed down to the islands. When I posted my IG story, I was home in Delaware with my parents. I was sitting at the kitchen counter right before dinner when I hit send. A few minutes later we sat down to eat, and I had my phone on the table. Suddenly, we all heard *cha-ching!* from the phone.

"What's that?" my mom asked.

I explained that the app we used for the online store made that cash register sound every time we made a sale.

Cha-ching!

"Sorry," I said. "I'll turn it off."

Cha-ching!

"No," my dad said. "Leave it on."

Cha-ching!

"You sure?" I asked.

"Yes," my mom said quickly. "Let's hear it."

Cha-ching!

And so we ate our dinner huddled around my phone that evening, listening to the sales coming in. My parents were aware that the business was off to a steady, if not stellar, start. But what I think they wanted to hear was that their son's company was doing something good for the world. Every *cha-ching!* was another fifty-eight dollars that was going to go help someone. Every sale was confirmation that I was using my platform for good; that I was finally on a road where I didn't see my celebrity only as a means to get into the VIP clubs, an excuse to sleep until four p.m., a crutch to avoid building something on my own.

Every *cha-ching!* was a sign that the hardship, the drama, the heartache, the sense of failure, had been worth it, because all of it had brought me to this point: sitting at the kitchen table with my parents, listening to my company make $30,000 in sales in one day. And so it went until, by the end of the month, we had hit $100,000.

8

WHAT'S A PILLOW PARTY?

When I was ten years old, I made my first sale. My childhood home backed up to a golf course, right between the fourteenth green and the fifteenth tee. Living next to the links tends to give one an appreciation for the game. More than that, it gives one a chance to talk with a lot of golfers and learn from them. Not only did I learn but I also saw an opportunity. It didn't make any sense to me that after a player shanked his shot into a pond he would just walk away, leaving the ball behind. *There must be hundreds of balls in those ponds*, I thought. Hundreds of *free* balls. And if they kept losing their balls in the drink, then wouldn't they need more balls? To my young mind, there could be only one answer, so off I splashed into the ponds to retrieve as many balls from the muddy bottoms as I could.

With my father pitching in for a stock of sodas, I set up my first retail shop right there in the backyard, with nothing more than a five-gallon Fisher's Popcorn bucket full of old golf balls and a cooler full of Coke. Then I'd wait and watch for the white roofs of the golf carts to appear over the ridge on the fourteenth fairway, and get ready to make a sale. The golfers would finish up fourteen, then pass my little shop on the way to fifteen, where I'd chat them up. Whether it was my age or my innate charm, the golfers got a kick out of this kid trying to earn a few bucks hawking old balls: fifty cents for one or three for a dollar.

Over the course of a summer I pulled in a few hundred bucks, which to a kid of ten (with no overhead) was an absolute fortune. It was all profit, since my father never asked for a reimbursement on the sodas. I was, however, too successful, and eventually complaints reached the course managers, who didn't take too kindly to a kid skimming from their golf ball sales. So they shut me down, but not before I learned a thing or two about business—and life.

The first thing I learned was that I was good at talking to complete strangers. Not because I was trying to get something from them (although I was), but rather because I genuinely enjoyed it. Even from a young age, I loved to meet new people, and I learned then that this trait—well, skill, actually—helped me make more sales. I also learned that I would get a physical response to making a sale. You could call it a high, or a rush, whatever it was, but damn if it wasn't exciting. I'd make a sale, then immediately want to make another one. I'd stay at my spot in the backyard all day, overlooking the course, just waiting for the sight of that white roof of a golf cart to peek over the ridgeline.

A lot of newer business owners sometimes see sales as

something that is a bit deceitful—as if you're tricking a customer into giving you money. But when sales are done right—face-to-face—it's really the creation of happiness. I know it sounds a bit sentimental. But those golfers left my stand with a new(ish) ball, an ice-cold Coke, and, most important of all, a smile. It didn't matter if they were happy because they got something they needed or whether they just enjoyed a brief chat with some precocious kid. They left happy. And, naturally, I was happy; not just for the money, although that was exciting enough, but because I gave someone something they wanted: I made them smile.

It wasn't always about making the sale, either. One day a guy finished up at the fourteenth and walked by my stand. He smiled at me but continued on without stopping. I noticed he was sweating pretty hard, so I asked if he wanted a soda.

"I'd love one, kid, but I don't have any cash on me," he said.

"That's okay," I replied. "Have one." I handed him a Coke.

He took the soda and thanked me, and we chatted for a bit. Then he went on his way. I didn't think much of it, and I was happy to give someone a cool drink, even if I didn't technically "make the sale." Later that day, after I had closed shop, a man in a Porsche showed up on our driveway. My dad greeted him at the door, and the man told him all about this kid who gave him a drink when he was thirsty, and he wanted to pay for it. He reached into his wallet and handed my dad a twenty-dollar bill—surely the most expensive can of Coke ever sold. Sometimes, happiness pays.

DOWN TO CAMDEN

In the summer of 2019, I had attended the grand opening of a small boutique in Camden, South Carolina, to help promote Sewing Down South. The store owners had purchased our first wholesale order and had asked my business partner Jerry if I would attend their party. Jerry jumped at the idea and called me immediately.

"You need to go, man," he told me. "They're having a grand opening party and you need to be there to sell the shit out of our pillows."

Attending parties and meeting absolute strangers was one of the perks—or hazards, depending on your point of view—of my television career. Fortunately, I enjoyed that part of my celebrity and got a huge rush out of getting to know my *Southern Charm* fans. So I didn't have a problem going to a party in Camden. What I had a problem with was whether anyone would care that Craig Conover, reality TV star, was at a furnishing store hawking his pillows. The owners certainly seemed to think I would be good for business; but would I be good for my own business? Or, put another way, was the only reason anyone had bought a Sewing Down South pillow was because I was on television? There wouldn't be any cameras. None of my costars would be with me. No reality TV drama or hijinks. Just me, pillow maker, utterly exposed and absolutely terrified of falling flat on my face.

As it turned out, I had a blast. When I got there, the owners of Swanky Southern showed me to a table where there was a bunch of Sewing Down South swag—hats, T-shirts, etc.—and a bunch of my pillows. I thought I would be working the crowd, but instead I mostly sat behind that table, signing autographs and talking to customers, who ended up buying a lot of pillows. A hundred or so people showed up, and we sold out in two hours. Afterward, I went out with the owners, a married couple and my new friends, finding ourselves at Waffle House in the small hours of the night. I might have crashed on their couch later . . . to be woken up by the husband at one p.m.

Anyway, on my drive back to Charleston, I was jazzed up. Excited is an understatement. I decided right then to announce to the world, on Instagram no less, that Sewing Down South would begin a "pillow party tour." I wasn't even sure what a pillow party tour would look like, but in my mind, I saw a repeat of the experience I just had in Camden. Three minutes after hitting send on the IG post, Jerry called me.

"Um, what's a pillow party," he asked, "and why are we having a tour of them?"

I explained what had happened in Camden and laid out, as much as I could in the car, my vision.

"We'll go around to these little shops and sell our pillows," I explained. "We'll have drinks, and music, and I can sign merchandise. It'll be awesome!"

I should have told him the story of my golf ball business: Like that ten-year-old kid I had been, we were going to put smiles on people's faces—and make a whole lot of money doing it. Instead I tried to explain to him what had happened at the store in Camden, although I fear something was lost in my explanation. Jerry knew it had been a successful event, but what he didn't understand was why we would want to spend time and resources replicating it elsewhere. (And he was doubtful that we could.) I'm also sure that the five texts he had sent me that morning, which I didn't answer, made him think that the Swanky Southern event was about me having fun. (He wasn't wrong, but it was definitely business *and* pleasure.)

Besides, in the whole history of pillows, no one—as far as we knew anyway—had ever gone on a "tour" to sell them. Bands go on tour. Comedians go on tour. Authors go on tour. But pillow-makers? They don't fucking go on tour. My partners were worried about the logistics and the optics. They just didn't know how to organize a single pillow party, much less enough of them to constitute an entire tour. And what if it failed? What if no one showed up? What if the very businesses we wanted stocking our pillows suddenly realized I was not as popular as I thought I was?

The other problem was that our sales weren't exactly the greatest. Instead of focusing on the business, we'd be diverting attention and resources to something that might blow up in our faces. While selling wholesale to third-party sellers had been a goal of ours from the beginning, we were still trying to get the online site going. Now I was asking everyone to stop what they were doing and focus on this crazy idea. But I stood my ground and made my case. Jerry had been urging me to get more involved in the day-to-day operations. Well, here I was, trying to get more involved and think of ways to boost our brand and sales. He relented.

I think there's a lesson here for budding entrepreneurs. Some moments simply defy acceptable business practices. From his sports-management firm, Jerry had seen meet and greets fizzle out, either because the sports star got bored or the fans failed to show up. Especially if the talent isn't good with meeting strangers, these kinds of events can quickly become humiliating mistakes. Despite my experience in Camden, Jerry wanted to protect the company (and me) from the same embarrassment. It might have helped his anxiety had I at least waited until talking with him and Amanda before committing the company to a series of events that could suck up valuable time, energy, and resources.

It's simply hard to capture the energy, the community, the sense of celebration that filled me—as well as the owners and the guests—at Swanky Southern and communicate those feelings into a business-friendly elevator pitch. And the truth is, I hadn't given the idea of pillow parties any deeper thought than: *I want to do this again.* Now I can look back and understand better *why* I wanted to do it again; *why* that party in Camden resonated so strongly with me that I would commit our young company to holding several of them. The reason why is that I was that kid again, hawking golf balls and Cokes between the fourteenth green and fifteenth tee, putting smiles on people's faces. That thrill that I felt then was in me that next day, driving home to Charleston, impulsively sending out an Instagram Story announcing the first great Sewing Down South Pillow Party Tour to the world.

That still didn't answer Jerry's question: What *is* a pillow party? But it was almost too late now. The emails and the DMs started flowing in with requests to host the next pillow party.

"You said it, what is it?" Jerry quipped, half-joking, half-serious.

We were about to find out.

CREATING SMILES

The first hurdle to overcome was Jerry and Amanda's hesitancy in committing our company—and themselves—toward planning and executing a half-baked idea. But by putting the cart before the horse, so to speak, with my Instagram Story, I had put all of us in a position of either figuring it out and doing it—or canceling it and looking like jackasses. Whereas before, we would get something like twenty emails a week to our customer service account, we got more than two hundred in the first couple days following the IG story. This number doesn't include the DMs from stores that were flooding my IG account. This overwhelming response helped convince my partners that there was *something* there—that there was a demand for these pillow parties, whatever they were.

But I also knew that Jerry and Amanda wanted me to show more confidence in my role with the company. I was the "face" and main designer, but they knew I could be more. I knew I could too. When the three of us entered into a partnership, the company was split into thirds, but the bulk of the finances, web, and operations of the company fell to Jerry and Amanda, for no other reason than because they were the pros at that stuff. Early on I was happy to let them carry the major lifting of the business, but I was never comfortable with being just the name and face of the company. It wasn't that Jerry didn't want me taking more ownership in the business; he just was waiting for me to assert myself.

So, this was me asserting myself. The excitement for the pillow parties didn't wear off after I had a chance to get a little sleep and consider everything. In fact, I was more pumped as the emails continued to roll in with enthusiastic stores and boutiques all but begging (and sometimes actually begging) to host a party. It was just like when I had started making pillows and would receive hundreds of emails from *Southern Charm* viewers asking where they could buy one. I had the same feeling that something special was going to happen with the pillow parties. Even if Jerry and Amanda couldn't see it yet, they also didn't want to pour cold water over my idea. We forged ahead and held on to the vague hope that we would figure it out as we went along.

Then I got a message from my old high school friend, Courtney, owner of Perfect Furnishings in Bethany Beach, Delaware. I have already recounted what happened at that first party, but now I'll add a bit more of what went on with the planning, as well as the aftermath. One of our problems with the hundreds of messages we were receiving was how to decide which ones were serious or not. It seemed an overwhelming task for a company of three people, and frankly, if that's the way things had remained, we likely would've just dropped the idea completely. Shaking his head at the absurdity, Jerry dreaded diving into those hundreds of emails, and I didn't blame him.

But Courtney's message gave us a single, legitimate store on which to focus our experiment. Our friendship meant that we could go in trusting that she would follow through on her end, if we could get our act together on ours. Besides, it was in my hometown. We had to know if the appeal of Sewing Down South extended beyond the South Carolina region where the show— and me—was most popular. Otherwise, our "tour" would consist of driving around Charleston and the surrounding towns. Holding the first pillow party in Delaware seemed like a good way to find out if this idea had legs.

As we had done in Camden, we had Courtney purchase a bulk order of pillows at wholesale prices, which she could then sell back to the guests. We also put the onus of providing refreshments and other entertainment on the store. Our value-add to the entire operation was me, the fact that I would be there, which we said (hoped) would be enough to make it all worthwhile for the owner. Otherwise, our loose idea was that the party would look like a book-signing event. I would be seated at a table, greet guests, take pictures, and sign merchandise. Simple. And so it was, in theory. The reality is that none of us—not me, not Courtney, and certainly not Jerry—could have imagined the turnout. At least two hundred people showed up to Perfect Furnishings that day, which was manageable enough, if also entirely unexpected. Our only promotion of the event was an Instagram message I had posted a week before, meaning we had spent zero dollars on marketing or promotion.

Thousands of dollars in sales, a line down the block, almost zero overhead—these things tend to have an impact on business-minded people like Jerry and Amanda. "I get it now," Jerry said to me after the party. It was a wonderful moment, equally as good as all those other wonderful moments I mentioned earlier, and perhaps the validation I had been seeking all along. It wasn't just that the party had been an unexpected success. I think even a slightly less successful event would still have convinced him of the value these parties had for the company overall. But Jerry also saw how this particular party—in my hometown, with my family in attendance, and the words of encouragement I received from fans—affected me in a way that he hadn't seen before. I too measured the success of Sewing Down South by dollars and sales—after all, if you don't have these things, you don't have a company. But you also measure success by the goals you reach and the joy you attain along the way. Selling Sewing Down South pillows through our Shopify app and website proved we had a real company; but there was something about selling those pillows out of a storefront, where one is able to talk with customers, that has always sent my heart soaring. Getting into stores had been one of my goals from the beginning; and not only had we gotten into stores, but it was I who was doing the selling. Few things compare to that rush I received during that first pillow party. Few moments will be as impactful for me in my life. That thrill fueled me to talk with every single customer in line that day—and every single customer who has ever stood in line for an SDS Pillow Party. It fuels me now, chasing that joy I experience in sharing my passion with others.

Aside from the dollars and sales, Jerry saw all of this, and it was as if he had been waiting for this moment to arrive: the moment when the whole thing finally clicked for me, when the joy in sharing something I've created with the world makes all the previous and current struggles seem infinitesimally small by comparison. I hesitate to say that Jerry treated me as anything less than a full partner prior to Bethany Beach, because that's not the case at all. I think he had been waiting for me to find my own confidence, my own joy in leading Sewing Down South, not as a face and a name, but as the guiding force behind all that we could achieve.

I don't think either of us stopped smiling throughout the entire party. Even now, as I write this, I'm smiling and teary-eyed at the memory of that moment, that magical moment when a dream was realized. What made that moment all the more special was that I was able to share my smile with others. I was able to smile at someone who had been waiting in line for hours and see that smile returned, whether that person was just a fan of *Southern Charm* or a high school football player who shares my passion for sewing. If there's a reason behind this book besides inspiring readers to turn their own hobbies and passions into something they can share with the world, then it is the hope that you too can experience that same smile one day.

AN UNEXPECTED TRIUMPH

Of course, the honeymoon was short-lived, and reality came crashing through the door—hard—during a party outside Annapolis, Maryland. The success of the first few parties had caused Jerry to rethink our logistics. If hundreds of people were showing up to buy *our* pillows, then why would we sell those pillows wholesale to the store? Why wouldn't we sell those pillows directly to the customer *from the store*? The store owners wouldn't like it, but then our value-add was the same as it had always been: my appearance would get customers into the store. The flood of shoppers through their doors—remember, these are small boutiques meant to accommodate maybe a dozen customers—was more than enough to keep the stores playing along with our new "pop-up shop" model. But the change also made us more vulnerable to catastrophe. If people failed to show up at a party where the store had purchased wholesale from us, well, that's embarrassing, but we don't lose anything except our time—and the goodwill of the owner. Going directly to the customer now meant that if those people failed to materialize, then we would be out the cost of the inventory we had set aside for the event. We'd lose money *and* the store would hate us.

It was a sign of Jerry's commitment to the pillow party idea that he, who was notoriously hesitant in committing SDS resources anywhere, decided to forge ahead with the new payment model. And it worked great for the first couple of parties that we held after making the change . . . but then came the Painted Cottage in Edgewater, Maryland.

We spent the night before the party, August 31, 2019, at my parents' house in Ocean View, after I'd had a very successful party that day at Casual Design Furniture with several hundred people showing up. The party had exhausted me, and I was ready to hit the sack, when Jerry suddenly learned that the inventory for the next day's party—specifically, the pillow covers—hadn't been delivered yet. This was a disaster. Without pillow covers, we had nothing to sell to the customers. We would be out thousands of dollars in sales. Jerry frantically worked the phone all night trying to track down the location of the UPS truck and had one of those all-too-familiar games of "pass the customer" that call centers love playing. By the time Jerry found himself talking to a guy in Pakistan, he was about to lose it entirely. No one knew where the shipment was, and UPS customer service was most definitely failing to service the customer. Finally, Jerry got an answer—or at least a partial answer. He found out that the shipment would've passed through the UPS Distribution Center in Philadelphia—that is, if it was on the way to Edgewater at all. Otherwise, it still might be at the distribution center—maybe. Unfortunately, that was about as much as we had to go on. It was now early in the morning and we realized that the only thing to do was drive to Philly to check on the shipment personally—or find someone there who had a clue.

At five a.m., Jerry jumped in his car to drive the three hours from Fenwick to Philadelphia. We weren't about to cancel, so I stayed behind to get ready to go to the party that afternoon. I learned from Jerry later that when he showed up at the Philly UPS distribution center around eight thirty a.m., he spent an hour trying to find anyone who might let him in. He finally located the manager, who confirmed that the shipment should be in the center.

"Great!" said Jerry. "Let's get it."

"We can't," said the manager.

"Um, why?" asked Jerry.

"We don't know where it is."

If you're familiar with the last scene in *Raiders of the Lost Ark*, when the Ark itself is wheeled into some nameless, generic warehouse the size of a city block and filled to the ceiling with nondescript boxes, you can appreciate Jerry's dejection at that particular moment. An hour after arriving, Jerry got back in his car, empty-handed, and drove back down. Now, Jerry didn't tell me any of this, probably because he knew I get nervous enough before a pillow party and there wasn't anything I could do anyway. I only learned that we were about to have a pillow party with no pillows when he finally arrived—after being in his car for six hours. I nearly lost it, but one look at Jerry, and I kept my cool. He'd had a far worse day than I'd had. We decided to forge ahead—and once more have one of those moments that defy business sense.

Six hundred people showed up to the Painted Cottage that afternoon. Six hundred people who came there to see me and buy a damn pillow. And now we had to tell these six hundred people that they could still see me, but there weren't any pillows to buy. Or at least, there weren't any pillows they could take home that day, because our solution to the crisis was to sell orders for pillows, which we would fulfill (and I would sign) later. Had the whole crowd of six hundred risen up at that moment and smashed the place to bits, I don't think either Jerry or I would've blamed them.

Only they didn't. They took the bad news as if it wasn't bad news at all, and we went on to have a ten-hour pillow party, complete with drinks and live music. Despite everything, the party was a smashing success, and we made twenty thousand dollars in sales. Even now, I don't rightly understand why we sold that many pillows without giving anyone a single pillow. Once again, during the party, Jerry gave me that "What the hell is going on?" look that I remembered so well from the first party.

And if that was the entirety of the Edgewater Pillow Party That Almost Wasn't, then I think it would go down as one of the most memorable we had. But there is another reason I remember Edgewater so fondly, and which I believe helps explain why the party defied explanation. If I had made a point before to greet and chat with everyone who stood in line at any of my parties, my resolve was only hardened at this particular party, for obvious reasons. If they couldn't get a pillow, well, they sure as hell were going to get a chance to meet me and get their autograph and picture, no matter if I stayed there all day—which I basically did.

It was sometime during this ten-hour line that I saw a young woman in a wheelchair, accompanied by her mother. I walked out from behind the desk to greet her. The young woman looked sick, and I learned that she was suffering through stage four cancer and that her prognosis was terminal. I talked to her as I talked to everyone who stood in line, and we took a picture together. I spent more time with her than I did most of the other guests, although I didn't think much of it. It was just the natural thing to do. I was touched by the young woman's desire to support me and Sewing Down South, but I certainly didn't expect what that moment meant to her. Several months later I received a letter from that young woman's mother. Her daughter had already passed, but she wanted to thank me for spending some time with her, which she said had been one of the happiest moments in her life.

She wasn't there for a pillow. She was there for a smile; and it was one of the happiest moments of *my* life that I could give her one.

ON THE ROAD

The shipping fiasco in Edgewater forced us to look at our supply chain with greater care than we had been giving it, and we managed to avoid that disaster again as the tour continued. Part of the issue was that this was when Hurricane Dorian hit. The moment with my parents that I mentioned in the last chapter happened the night before the Edgewater party. I didn't mention it then, but the success of the charity drive basically broke our supply chain. Some customers weren't going to get their pillows for six to seven weeks. And that was on top of the shipping crisis we had in Edgewater. Our solution was to change manufacturers, from the one in North Carolina that printed on demand to one in South Carolina, closer to Charleston. The company was family owned, and was originally from Chicago, but had moved its operations to South Carolina in 1978. The new manufacturer allowed us to make a decision I had been pushing for since our launch: We would start holding inventory.

Otherwise, the tour continued, and picked up speed. By this point, Jerry had fully bought into my vision and was spending most of his days doing nothing more than planning, booking, and organizing logistics for the upcoming parties. When we started, we figured we could do one party a weekend. That plan lasted for a weekend, when we bumped it up to two, and even managed to squeeze a third in from time to time if the travel allowed for it. The Sewing Down South 2019 Pillow Party Tour ended up looking like this:

Aug. 24: Beaufort Linen Co., Beaufort, NC

Aug. 30: Casual Design Furniture, Fenwick, DE

Aug. 31: The Painted Cottage, Edgewater, MD

Sept. 7: 4 Rooms, Greenville, SC

Sept. 27: The Lucky Knot, Alexandria, VA

Sept. 28: For Posh Sake, Mechanicsville, VA

Oct. 13: Kittenish, Nashville, TN

Oct. 19: Eloise Trading Company, Aberdeen, NC

Oct. 20: Sweetgrass Home, Charlotte, NC

Nov. 8: The Community, Charleston, SC

Nov. 9: J&K Home Furnishings, Myrtle Beach, SC

Nov. 13: Donna Donaldson Interiors, Summit, NJ

Then came the Holiday Pillow Tour, complete with an exclusive holiday pillow I designed specifically for the tour:

Dec. 14: Draper James, Atlanta, GA

Dec. 15: At Home Furnishings, Birmingham, AL

Dec. 20: Details For the Home, Haymarket, VA

Dec. 21: Calico, Lutherville, MD

Dec. 22: Ellie Main Line, Wayne, PA

If Sewing Down South ever goes bankrupt, Jerry could easily find another job as a manager for a rock band. The organizational skills he brought to the tour were nothing less than awesome. Indeed, the whole thing felt like we were a band on the road, which was both good and bad. As word spread throughout the boutique and home furnishing community, demand for our parties far outpaced our ability to book them. Jerry floated the idea of selling tickets to the parties, which I quickly squashed. If we had to sell tickets to see me, then that money was going to go to a charity. Instead of tickets, we decided to cap the number of guests at two hundred people. It wasn't something I wanted to do, but as much fun as ten-hour pillow parties are, they aren't sustainable. These were energy-draining events, for both Jerry and me. And let's not forget that Jerry was still running operations for Sewing Down South as well as his other business, ProVentures. Since I insisted on meeting everyone in line, a two-hundred-guest party still would take three to four hours. But we did have to make certain arrangements, given the size of the crowds that were coming. For example, we started asking the stores to hire security guards, not to protect me so much as to keep order in the lines. When you're standing in line for several hours, being plied with drinks, sometimes better judgment goes out the window and tempers fray.

One of the most remarkable things we noticed, as we set up shop in these small boutiques and stores, was how appreciative the owners were. After the party in Edgewater, the owners of the Painted Cottage met me the next morning in the parking lot picking up my car. With tears in their eyes, they told me that they had decided to close the store, but now, because of the success of the pillow party, they were going to keep it going. (And they're still in business today.) But it wasn't just the stores themselves that were grateful; sometimes it was the entire town. In small towns like Edgewater (population: 9,000); Aberdeen, NC (population: 7,500); or Haymarket, VA (population: 1,500), our arrival was greeted like a major event. "Nothing like this has happened here for years," was a common refrain I heard from guests. While no national media outlets bothered to send reporters, local newspapers and stations would cover our pillow parties as if they were newsworthy events—which in a way they were for these small towns.

Looking back, what strikes me today is the enduring value that small stores, those mom-and-pop joints that once dotted the American landscape, have in their communities, and how they've been suffocated and driven out of business by the emergence of online retail. I'm a realist in these matters, and Sewing Down South hasn't shied away from doing business with the big-box stores like Thomasville and Bed Bath & Beyond. I also know that my company's long-term future is tied to online retail. But it wasn't until the tour that I understood the impact that these stores could have on a community, and how their disappearance in recent decades has profoundly affected the towns they served. One reason the pillow parties were such a success is that they were able to recapture a bit of that old-town spirit; the sense that a single store is as much a community center as a town park. It's the power of face-to-face commerce that leads the buyer and seller to bring a smile to each other's faces. To this day, I still receive messages from owners on the anniversary of the party we held at their store, reminiscing about the great time they had, updating me on their success (or struggles), and asking when Sewing Down South will be ready to do it all again.

Soon, I reply. As soon as we can. If these stores had been hurting before our parties, one can only imagine what has happened since the devastation wrought by Covid. While I hear from many of the owners from time to time, I don't hear from all of them, and some have stopped sending me messages. When I think about that, I'm reminded that the value of in-store retail is more than simply commerce; in many communities across the United States, in-store retail is an essential element of daily life. I'm proud that Sewing Down South can claim that its first major success was tied to in-person retail, those small stores and boutiques that gave us life in those early days, when I had little more than a crazy idea to start throwing pillow parties. Our success depended on them, and to them I say thank you. We'll be back on the road as soon as possible.

LIVING WITH MY DARKNESS

"I don't want to go out anymore," I said to Jerry. Well, more likely, I screamed it at him.

We were in the middle of a pillow party at For Posh Sake in Mechanicsville, VA, close to Richmond. Five hundred people had shown up, which meant several hours of me standing behind the table greeting guests, taking pictures, signing autographs, and being handed drinks. And more drinks. And a shot here and there. Eventually, it caught up with me, and during a break in the party, I went to a back room to take a breather, only I didn't want to go back out.

Jerry tried to reason with me, but I was beyond reason at that point. "I've been here for five hours!" I said, and kicked the wall. I wasn't lying. I had been there for hours, and I was shit-faced. I was beyond exhausted. This was our second party of the weekend, our third of the month, and our eighth since the tour began. It's not like I had abstained during the previous parties, but I think there comes a point on any tour where you just break. I had broken.

But Jerry wasn't letting me off the hook so easily.

"Dude, you're going to shut up, first of all," he said to me. "Then you're going to pull up your big-boy pants and go back out there and talk to the last thirty people who have waited all day to see you."

It was the kick in the ass that I needed just then. I went back out and finished what I was there to do. I met my guests and shook hands and signed autographs and took pictures with those last thirty people, as I had done with the hundreds before them. I did my job.

It's a cliché to say that life on the road can be hard. Spending several hours at a party is tiring work, and to get up the next morning to do it all again took its toll on both Jerry and me. We'd hop in the car, slug down our daily dose of Monster Rehab energy drinks, and drive to the next one. You'd think that after doing a few of them, I would have settled into a rhythm, but the truth is that my old fears and anxiety wouldn't leave me alone. I was a nervous wreck before each party, and even the soothing sounds of my favorite Taylor Swift mix (don't laugh, but yes, Taylor Swift is my go-to artist to get my head in the game) couldn't alleviate my anxieties. Often, the schedule was so grueling that we'd roll into the next town with no time to prepare. So you make do with what you have. Jerry certainly won't let me live down the day I ran into a CVS to purchase some self-tanner but didn't have any time to apply it before the party. My only option was the CVS bathroom, where I absconded for about a half hour to apply the tanner, fix my hair, and get into some fresh clothes, slugging a Bud Light while a CVS employee was banging on the door to ask if I needed any help.

Looking back, these are funny moments, but life on the road brought out that dark side that has lived in me for years. The constant strain of "being on" for several hours makes me turn to behaviors that I know can be destructive. When combined with my innate love of meeting new people, and sharing with them the joy of celebration, I sometimes lose sight of the reason I'm there in the first place. That first drink that is handed to me when I arrive acts like the trigger that allows me to turn my job into just another day out with friends. If I'm "working," then I'm stressed and withdrawn; but if I'm partying, then I can just be myself. I'm best when I'm myself, when I'm genuine and not trying to play a part. But that doesn't mean I'm not still working. The blurring of these lines has sometimes led me over the edge, with alcohol providing the gentle push that allows me to forget that I'm still the name and face of this growing company.

After one potentially embarrassing moment, Jerry sat me down in the car.

"You're allowed to have fun, but you need to remember what we're doing here," he said to me. "Don't ruin everything we're trying to create."

If there's anything I hate more than being addressed like a

child, it's knowing that I have been acting like one. Jerry was right, of course. On the show, if I or one of my friends does something absurd or embarrassing while drunk, well, that's what viewers tune in to see. But when I'm out there representing Sewing Down South, the rules are different—and I must be different too. I have known for many years now that I can slip too easily into an escapist mindset. I know what calms my nerves and what lets me forget the fears and anxieties that constantly plague me: it's spending time with friends, enjoying a drink, and cutting loose. That's my escape, and for the most part, there isn't anything wrong with that. But I've since learned that my need for escape has a darker side that brings out the very worst parts of me. Indeed, it turns me into the very person I have struggled hard not to be.

When I finally quit Adderall, I rode that wave of feeling like I had accomplished something very big in my life. Hearing about others' experiences, I know how hard it is to kick such a deep-seated habit. What I didn't realize was that that need for comfort from outside substances would stay with me, Adderall addict or not. Like water finding its own level, the need to seek oblivion will come out if I'm not careful. The Pillow Party Tour gave me such a natural high of meeting my customers and supporters, one that I remembered quite distinctly from my childhood selling golf balls. But behind this natural high lurked those old fears and anxieties; the self-defeatism that said, *I'm not good enough the way I am*. Something is wrong with me, and so even while I'm in a moment that provides healthy fulfillment and validation, I sometimes can't quiet that dark voice.

One of my greatest joys in being on the road and visiting with fans of the show and the company is to hear their . . . well, surprise that I'm not the person they thought they knew. For seven seasons, they've seen a young man struggle to find himself in a world full of decadence and wealth. They've seen me fall short of my potential time and again. They might think that my sewing or even my company are little more than platforms that I have invented to give the appearance of success; that, in the end, this Craig Conover guy is just a reality TV star who has fallen assbackward into a successful company. It only takes a few minutes of talking to me to overthrow these assumptions and show them that the guy they thought they knew is decent, hardworking, and above all, interested in them. It's a validation of a different sort, not the fawning adulation of strangers that I sought when I was coming to grips with being a public figure; but the enlightening moment that the two of us aren't that different, and that indeed we can share similar interests and dreams. I revel in those moments, because they give me such a surge of confidence and joy that I am that person after all.

But that person they saw on the show does exist inside me; he's the person that I have struggled to overcome, whose constant presence haunts me and whispers: "I am the real you." And when I fall too deeply into my escapism, when the drinks and the music and the joy give me just the nudge I need to jump off that cliff of responsibility and into that dark sea, I realize that I will likely always struggle with him. I don't think I'm unique in that regard. In fact, in talking to others at the pillow parties, I know I am not. Everyone has the worst version of themselves waiting to come out; waiting for the moment when the strain and the pressure become too much and the only thing that makes any sense is to say "Fuck it." That siren song is in everyone's ears, and if my journey these last several years has taught me anything, it's that that song will never stop playing. We cannot quiet it entirely, but we find our true selves, and we realize our full potential, when we fight against it, when we ignore the insecurities and the fears that we don't deserve to do what makes us happy.

When Jerry told me not to destroy all that we'd worked so hard to create, he wasn't just referring to Sewing Down South. He was talking to me, and the man I am today, the one who has overcome all the struggles and inner demons to finally live the life that makes him happy. His words are also a warning to remember that boy who got such a thrill selling golf balls in his backyard and putting smiles on people's faces.

THE NEXT STEPS

In August of 2019, Sewing Down South did $67,000 in sales, with $25,000 coming from the pillow parties. In September, we did $105,000 in sales, most of which was the result of our charity drive for Dorian, but made $40,000 from the parties. In October, with the pillow parties in full swing, we made $135,000 in sales, with again $40,000 coming from the pillow parties. Word had started to get out, the fire was spreading, and all three of us felt it. Something had started to happen. The pillow parties had unleashed this energy around what we had created. Something special was going on, although even I—ever the optimist—was unsure about what it all meant. But other players in the market had started to take notice of this little pillow company out of Charleston. We had crashed through the doors and surprised everyone, including myself. I'll detail these opportunities more in the next chapter, and I don't want to dismiss their importance. But when I look back on that amazing autumn of 2019, I see the beginnings of something great. We had done it *our* way, and we had succeeded. The parties represented the turning point for Sewing Down South, and for me. My instincts had been right. My vision had been realized—even beyond my wildest dreams. Now, it was time to take the next steps.

9

THE PARTY CONTINUES

*I*n August 2019, right before we set off on the great Pillow Party Tour, we got an email from someone from Authentic Brands Group. Two things to mention here: The first is that when I say we "got an email," I mean that all three partners shared a single email address for Sewing Down South at this stage in the company. Otherwise, we just used our personal email addresses—and sometimes I would do business over my social media channels. The second thing to say is that Authentic Brands Group, which probably doesn't mean anything to the average reader, meant the fucking world to Jerry and Amanda. I had no idea what it was, but Jerry and Amanda, as people who know business, could barely contain their excitement.

Authentic Brands Group is a company that owns more than fifty consumer brands, including Barney's, Reebok, Brooks Brothers, Forever 21, Nine West, Hickey Freeman, Juicy Couture, Nautica, and *Sports Illustrated*. It also "owns" the estates or likeness of many deceased celebrities, such as Muhammad Ali, Marilyn Monroe, and Elvis Presley. What I'm saying is that this company is a freaking titan in the business world. Everyone in America has done business in one of their stores. More relevant to us, in 2018, ABG had acquired the furniture-maker Thomasville.

So when this email from ABG came into our single company email, hiyall@sewingdownsouth.com, Jerry was freaking out. I knew nothing about what it meant, so thank God Jerry was managing the company email. I probably would have forgotten to reply back. Jerry did reply back, which was how he found himself on the phone with Nick Woodhouse, president of ABG. Nick's pitch was simple enough: ABG was trying to relaunch the Thomasville brand and they felt that Sewing Down South would be a perfect addition to their lineup of products. Sounds great, but Jerry had one question.

"How did you hear about us?" he asked.

"Well now, I don't quite remember how you got on our radar," said Nick. "But we love what we see."

Fair enough. If also a little mysterious. The Pillow Party Tour definitely led to some wonderful opportunities, as the home décor world suddenly awakened to this little upstart company. But the tour hadn't happened yet. Our marketing, for better or worse, was tied to my supporters, which means it was tied to *Southern Charm* viewers. They had proven to be a solid foundation on which to start a business, but all three of us knew that for Sewing Down South to be what we all wanted it to be—a brand in its own right—then we had to expand our reach beyond *Southern*

Charm. We hoped that we could do that organically—in other words, cheaply—but it came as a complete shock to us, especially Jerry, that word had spread far enough to attract a brand like Thomasville—and a company like ABG. However Sewing Down South entered ABG's orbit, we were glad to be there. Associating our brand to Thomasville's, one of the biggest home décor brands in the country, was exactly the validation our little upstart business needed to reach beyond our core demographics.

We sent ABG some pillows so its team could inspect the quality. When they passed muster, it was time to get down to business. We scheduled a meeting with the ABG team in New York City in November to coincide with my appearance at BravoCon, a three-day convention celebrating all things Bravo. I don't want to minimize how much meeting all the *Southern Charm* fans has meant to me. As I hope has been made clear by now, I take my place on the show very seriously and I know that I'm where I am today because of my supporters from the show. I met viewers often enough in and around Charleston as well as during my travels, but BravoCon was the first time I had met them en masse. It would have been a unique experience—if I hadn't already had very similar experiences during the Pillow Party Tour. Nevertheless, I had even more to be thankful for now that their support had led directly to this unique opportunity with Thomasville.

Even then, I didn't know how much I owed my supporters until the meeting with the ABG people started. The two-floor offices were right on Avenue of the Americas, and the entire team treated Amanda, Jerry, and me like VIPs. During the meeting we discussed how to create designs to elevate the new Thomasville brand and still stay authentic to SDS. They were to be more elegant, less whimsical, and beach-house oriented. They were looking for designs that were sleek, colorful, and upscale. It was certainly a departure from what we were doing at that moment, but also an opportunity and a challenge to expand our offering. The nature of the deal was that Sewing Down South would partner with Thomasville and have a display in all the rebranded big-box stores that were coming. The designs would also be available on both companies' websites. Even more exciting, we were going to get our own showroom at the High Point Market Authority in High Point, North Carolina. High Point was the largest home furnishings industry trade show in the world, with more than two thousand exhibitors scattered around 180 buildings. Just being there, and being connected to Thomasville, would solidify our presence as the company to watch. We were now playing with the big boys. Our little three-person team had suddenly arrived.

At the meeting was ABG president and CMO Nick Woodhouse. As we got to talking with him, he mentioned that his wife was a "huge" *Southern Charm* fan.

"In fact," he said, suddenly remembering, "she was the one who suggested that we partner with Sewing Down South for the Thomasville relaunch."

Did she? Well, mystery solved. Thank you, Mrs. Woodhouse.

Three months later, on February 2, 2020, Jerry and I found ourselves at the Sports Illustrated Super Bowl LIV Party, invited by our new friends at ABG. There was a moment during the party, as I was chatting with Elon Musk and Jerry Rice, when I had to ask myself the question I had asked often in the past year: "How did I get here?"

The arrival of Covid delayed a lot of the plans we had made with Thomasville, including showcasing at High Point and the opening of the newly rebranded Thomasville locations. While unfortunate, we weren't dependent on these new sales channels opening up. If anything, the Thomasville partnership confirmed that we had moved beyond being simply a small start-up pillow maker whose popularity was tied to the show. We started to feel confident that even if the show ended, Sewing Down South wouldn't just survive, but continue to thrive. We had a brand now, one distinct from *Southern Charm*. And while the show will always hold an important place in Sewing Down South's history—for which I was and remain grateful—our destinies were on different paths.

BACK ON TV

It was during the Pillow Party Tour, in the fall of 2019, when I was driving home from my parents' house in Delaware, that I read a message that came through the Sewing Down South IG channel. It was from HSN, just a simple message explaining that they'd heard about our tour and would love to talk with us. I nearly dropped the phone. Setting the car to cruise control, I blasted whatever music was coming out of the speakers (likely Taylor Swift), jumped on the driver's seat, and started dancing and yelling. Not very safe, and I apologize to my fellow motorists on the road that day, but damn, it's not every day that you achieve one of your lifetime goals. I was one of those kids who would watch HSN and its then-competitor QVC fanatically. I also loved infomercials. There was something about the whole production that pulled me in and kept me rapt on every product being sold. I'd run to my mom and say, "We need this!"

"No, Craig, we don't," she would reply, to my eternal disappointment.

In any case, when we started Sewing Down South, in the back of my mind—and I mean, way back—I harbored this dream to one day be on HSN selling my pillows. It was a far-off goal, like my dream of opening a store, that I wanted to hit within the company's first five years.

It was Jerry who picked up the ball next, while he was at a casino, no less. I had responded to the IG message with Jerry's contact information. I didn't know that HSN's head buyer would call him immediately, but she did. Which was why Jerry, who was letting off some tour steam at Washington's MGM National Harbor casino, answered a call without knowing who the hell was on the other line.

"Jerry Casselano?"

"Yes? Who is this?" said Jerry, the *ding-ding-ding* of slot machines echoing in the background.

"Hi, this is HSN calling you."

"Who?"

"HSN."

"Give me a second, please," said Jerry, who left his table to find a quieter spot away from the casino racket. "I'm sorry. I thought you said HSN."

"This is HSN."

"Wait, seriously?"

The gist of the call was that HSN had heard that this pillow company started by some reality TV celebrity was making a fortune going on the road to small boutiques.

"We've never heard of anyone doing something like that, and, well, we're impressed," said the buyer. I'm sure the hundreds of supporters who turned out were equally as impressive.

That call kicked off a partnership between Sewing Down South and HSN that continues to this day. Several months of back-and-forth happened, before Jerry, Amanda, and I visited the HSN campus on January 12, 2020. Sewing Down South was less than a year old. So much for "five-year dreams."

The sprawling, sixty-six-acre campus is a true modern marvel in corporate retail, with multiple studios, huge warehouses, and gorgeous grounds all designed to awe and inspire the visitor. It's like its own city, nestled in this beautiful part of Tampa. We walked around gawking at everything—and ended up getting lost on our way to a meeting with HSN top brass. That didn't stop us from snapping a pic next to the HSN corporate logo and posting it on IG, teasing supporters about what was coming up. It was a bit premature, since we didn't have a deal yet, but I've never been known for my patience.

We made it to our meeting, but judging by the smiles we got when we explained our lateness, I don't think getting lost in that place is all that rare for newcomers. We found ourselves in a conference room with the very people that other business owners spend years trying to meet, and most never get the chance. The meeting itself boiled down to the designs we were going to choose for our exclusive HSN lineup. We ended up picking twenty-three of them, which, in hindsight, was far too many. But what did we know? More is better, right? When we left, all smiles and handshakes, we had a six-figure deal for around six thousand pillows.

Before leaving, I dragged the rest of my partners to one of the studios. I had no idea if this was the one I would be filming at, but I didn't care. It looked just like I remembered from all those hours I spent watching HSN as a kid. Now it was my turn. Now I would be the one in front of cameras in the HSN studios, possibly inspiring another kid somewhere who would annoy his mom about buying products that seemed life-altering.

And that's pretty much where the honeymoon phase ended. From a manufacturing standpoint as well as a presentation standpoint, we learned twenty-three designs were simply too many. The design of so many unique covers stressed our production limits, which is to say nothing about how I was supposed to sell twenty-three separate pillows on the air. Especially when we learned the diligence that HSN gave to inspecting the products, we should have settled on less than ten. Oh well. These are good problems to have.

Jerry then learned the hard way what it means to appear on HSN to sell your products. He found himself buried in over forty documents, each one thirty to forty pages long, setting out legal matters, standards, shipping protocols, etc. I don't know how he managed it all. At one point, I heard him grumble about "blowing his head off." But the biggest headache proved to be our claim that Sewing Down South products were "made in America." It's true enough; all of the pillows we sell are made right here in the United States. Except . . . some of the raw materials for those products come from abroad. That's a problem, at least from HSN's viewpoint.

To pass HSN's rigorous inspection, we couldn't claim that our products were "made in the USA." Jerry fought about it, but it wasn't a fight he could win. This wouldn't have been much of an issue if we hadn't already manufactured all six thousand pillows and had them waiting on the pallets at our factory, ready to be shipped down to St. Petersburg. Two-thirds of these pillows had been given the "Made in the USA" tag. As long as they had that tag, HSN wouldn't sell them. So Jerry traveled to the factory and, with the help of the team down there, personally went through roughly four thousand pillows, removing the tag and sewing in the right one stating: *Made in the USA of domestic and imported materials.* The job took several days to finish. We ended up passing the eight-hour virtual inspection, but it was an experience that Jerry never wants to repeat.

By April, we had another problem: Covid. Because of the lockdowns, I wasn't allowed to film from HSN's studios anymore. We scrambled and came up with an alternate venue: my house, where we'd stream over Skype. The only good part about this new protocol was that now my appearance on HSN could be filmed by the *Southern Charm* crew. My time on the network was scheduled for early July, well after the time when production usually had wrapped. But because of the stoppage over Covid, filming was still going on. Which was how viewers were able to watch some of the behind-the-scenes of the HSN shoot on episode 6 of season 7. I think it was a blessing in disguise. As much as I really wanted to shoot at the HSN studios, doing it at my house allowed the show to finally give some viewers an inside look at Sewing Down South and its success.

In the end, we sold 40 percent of our stock that day during my live appearance, so, despite the headaches, it was all so very much worth it. Younger me, the one who obsessed about HSN and infomercials, was surely smiling. It does feel very satisfying when a dream is realized.

TAKING CONTROL

Season 7 was bizarre for the whole cast, and not just because of Covid. It was the first season that Cam wouldn't be on the show. In response, the producers tapped me to be the new narrator, the one who catches everyone up on what's been going down with the crew in Charleston since the last episode. Of course, it was more than just being the new voice of the show. We were all going to miss Cam, but when perhaps the most "normal" and certainly one of the most popular cast members leaves, it's an opportunity for others to step up. I have no doubt that the success of Sewing Down South was a factor in the producers' decision to make me the new "voice" of the show. I believe there was an awareness within the production team that they had missed the story about my little sewing company. Unless you were following me on Instagram, most viewers probably had some proverbial whiplash at my sudden success. Yes, they had shown Jerry and me discussing working together in the previous season, but how the hell does that lead to HSN? The launch of the company; the Pillow Party Tour; the Bahamian charity drive—viewers saw none of this.

I'm sort of torn about this. On the one hand, it would have been quite the middle finger to everyone who had dismissed my sewing to have shown the crowds that turned up at the parties. I know that's not a noble motivation, but I'm also not above gloating a bit, especially when so many just assumed I was going nowhere with my little passion project. On the other hand, I think it was good to be with my supporters and customers without the show intruding. The cameras would have put up a wall and vastly complicated the logistics. I would also have wondered if people showed up for me and my pillows, or because cameras were there. As it happened, I didn't have to wonder. They came for Sewing Down South, not for *Southern Charm*.

But with season 7 approaching, I felt like the production wanted to make up for lost time. Suddenly this "loser" had achieved incredible success. Suddenly I had this company that wasn't dependent on the show. Which meant *I* wasn't dependent on the show. On this point, let me make something very clear. I love *Southern Charm*. I want the show to continue to succeed. I want to be a part of its success because I know I have helped to make it a hit. But it felt so good to get to a point in my professional life where I had something that was entirely mine. It was liberating. Sewing Down South gave me the freedom—finally—to be just who I was, damn the consequences. I could relax and enjoy being on the show without constantly questioning whether the person viewers saw would be someone they wanted to see next season. If they liked me, great. If not, well, I had a pillow empire to build.

What I'm saying is that Sewing Down South gave me confidence in a way I had never felt before. The confidence to enjoy being on television; the confidence to be who I was; the confidence to negotiate from a position of strength; and the confidence to take control of my life. It was a brand-new experience for me. A brand-new world—in more ways than one.

Since breaking up with Naomie two years earlier, I had not had a serious girlfriend. Several flings, some extended periods of dating the same girl, but no one I would have called someone special. I had certainly moved on from Naomie—I wasn't holding a candle for her—but I just hadn't met anyone who blew me away. Then I traveled to Aspen for New Year's at the end of 2019 and met Natalie Hegnauer. She was part of a group of women that we had met on the slopes, and I remember hanging outside the bar at the ski resort and seeing her sitting at a table. I introduced myself and we started chatting and I recall being mesmerized by her eyes. In fact, I even said that to her: "You have really pretty eyes." Smooth, I know. But hey, it worked.

I left Aspen to go to New York City for our Sewing Down South meetings, but kept in touch with Natalie over IG. We hadn't even exchanged numbers by this point; it was just a little harmless flirting, but obviously leading somewhere. I think we both were playing the game of who was going to ask for a number first. I don't remember who won, but I do remember that when, at one point on the phone, she asked me what she should do for her birthday, I blurted out: "You should come here."

Natalie was splitting her time between New York and Florida, but she agreed to my offer and came up in March 2020, right when filming started. She arrived with a friend, and I picked them up at the airport—a move which kind of shocked her. Apparently, in New York, picking someone up from the airport is some sort of Herculean task. We all went out to dinner that night, and that's when she and I had our first kiss. Not long afterward, she extended her stay in Charleston a week, then another week. All of this was before Covid hit, when we were going on the boat every day and just enjoying dating one another. Natalie never intended to stay for as long as she did, but then we all came down with Covid, which is how she ended up quarantining with me, but more on that in a bit.

One of the new additions to the show that made me extremely excited was Leva Bonaparte. I have known Leva since the very early years of the show, as did most of the cast, because we often hung out at her restaurant, Republic. I remember I would sit at a booth in the front of the restaurant, next to a curtain that separated the tables from the front door, where Leva was often working. She would pop her head out from behind the curtain and we'd talk life, girls, anything. She became like a big sister to me over the years, and I would often work with her on her new restaurant ventures. Nothing major, mostly just suggestions based off my knowledge of the night life in town, menu options, and stuff like that. But to Leva, my suggestions proved valuable. She implemented many of my ideas, boosting my confidence as well as deepening our friendship.

So I was overjoyed when Leva agreed to join the cast, to fill in the big vacancy left by Cam. By this point in their career, Leva and Lamar were powerful players in the Charleston business community. Their many restaurants bring in a lot of money for the city, and they are two shining examples of the "new" Charleston—one defined by outsiders, in this case, minorities, coming to town and remaking it for the next generation: younger, hipper, and more in line with the values and ethos of those who have made Charleston the city it is today.

Of course, the real story during season 7 was the onset of Covid. We had started filming in March of 2020, which meant we didn't get very far before production shut down. Admittedly, I was annoyed, and dubious about the severity of the situation. I wasn't the only one, either. There's an early moment when Shep shows up to my house with a case of Corona. Still, I was a bit in denial about just what was going on. Looking back, I think this stemmed from panic; I simply didn't want production to shut down. I thought it might mean there wouldn't be a season 7 at all. We had already gone much longer than usual since our previous season (for reasons that are above my pay grade) and, while I was happy with where I was with Sewing Down South, I wasn't quite ready to say goodbye to *Southern Charm*.

Then we got the news in the middle of March that we were all dreading: production paused. None of us knew for how long. The immediate effect of the stoppage was that the St. Patrick's

Day Party that was to be held at Patricia's was canceled. *Screw that*, I thought. *I'll have one myself.* Madison LeCroy and Austen Kroll, then still dating, had been at a wedding earlier in the day with a bunch of out-of-towners from New York. The two of them hit my party after the reception. We learned later that many of those New Yorkers soon after came down with Covid, which meant they either had it at the wedding or they got it at the wedding. The fact that I threw a huge party during the middle of a deadly pandemic reveals that I wasn't quite taking the whole thing very seriously. I knew some parts of the country (and world) were getting hit hard by the virus, but the whole thing seemed so far removed from my life. The shutdown was an extreme annoyance for me; not a lifesaving move. Fortunately, none of us came down with it—yet.

And that was the last real blowout we had before we all retreated to our homes and hunkered down. During all this, my house was still under construction. Basically, I had severe water damage and it wouldn't be fixed for some time. So Anna Heyward had found me a long-term rental downtown, which was just fine with me, since I was at least near Austen. If anything made us closer friends, it was Covid. With nothing else to do, he and I would use our golf carts to shuttle between our places. We spent a lot of time together, playing videos games and screwing around on Instagram. This was what led to our Instagram Lives, where he and I would just talk and answer questions as they came in. I mean, there was nothing else to do, so why not have fun? I remember getting a message from Andy Cohen during this time telling me that our live shows basically kept him sane during the lockdown.

By June we were informed that filming would begin again, and that we all had to be tested. I felt confident that I was negative, since I hadn't done much of anything for the previous six weeks. Only I never found out. Somehow the lab lost my test, which meant I had to take another one. And that's when I made my mistake. Now that the city was opening up again, I went to a concert with Austen, Shep and his girlfriend Taylor, and Natalie. We sang; we partied; we drank. A day or two later, I did my test again, then headed out on a boat I was renting. It was Anna Heyward who finally got a hold of me.

"Craig, where have you been?"

I could tell by her tone that something was up.

"You've tested positive," she said.

Fuck.

The show already knew, and damn, were they pissed. But I knew I wasn't the only one. I couldn't be. "Just wait," I told them. "You'll see." Then Austen's test came back. Positive. Natalie. Positive. Taylor. Positive. The only one who had been with us at the concert who wasn't positive was Shep, and he essentially stopped seeing us, which was why Taylor ended up quarantining with me and Natalie. In the end, filming was delayed for two weeks because of us.

I'll admit that that's when the full severity of the pandemic really hit me. My symptoms were for the most part mild. I remember waking up several nights in a row soaking wet with sweat. I also lost my sense of smell for a couple days afterward, but I never really felt sick or flu-like. Austen, on the other hand, was down for several days. Still, I felt dirty, like I had acquired an STD. But at least I stopped being so glib about the whole thing. And much like with filming HSN at my house instead of in St. Petersburg, there was a silver lining too.

The friendship that Austen and I forged during this dark period continues to this day. We discovered that we had a natural rapport with each other, one that audiences really liked. We had been friends for several years, but it wasn't until the lockdown that we started working together on ventures beyond the show. The Instagram Lives eventually led to us starting our own podcast, Pillows and Beer. I also watched Austen get his beer company, King's Calling Brewery, up and running. And yes, I witnessed the manipulations that Madison put Austen through both during and outside of filming. The reason I appeared so angry toward her during the reunion episode of season 7 was because I saw how she treated my friend.

Meanwhile, I was trying to manage a company. Being primarily an online brand, Covid didn't have a strong effect on our sales during the lockdown. If anything, our sales continued to increase month after month, likely because everyone was home with nothing to do but shop online. We lost some in-person opportunities, such as the High Point showcase, which was hard, and planning for a second Pillow Party Tour had to be put on indefinite hold. I also had to set aside my other dream, now that I had checked off HSN: opening a retail store. The pandemic would pass, and I had to be patient. The one thing we did differently was augment our lineup with face masks. Once in a while we'd survey our followers on social media, asking them what other products they'd like to see in the Sewing Down South lineup. By a country mile, the overwhelming response was to start producing face masks in our designs. Jerry and Amanda were enthusiastic about the idea and thought it was worth a try. If the past year of business had taught us anything, it was that the Sewing Down South brand was bigger than just pillows. Yes, pillows were and are our bread-and-butter, but other branded merchandise, such as aprons, oven mitts, hats, and T-shirts, were doing just as well. So we tried out the face mask and, dear God, they were a smashing success. Not knowing how much we'd sell, we put them on the website, and within twenty-four hours we had sold four thousand three-packs of masks. So we did more, including designing a flamingo-themed mask to coincide with our flamingo pillow design, and sold out of those fast. Within a few months, we had sold about $100,000 in face masks. Thank you, Instagram followers. And just so no one thinks we simply profited off a deadly pandemic, we gave most of that money to various causes and charities and donated a free mask for every one we sold.

If I had to look at how I—and Sewing Down South—grew during those dark months in the spring of 2020, it was by learning how to roll with imperfect conditions. This was a big step for me. In my early attempts to make a company out of my sewing, I was often paralyzed by indecision. Before Jerry and Amanda came on board, I would let opportunities slip through my fingers because I was incapable of doing anything unless things were absolutely perfect. By the time they were (if they were), the opportunity was often gone. Or, more likely, I simply gave up on it. Part of this behavior was due to the Adderall, which might have made me more productive, but stole my ability to act decisively. What I've learned is that circumstances will never be perfect. While you're waiting around for the perfect time to arrive, others are acting; and it's action, not perfection, which builds businesses and—incidentally—builds character and confidence. My greatest fear was things wouldn't work out if they weren't perfect at first. But when you act, and things don't work out, you learn to move on. You act *again*. Continual movement. Don't stop, not ever. Just keep going and pushing and imagining and creating and you'll steadily move toward your goal. And then when you reach it, you'll keep moving to the next one. Which is what we did.

A PERMANENT PILLOW PARTY

During Covid, I kept my mouth shut about wanting to open a store. I knew it was a conversation that Jerry, ever the accountant, didn't want to have. Besides, things were going well. In November 2020, we did $250,000 in sales. Things were moving in the right direction, so why not keep going in that direction? But, man, I really wanted a store.

Why? To answer that I'd have to go back to that kid on the golf course hawking used balls. I'd have to go back to sitting behind a desk at some boutique in some small town, greeting customers and making sales. Because there is something about the face-to-face interaction in business that has always given me such a rush. For many reasons, we launched Sewing Down South as an online-only store. It made the most sense for what we were capable of doing at the time. Jerry and Amanda would never have agreed to partner with me if I said I only wanted to open a storefront. Well, actually, they would have laughed at me, then they would have hung up. Their strategy of slow but steady growth was the right one. But *my* strategy of taking our online brand directly to the customers during the Pillow Party Tour was also the right one. The success shocked my partners, because it defied everything they knew about starting a business. I was overjoyed at the tour's success, if not quite as shocked as they were. I simply *felt* that the Sewing Down South brand was and should be primarily a brand that customers could interact with; with me, with the products, with the whole lifestyle we were selling. The tour was the first bit of evidence we received that I was onto something. HSN, and the success I had selling our products live on air, was another piece. Now I wanted a permanent pillow party.

The third and final piece—the one that convinced Jerry and Amanda that opening a store was our next logical step—was a deal we signed with Beachly, a subscription box service specializing in beachwear. The company reached out to us in October 2020, asking if we were interested in designing a couple of pillows that they would include in an upcoming box. At first, Jerry sort of dismissed the idea. He just didn't think that the subscription box market was where we should be, particularly now that we were aligned with Thomasville and HSN. Why would we go in with this company? And then they talked numbers. Beachly wanted to order twenty-five thousand pillows, an order that came out to roughly half a million dollars, potentially the largest order in SDS history. That caught Jerry's attention, and suddenly Sewing Down South was very much into the subscription box game. After months and months of back and forth, we came to tentative terms and designed a couple pillows that would cater to two markets—one for the West Coast and one for the East Coast, and they would all be shipped out in October 2021.

It was the Beachly order that allowed us to start seriously considering opening a store. The money from the order gave us some breathing room with our finances to take some risks—even though opening a retail store is probably the biggest risk a company can take. The order came in February 2021, the same day as my second HSN collection launched. Amanda, Jerry, their significant others, and I were renting a beach house at Isle of Palms for two weeks for photo shoots and my HSN appearance. Once I wrapped with HSN, Jerry turned to me and told me the Beachly order officially came in along with their deposit, and I was in Jerry's ear every day after that about getting a brick-and-mortar operation up and running. He and Amanda relented. Never mind that none of us had any experience opening a retail store. When had that stopped us from doing anything? Forward motion.

"Okay, Craig," said Jerry. "I guess we're opening a store."

And that's how we found ourselves looking at properties in downtown Charleston starting in February. We didn't have a shortage of places to pick from, unfortunately. Covid had done to Charleston small businesses what it had done to small businesses all over the world—shut them down. Up and down the once-busy streets of Charleston, empty storefronts were a stark reminder of the real toll that the pandemic had exacted on my city. People thought we were crazy for even considering doing a retail space while the pandemic was still going on. Perhaps. But as with stocks, so with stores, buy when the price is cheap. The first place that caught our eye, mine especially, was a corner location on King Street. I was sold on it, even if Jerry and Amanda had reservations. The problem, in their view, was that the interior needed a lot of work. In its current shape, it was wholly unsuited to our needs. We might get a good price for the place, but whatever savings we managed would be sunk into modernizing it. I let my enthusiasm get the better of me and couldn't be budged from my desire to take the corner. Not even when Jerry told me about another place, also on King, that a retail business had vacated eight months prior, which meant it didn't need as much upfit. But I was adamant.

"Just shut up and go look at it," Jerry scolded me.

Fine.

Okay, Jerry was right. It wasn't a corner lot, but it was 2,300 square feet, with about 1,300 of that dedicated to the storefront, and located in the heart of Upper King. The rest was for back-of-the-house stuff, like storage. The interior was a mess, but it had all the right wiring. All that was needed was some remodeling: floors, paint, walls, shelving. Best of all, from my point of view, were the huge windows that looked into the store. They were beautiful, or would be once we gave potential customers walking by something to look at. I called Jerry back.

"We have to get this place," I said, my corner-lot baby all but forgotten. One of the things I loved about the location was that it was across the street from the bar Jerry used to bounce at in college.

Jerry laughed and told me to relax, that he was working on the price. He worked on it for three weeks, much to my annoyance and fear of losing the place. But Jerry's patience and persistence paid off and we got an incredible deal. Even today, other business owners are amazed at how well Jerry negotiated. Then, on March 23, we signed our lease. The three of us got together then and discussed an opening date. We decided on May 15, less than two months away. We wanted to move quickly, because in Jerry's and Amanda's minds, time meant money and the longer we delayed opening, the more we were sinking money into something with no return. Perhaps if we had had *any* retail experience, then a six-week window to entirely remodel the interior, get the necessary business license from the city, pass safety and fire inspections, hire staff, organize the product lineup, order inventory during a pandemic, and plan a grand opening might not have been a realistic timetable. But none of us did, and maybe *that* is why we thought we could do it. Whatever. Let's do it.

On April 1 we received the keys to the storefront and immediately got to work. As we were working away on the exterior of the location, a woman walked by. She stopped, put her hand on her hip, and just looked at Jerry. Jerry looked back.

"Can I help you?" he asked.

"Who are you?" she responded.

"Who are *you*?" Jerry shot back.

This was going well.

"How did you get the keys to this place?" she then asked.

"Because I paid for them," Jerry replied.

"Well, you're not supposed to have them," she said.

"Hold up," Jerry said. "Who are you?"

"I'm the property manager."

And so began an often tumultuous, if also humorous, relationship with our landlord, Tammy. I think the best way to describe Tammy, as we would all learn over the next few weeks, is that there is no better friend and no worse enemy than her. I guess you could say we started out as enemies, not in a strict definition of the term, but she seemed to delight in making our lives more difficult at precisely the moment when we needed things to be easy. She'd tell us we were parked in the wrong spot. She'd tell us we couldn't play our music while we worked. She'd pop in whenever she felt like. She'd tell me I was too hard on that poor woman (Madison) during the reunion episode. I mean, everything.

Meanwhile, we're kicking our asses to get the interior of the store set up. There were a million little details, from the floorboards to the walls to the display cases to the minibar I wanted to set up (complete with a kegerator), to the "Instagram wall" that Amanda wanted to decorate with yarn and a neon light that said *Sew What?* We would spend our entire day at the store, often getting there at dawn (well, okay, not me, but Jerry would), and working till well past midnight. Jerry even decided that he couldn't stay in Washington, DC, anymore, and had to move— permanently—to Charleston. We eventually hired a consultant to help us with all the things we hadn't thought of. She was a master at opening stores, and she saved our asses during these critical weeks. It was her who, in addition to helping with the physical layout of the store, also took on responsibilities for hiring staff.

None of the partners had any experience here, and this was one area where we didn't want to just wing it. Our staff had to be the face of the store. We needed people who weren't there simply because they liked *Southern Charm* and thought they'd get on the show or wanted the exposure to advance their Instagram careers. She handled it and, I must say, she did a fantastic job, which I'll explain more in the next chapter.

As opening day approached, we started to deal more with the city. First there were the fire inspections, which concerned us, but we ended up passing just fine. Then, Jerry went in to purchase the business license and receive our occupancy limit. He had all the paperwork ready to go, and handed the clerk a check. The clerk then handed Jerry the license, which included the occupancy limit. And right there in bright red letters was written: 15. We had invited *150* people to the private opening we were planning to have on May 14, the day before the grand opening.

"Fifteen?" Jerry said. "Does this mean just staff?"

The clerk looked up. "No, it's staff and customers."

And that's when Jerry lost it.

We knew someone had screwed up, but there was simply no way to change the occupancy limit in two days. So we ignored the limit. The pandemic was coming to an end (at least we thought it was until the Delta variant arrived during the summer of 2021), the city was opening up, vaccines were available, and we were going to celebrate with a massive party. What else could we do?

On the day of the private party, all of us, including staff and spouses, got to the store early to set up for the night. We had Austen's beer on tap; we had Orange Crushes ready to serve (a nod to my favorite drink from the beaches back in Delaware); we had the merchandise all set up. One addition to the products we were selling was scented candles, a passion project of mine that I had started working on while at Winter House. The smell of scented candles reminds me of my home back in Delaware, where my mother had literally dozens of them throughout the house. With Amanda's help, I created the scents and chose the names of each candle. Jerry thought they wouldn't sell—who comes to a pillow party to buy candles?—but I didn't care. It was a little touch of home right here in my store, a nod to a mom whose love and support has been a constant in my life.

Then the party started, and the 150 guests started to cycle through the store at regular intervals. We didn't have all 150 inside at one time, but we certainly had more than fifteen! Oh well. If there were going to be consequences for going over capacity, we would deal with them later. At that moment, it was like I was in the middle of a dream. My best friends had all shown up; even the Swedish ambassador, Karin Olofsdotter, who was in town, made an appearance. Perhaps the only people not there who should have been were my parents, Marty and Big Craig. Of course they wanted to be, but they had decided to stay away during this weekend so as not to overly stress me out. Besides, they preferred to be there when I wasn't so busy with everyone else (and they had been there a week earlier helping set up).

The bar was supposed to end by eight p.m., but one look around the store told us that no one was ready to leave. So we extended it to nine p.m. Then ten p.m. Then eleven p.m. Finally, we decided that that was about as far as we could push it, and closed down the festivities. Once everyone had said their good-byes, we noticed a fire inspector outside the doors. Jerry walked outside to ask what was the matter.

"We got a tip that you had more than fifteen people inside tonight," said the inspector.

Jerry didn't even try to deny it. "Yes, we did, because the fifteen-person limit is bullshit," he said.

"Perhaps," said the inspector, "but I still need to inform the city."

We had a good relationship with the inspector, who had already cleared us in her report weeks earlier. Jerry wasn't afraid to tell her the truth, because he knew she agreed that something wasn't right with the capacity. There was no good reason for it. Still, the inspector had to do her job. Our attitude, mature or not, was that we'd deal with it when we had to.

After that little hiccup, the staff, Jerry, Alexis, Amanda, Ben, and I decided to go out for one last drink. It was supposed to be a nightcap, but it turned into something a bit more. I'm not sure when I finally collapsed on my bed, probably around one or two a.m., but it was well later than I had intended, especially since our grand opening was scheduled for ten a.m. the next day and Jerry wanted everyone there by eight a.m. to get ready.

I might have set my alarm; I might not have. All I know is that I was shaken awake by Jerry around eight thirty a.m. I opened my eyes to see him standing over me. In the corner of the room were Graham and Anna Heyward.

"What's going on?" I mumbled.

"Dude, get up," he said, while shaking me vigorously. "Craig, you gotta get up and see this."

"See what?" I moaned.

"The store, man. You gotta see the store."

Suddenly, I remembered. It was opening day. Only two things could have gotten me out of bed that morning at such an ungodly hour (for me): Armageddon . . . and my store.

"What?" I said, slowly rising from the bed. "Is there a problem?"

"Just get ready," said Jerry.

I remember thinking that, although I had to be up anyway, whatever had sent Jerry to shake me awake had better be good.

It wasn't good. It was better.

10

FIND YOUR STORY

*W*hen the dust had settled after our opening weekend, things slowed down, even to the point where sometimes there wasn't anyone in the store besides staff. That's the way it is with stores sometimes; not every day can be opening day. However, during one of these quiet moments in our first week, an older woman walked into the store while I was behind the counter. By this point, I was used to first-time customers immediately approaching me, introducing themselves, and asking for a picture in front of the IG wall. Only then would they start to look at the merchandise. But this woman didn't even look at me. She went immediately to the pillows. I walked out from behind the counter and asked if she needed any assistance.

"This is wonderful," she said, holding up one of the pillows. "Who owns this store?"

"I do," I said. "I'm Craig Conover."

"Well, you have very nice pillows, Craig," she said. "I'm going to tell my friends about them." I thanked her and helped her check out. She had no idea who I was, and I couldn't have been happier.

AN OPENING TRIUMPH

I soon learned why Jerry had been so eager to get me out of bed the morning of opening day. At eight a.m., he and Amanda had driven down to the store to prepare. As they were driving, they each wondered to the other what would happen if no one showed up. It was the biggest risk that our young business had made. But unlike a lackluster pillow party, this was an investment that we couldn't just walk away from. We had signed a multiyear lease. We had invested in inventory, not just pillows, hats, aprons, oven mitts, and shirts, but also my precious candles, which could only be bought at the store. We had blanketed social media with announcements. We had even bought hundreds of tote bags that first-day customers could take home with them as a souvenir. We had put ourselves out there in the most vulnerable way a company can, and now we were about to find out if it had all been one huge mistake.

"Oh my God," said Amanda, as she and Jerry turned the corner onto King Street. They were still several blocks from the store, but the line already stretched for a quarter-mile.

Jerry, stupefied, asked, "How many do you think there are?"

Amanda shrugged. "Four hundred, five hundred?"

And more kept getting in line as they parked the car. The rest of the staff was already there, and Amanda had them go out to those who had been waiting in line, some as early as six a.m., with some knickknacks, gifts to reward them for their patience. Jerry then recognized the first person in line. It was the same man who had approached him the night before, ahead of the private party. He had asked Jerry if there was "any way" he could get in line for the party that night. Jerry said it was just for invited guests.

"How much?" the man pleaded. "I'm here for my wife, who couldn't make it. She just wants a pillow from the store."

Jerry still had to refuse. We were already pushing the city on our capacity limit; Jerry couldn't start charging people to get in a line that was invitation only. The man took it well and said he would get in line early the next day. He was the first in line. And that's when Jerry looked at Amanda: "I need to get Craig's ass out of bed."

I eventually made it down there before the store opened. With Jerry behind the wheel, we did a lap in front of the store to take it all in, as they couldn't see me through the tinted car windows. I stared, stunned, at the line, before I hustled in through the back door. Inside, the whole staff was buzzing. Most of them thought they understood what they had signed up for, but I don't think even in their wildest dreams they imagined an opening day like this. I tried to play it cool, as if this was what I had been expecting all along. I had expected large crowds, but not *these* crowds. The plan was for me to cut the ribbon to the store at ten a.m., but I was impatient and couldn't get the scissors to slice. So I slowed down, took in the moment, and opened the store to loud applause and cheering. The first thirty people rushed in, starting a madhouse kind of morning. But the pillow parties had prepared me for this. While the staff worked frantically, and while Jerry and Amanda did their best to maintain order, I settled into a comfortable rhythm of meeting guests and taking pictures.

At some point that morning, I managed to catch Jerry and Amanda's attention from across the room. I had nothing to say, and neither did they, but we all just smiled together. We could breathe. At least right now, everything was all right.

A member of the town council showed up take a picture with me, as did the head of the visitor's bureau. The latter pulled me in and said, "This is so amazing for the city. Just to see King Street alive again is amazing." Indeed it was. Sewing Down South was now part of Charleston. A city that hadn't always felt the most welcoming to those of us on the show could no longer ignore our contribution. We were here, and we were going to stay.

After a year of uncertainty and fear and lockdowns and store closures, the opening of Sewing Down South was a celebration for the city. We weren't the only ones who were going to be all right; Charleston was going to be all right too. Life had returned to the city that I love, and Jerry, Amanda, and I had played a part in bringing it back.

After forty-five minutes of being open, Jerry (ever the CEO) found me to say that we had so far done $9,000 in sales. His goal was $15,000 for the day, but I knew he had allowed himself to hope for $20,000. We were almost halfway there, and it wasn't even noon. When noon did roll around, we had passed the $25,000 mark, not that I was paying much attention to numbers anymore. I was back in the zone, out there with my supporters and customers for three and a half hours, then a twenty-minute break, then back out for another three and a half hours. I met local fans of the show; I met tourists who had come down just for the opening; I hugged bachelorettes; I talked to fathers who wanted something for their little girls; I met grown men who asked me about stitching and embroidery.

Finally, around nine p.m., we decided it was time to close it down. After everything was put away and we could finally relax, the whole staff headed to Hall's Restaurant down the street for the after-party. But I was near exhaustion and could only think about my bed. Even when Jerry told us the day's final tally—$41,000— I managed a very weak smile and asked about the candles. Jerry said we sold half our stock. That made me happy. I then said my goodbyes and took an Uber home, where I collapsed on my couch. Before drifting off into one of the most contented rests in my life, I stared at my ceiling and smiled.

And here is where I want to thank our amazing staff, who brought their expertise and skill to showing just how much Jerry, Amanda, and I didn't know about opening a store. There is Kelly McGinty, whose boyfriend, Alex, worked as our main contractor during the remodeling. Kelly M. is our director of operations and organizes the back-of-the-house responsibilities. Also working as our sales lead is Jack Gilchrist, who delayed law school for a year to work for us (a decision that I clearly understood). Jerry jokes that Jack will learn more about law working at Sewing Down South than he would in three years of law school anyway. Leading the front of the house is Marissa

Connors, who came to Charleston by way of Los Angeles. Helping in the front is Madison Carlson, who quit her job in Alabama to move to Charleston with her boyfriend. Together, the staff call themselves the Sew Crew. I never considered that I would one day be in charge of employees, but I couldn't have asked for a better bunch of young people to take this crazy journey with us.

After that opening weekend, Jerry, Amanda, and I were inside the store going over numbers. We heard a knock and looked outside. It was the fire inspector again. She sort of shrugged as we rolled our eyes. *Here we go again.*

"Look, y'all," she began, "you have the whole government of Charleston following you on Instagram. They're pissed and they're going to shut you down."

"Can they do that?" asked Jerry.

"Of course they can," she said. "You've been rubbing the occupancy limit in their faces all weekend."

"Come on, you know that number is bullshit," said Jerry. "They're trying to stop us from doing business."

"All I can say is that they're going to shut you down if you don't follow the limit."

It wasn't her fault; she was just the messenger. I'm sure she could have shut us down and revoked our business license right there on the spot. But she was giving us time to figure it out. Only we were out of ideas. However—and whyever—it happened, the city was convinced that this 2,300-square-foot store could only hold fifteen people at a time. We all knew that we couldn't do business that way; at least not the kind of business we wanted to do. My whole concept of the store was that it would function like a permanent pillow party. But a pillow party of fifteen people, almost half of which are staff, just doesn't work.

And that's when Tammy, our property manager, walked in.

"What a party, huh?" she said, marching into the store as she usually did.

She saw our faces and immediately discerned something was wrong. Jerry explained about the occupancy limit.

"Well, that's wrong," she said matter-of-factly.

In unison, the rest of us cried: "We know!"

Then she smiled. "I'll take care of it." She stormed out of the store.

To this day, none of us know how Tammy took care of it. What we do know is that she went down to city hall and raised hell. And I don't want to be within fifty miles of Tammy raising hell. Apparently, no one at city hall wanted that experience again, either, because soon after, we were told that the "mistake" had been corrected. Our new occupancy limit was now forty.

Like I said earlier: No better friend, no worse enemy.

The first weekend of Sewing Down South's storefront couldn't have been more different than the first few days of our website. The weekend total came to $72,000, bursting Jerry and Amanda's $40,000 target to smithereens. We knew that past sales were no guarantee of future success, and that the novelty of the opening would eventually wear off, but for those first days, we could congratulate each other on opening a successful store in less than two months.

LIFE NOW, HUSTLING

When I first considered writing a book, I wanted it to be a cookbook. That's another life goal of mine, and one day I hope to make it happen. But when discussing it with Jerry, he convinced me that I should tell the story you just read instead. I wasn't convinced. Who the hell wants to read a story about a thirty-something reality TV star whose company, while successful, is less than three years old? Memoirs and autobiographies are for those whose lives have been lived; I felt like mine was just getting started.

"That's the point, man," replied Jerry. "People should hear how you started your life."

That made me pause. I never rewatch old seasons of the show. I will watch when the season airs, then move on. It doesn't do any good to dwell on the embarrassing past moments. But I realized that there's a big difference between watching, say, season 2 and watching season 7, at least as far as my own story is concerned. I recall what Austen said when he thought back to the moment he first met me: "I thought you were just this skinny Adderall freak." Harsh, man, but not wrong. I'd also add that I was confused; I was lost; and I had no real plan for my life. I lacked discipline. I lacked passion. And I sought out validation from all the wrong sources. I see that kid who Austen saw in those first few seasons. I wanted to use this opportunity to correct some of the record—to fill out the story a bit with a little nuance and context—but the general impression that Austen and others had was mostly correct. I had talent; I had intelligence; and I could work hard when I was motivated, but in the end, I couldn't escape the cage that I had built around myself.

Then you watch season 7. Damn, but what a difference. Gone is that "skinny Adderall freak," replaced by a confident, successful, and hustling young man. With one or two exceptions, I am proud of the person I see now on-screen. I don't need to turn away. This isn't just because of my professional successes and kicking Adderall—it's because I know who I am and I don't tie my self-worth to what others think. My happiness isn't about whether I come off "looking good" on the show; it's tied to whether I got out of bed and got something done that day. Did I have a good meeting with Jerry and Amanda? Did we have a great idea? Did I put something toward a cause I'm passionate about? Did I put a smile on the face of a customer at the store? Did I talk to my brother? Did I call my parents? Did I create something *new*? These are the questions whose answers define my happiness today.

How I went from those early seasons to now—how I started to finally live my life the way I wanted to—is the purpose behind this book. For my supporters from the show, I wanted to fill in the gaps that *Southern Charm* didn't capture, the good and the bad. I wanted to tell you about my Adderall addiction in full. I wanted to recount my journey with the law in full. I wanted to take you through my relationship with Naomie in full. And I wanted to show how sewing was able to lift me out of my despair and set me on this current course. The show documented very little of this. This book is the rest of the story.

To fill in some other gaps that have happened after season 7, I'll add a bit more. First, with Natalie, I can say for certain that we fell in love during our quarantine. Perhaps it was the quarantine itself that formed this very strong bond between us, because once it was all over, and the world opened up again, we drifted apart. She did move to Charleston for a time, and once more the closeness began to diminish. We started to argue a lot more, especially after we had been drinking. And so, in August of 2020, I stopped drinking for two months. It was my way of showing her that I wanted to give us one more try. Truthfully, I enjoyed the respite from alcohol. I still went out with my friends to the bars and places I loved, where the servers and bartenders learned to stock non-alcoholic beer for me. My sobriety during these months certainly led to fewer arguments between us, but it didn't solve all our problems.

For Thanksgiving 2020, I was disappointed when she told me she was going on a ski trip with her friends rather than coming to Ocean View with me. She ended up changing her mind, although it was a sign of where each of us was. When I left to film *Winter House* in January 2021, we were still together, and despite rumors that I had started seeing Paige DeSorbo, nothing happened between us. However, I was also upset when I heard that she had had dinner with Madison while I was filming in Vermont, given that Natalie knew full well how I felt about Austen's ex. So when I returned, we both agreed that the relationship wasn't working anymore. What had happened between us during quarantine just couldn't last in the real world, and while that is unfortunate, I don't regret a moment of it.

Then there's Naomie. The gift of years—and a much clearer head—has allowed me to reassess our relationship, during which I experienced the happiest and saddest moments of my life up till that point. I think that's how it is with your first true love: You learn about who you are. After we broke up, I was bitter and resentful. I blamed the show for tearing us apart, and I blamed Naomie for going along with it. I could see what was happening, but she couldn't. And I can say that now because she's told me that. We have both moved on from the past and become close friends. I think she trusts me now more than she ever did when we were dating. There's a simple explanation for that: I am (again) that guy with whom she first fell in love. She has said to me how she regrets the way she discounted my dreams and ambitions. She regrets the things she said (as do I).

I don't feel vindication from this; I feel relief. I had to earn these words from Naomie. At the time we were dating, I felt entitled to her support and love. I could never understand why she wouldn't stand by me and be my "ride-or-die" girl. Perhaps there were moments when she should have been that person for me, regardless of the way I behaved. But in the end, I had to be the man I always said I was—and so often wasn't. We both carry a great deal of regret from those years, but at the same time we've both become different people. While I think it's good to face the person you were, and accept that you screwed up, I also believe that the things you do and say when you're young should be forgiven. We all make mistakes, and Naomie and I were very young. What I'm saying is that we have forgiven each other and ourselves.

Accepting that the past happened has played a major role in helping me face the future with optimism and joy. I can say for certain that I am doing exactly what I should be doing for the first time in my life. Sewing Down South is only getting started. We have plans for expanding our home goods line, even branching into an area dear to me, the kitchen and cooking. So far, our one store has been successful even beyond my dreams, and perhaps soon enough we'll be able to call the King Street location our flagship store. With Jerry and Amanda beside me, I feel like we haven't even begun to see the limits of our growth.

On a more personal note, I feel liberated in pursuing projects beyond Sewing Down South and expanding my television career. One of my lifetime goals was to achieve a level of financial freedom. What I mean by that isn't simply to make a lot of money; it's to make money *my own way*. For years, my main source of income was the show. It's been running for eight seasons, and while we have no plans to stop, it will eventually. While I never want to say goodbye, I'd be content with moving on to other opportunities. Despite Sewing Down South's success, I want to remain in television. In what capacity, time will tell, but I've always loved it—even when I was depressed. I owe so much to the producers of *Southern Charm*, to Haymaker, to Bravo for opening up this professional route for me. I couldn't have known it at the time, but I'm pretty good in front of the camera. And if I had my choice, I'd love to stay in front of the camera for as long as all of you want to watch this kid from Delaware move through life.

Now you know how it all started for me. If you want to stick around a little longer, then we can see where it goes.

Epilogue

WHAT THE HELL IS GOING ON?

During the course of writing this book, we received an email from a high school teacher from Missouri. He wrote:

> Hello Mr. Conover and Team:
>
> I am a high school Business Teacher from Kansas City, MO. I just want you to know that I use you as an example in my classroom, especially in my Entrepreneurship class. I have seen the episodes from your TV show when you were first starting to sew. I have seen some people roll their eyes, laugh, and who did not fully support you; however, it did not stop you from pursuing your new endeavor. I also use you as an example in my College and Career class . . .
>
> YOU ARE AN INSPIRATION to my high school students. Work hard, don't ever give up. THAT'S YOU! . . .

and yes, we will enjoy the products we purchased from your store. :)

Keep on stitchin! Thank you.

Another email came in from a man in Ohio:

Craig,

I've been binge watching *Southern Charm* with my wife. Honestly, it is the only reality series I've enjoyed watching. I am sure you have an office aid who answers your email [Yes, his name is Jerry Casselano], but I appreciate your dedication. The hard work you put into your company will be rewarded greatly. My wife and I started our business, a chiropractic office in northeast Ohio, with just six thousand dollars of our money and a small, ten-thousand-dollar loan from my parents.

In less than eight years we have grown to six thousand patients, serving communities from three states.

Your passion and personal growth (seen on television) inspired me to purchase a pillow for my wife's birthday. She is turning 36 and discovered she is pregnant with our third child—a total surprise as we were done having more children and our youngest is five. I know it will make her smile and will be a touching gift.

Keep up the good work, Craig.

God bless and I know you're going to be the male Martha Stewart persona you wish to be.

And this one:

Dear Craig:

I know you probably won't read this, but I wanted to let you know how proud of you I am! I know that sounds strange coming from a complete stranger. I've been watching *Southern Charm* from day 1 and you were always one of my favorites. It's like watching your little brother succeed!! Keep rocking it out, stay safe and healthy, and have a fantastic holiday season. I can't wait to purchase more products someday soon.

And there's this one from a mother:

So happy for your success . . . I've been watching *Southern Charm* from the beginning and watched you find your passion for sewing . . . our daughter, Sonni, worked at Sermets and always told us what a nice guy you were . . . she moved home to Birmingham in 2018 and we always watched *Southern Charm* together. Sonni passed away last year, but I continue to watch the show . . . always makes me feel she's with me.

I share these messages first because I am overwhelmed on a daily basis by them. To all my supporters and customers, I know I wouldn't be where I am without you. You believed in me when so many others didn't. Your words of encouragement during my darkest hours as well as my brightest are the fuel that continues to feed my passion. So, to all of you, I say thank you. From the bottom of my heart.

I also share these messages because I think I now understand the answer to the question that my friend Courtney asked me outside her store, Perfect Furnishings, before our first pillow party: "What the hell is going on?" Here's what's going on, Courtney. People have dreams, but many of us need inspiration to reach them. The story of Sewing Down South, which can't be told without also telling my story, inspires. At first, I thought that people only wanted my pillows because they were my supporters on the show. It was only later, after the company had started, that I heard from them how much they had been hoping I would succeed. At first, this confused me, until I started to listen to what they said. So many of them told me how they saw themselves in my struggles, and how they too wished they could make their passion into something real. By rooting for me, they were rooting for themselves. I now realize that the company I started with Jerry and Amanda proved something that we all want to believe but so rarely see: Sewing Down South is the triumph of passion, perseverance, and hope. The story of Sewing Down South, my story, inspires because it shows that sometimes all one really needs is a sewing machine and passion—and maybe some hurt feelings and wounded pride. Sometimes, these are enough to break the vicious cycle and steer your life onto the road to joy and fulfillment.

One doesn't need to experience a devastating addiction, or a heartrending breakup, or a moment of serenity in a tropical paradise to connect with my story. In fact, I think these are the things that people connect with the least about me. Rather, what they

connect with are the very normal moments of self-doubt, indecision, and procrastination that often blocked me from walking
that path of success. I'm not different in that regard from anyone
else. When we encounter these obstacles, we lose faith. We believe
we aren't worthy of the fulfillment we want to find on the other
side. And when we lose faith, we stop believing we are worthy. We
can't do it, not because we don't know how, but because we don't
deserve it. Passion, success—these are the things that are for *others*; but they're not for us.

And here's the thing: I still struggle with procrastination; I
still doubt myself; I still have a hard time making a decision. In
many ways, I am still the same person I was staring at the pillows
that littered my house without the foggiest idea of what to do
with them. I know I will always be that person, the one who can't
get out of bed on time; who wants to go for one more drink; who
feels like he has to prove himself constantly. I didn't suddenly lose
these personality traits. (Just ask Jerry and Amanda.) But whereas
I had previously used these unsavory parts of myself as an excuse
for why I couldn't succeed, now I have learned to live with them,
to—as Jerry once yelled at me—"pull on [my] big-boy pants" and
get out there anyway. We don't suddenly become different people
when we start to live our dreams. We just start to live our dreams.
The parts about ourselves that hold us back might be difficult to
overcome, but they can't be excuses.

And while this book might seem like a long list of my very
apparent character flaws, I hope that some of my more notable
traits also came through. I often cared what people thought about
me (too much, in fact), but I never cared what they thought

about my passions. Not once during all the times that someone snickered, rolled their eyes, or even broke up with me did I walk away from my passion. A lot of people, some very close to me, thought I was crazy for setting aside the law for pillows, but I never once questioned it. *This* is what I wanted to do; I had to get out of my own way to do it, but I never doubted that it was worth doing. Your passion is worthy. You are worthy. Let the haters hate, but keep going. Keep taking those steps. Ask for help when you need it and ignore those whose advice would divert you from your dream.

What the hell is going on? Just this: Trust yourself and do what makes you happy. You will find that fulfillment you seek, and you will even inspire a few others along the way. And when you do, come find me at the store. I'd love to hear your story too.

AFTERWORD

When *Pillow Talk* was first published, I read and listened to readers' reviews carefully. I was anxious to know how others would respond to my story—or not. Most of all, I wanted to know if my story was able to help those who might be suffering from an addiction or other personal demon that kept them from living the life they wanted. The reaction was tremendous. Readers from all walks of life have reached out to tell me how *Pillow Talk* helped them realize that they weren't alone in their darkness. I didn't necessarily set out to write a "self-help" book, but it's one of the greatest accomplishments of my life that by just telling my story, I was able to give hope to those who are still suffering. To them I say: Don't give in and don't give up. Your new journey is just beginning.

As for the criticism, well, you can't please everyone. Some readers were disappointed that I didn't include more gossipy "behind-the-scenes" tea on *Southern Charm*. I suppose there's an expectation that any book from a reality TV star *must* include juicy, scandalous tidbits that somehow were kept locked away from public view. But it was never my intention to write such a book. From the very beginning, my purpose was to tell *my* story, both on and off the show, and whatever "tea" I spilled would be tea that helped explain or illuminate that story. The gossip that is in these pages is in service to the story, not to titillate readers with others' dirty laundry. I do understand why some readers wanted more of it, but I make no apologies for disappointing them. I set out to write a book that stood above the other titles in the same genre, one that said something meaningful, one that I would be proud to call my own five, ten, or twenty years from now. I feel like I succeeded.

That said, there were some obvious omissions from the hard-cover edition, most notably my relationship with Paige DeSorbo, that probably confused readers. I also think enough time has passed to offer some updates on the status of my friendship with others from the show, particularly Madison LeCroy and Austen. The publication of the paperback version of *Pillow Talk* has given me the opportunity to fill in some of these gaps. My excuse for not including them in the first go-around is simple: In book pub-lishing, there is a lot of time from the moment an author stops writing to when a book comes out. Things can change. Things *did* change. Had I written down my feelings about, say, Madison in detail in the fall of 2021, then I would be using this oppor-tunity to offer apologies. And I wasn't about to write about my relationship with Paige, which had only just begun. As much as I wanted to shout my love for her from the rooftops, I wisely chose to stay silent and let the relationship take its course.

Now I'm ready to shout it from the rooftops.

But first, let's talk about Madison. Anyone who watched the season 7 reunion episode knows that Madison brought out the worst in me. Which is funny because the first time I watched the episode was more than a year after it originally aired—and I watched it *with* Madison. By this point, we had moved past our animosities and rediscovered a friendship. How, you're probably wondering, did *that* happen? Well, I give almost all the credit to Madison. In the summer of 2021, she and I found ourselves at the same party. That's not surprising, because we still run in the same social circles and Charleston just isn't that big. Per usual, however, I did my best to ignore her. Madison had no intention of ignoring me and jumped on my back at one point. "Hey, can we stop hating each other?" she asked, hanging off my back.

"Oh, thank God, please," I responded.

I was genuinely relieved. Almost all of our animosity toward each other was based on who we had been dating at the time our friendship soured. I still don't agree with many of her actions during the period when our feud grew heated, but those relationships are in the distant past; there is nothing between us that should still be causing friction other than bad memories. I've also learned that it takes a lot of energy to hold a grudge. It's exhausting to dislike someone with the fervor I disliked Madison. (I mean, just look at me in the reunion episode.) I've known Madison for a decade, and she and I have been friends through most of those ten years. Even if I still disagree with some things she did, it was time to bury the hatchet.

A few months later, my friend and business partner, Jerry, and I ran into Madison at a restaurant on King Street not far from the store. Madison was celebrating her birthday, and Jerry and I decided to send her table a couple bottles of champagne. When we walked over to give our birthday wishes, Madison asked when I was going to invite her to the store. So I did, and she and her now fiancé, Brett, came by a few days later. A friendship reignited from these small steps.

And so it went, on through filming season 8 and into the spring of 2022, when the network asked if they could film us watching the infamous reunion episode together. Sure, why not? She couldn't believe I had avoided it for so long. If I had to go through the embarrassment, might as well go through it with Madison and thousands of viewers. I had heard enough about my behavior from others to know that I had been pretty cringe that day. Even Andy Cohen—who knows how to handle drama—had to call me out in the middle of the episode with a cutting "Just calm down, dude." But I knew I had to face the music eventually, and who better to share the moment with than my one-time archnemesis, Madison? So, she and I got drunk watching the reunion, laughing and cringing—but mostly laughing. Dear God. I had been a hot mess. Every time I asked her if that was as bad as I would get, she would wag her finger: "Just keep watching." She was right. It always got worse. Even if you've seen the original episode, you should check out the watch party Madison and I had. Have a laugh at my expense.

Still, Madison fully admits she threw some pretty tough punches my way. We're both passionate people, and sometimes we fight dirty. We rarely back down, especially when we're pushed into a corner. Madison stuck up for herself—perhaps too harshly in some instances—but now it's all water under the bridge. Given my state that day, I really can't hold anything against her. I think what has also helped us reconnect is that Madison is a huge fan of Paige. There's a mutual respect they have for each other, and it's no wonder. They are two very independent, strong women who live life their own way.

As for Austen, season 8 was a whirlwind for sure, as our frustrations that had been simmering since *Summer House* spilled over. Many readers might think it's because of how Austen treated others, but the truth is that our squabble was about us, our friendship, and our expectations of each other. Under normal circumstances, I think Austen and I might have been able to settle our differences if we had just had some time off from each other. But season 8 filmed right after *Summer House,* meaning we never got that break. With these back-to-back shows, you sometimes find yourself thrust from the frying pan into the fire. So like a struggling married couple, we needled each other over petty spats, all the while ignoring the big issues. In fact, we wouldn't confront the big issues between us until a talk we had on the Pitt Street Bridge near Charleston in October 2021.

The background to this talk was the plan Jerry and I had

devised to promote the book. We wanted to revisit all the boutiques and stores we had visited during the Pillow Party Tour. More
than that, we also wanted to tie this publicity tour to the podcast
I host with Austen, *Pillows and Beer*. So we decided we'd do both:
We would hold a Pillows and Beer Tour, taking the podcast on the
road in front of a live audience, and squeeze in book promotions
at the stores. But for that to happen, Austen and I needed to clear
the air. Our discussion that day on the bridge was frank and open.
I knew from the Pillow Party Tour that going on the road was only
going to exacerbate the tensions between us. We'd likely kill each
other before we got halfway done with it. So I talked about what
had upset me with *Summer House*; it wasn't so much all the girlfriend drama as it was his running his mouth about me to anyone
who would listen. Austen talked about how he felt I was being
far too judgmental and aloof. Perhaps I was; I had just started
dating Paige when we began filming season 8 and I was focused
on moving on with my life and avoiding negativity. Our talk that
day didn't resolve all the issues, and we'd still snipe at each other
throughout season 8, but it had to happen for us to move forward.

   In March 2022, we went on tour . . . and oh man, was it a
cluster. Seven cities in a month. We started in Washington, DC,
traveled up and down the East Coast, and ended in Chicago at
the famous House of Blues. A cluster to be sure, but it was also a
smashing success. There's nothing to compare to that high you get
walking onto the stage in front of a live audience, answering questions from the fans and just having a great time. We both took our
fair share of criticism, and I know Austen for one appreciated the
opportunity to set the record straight. Which isn't to say that our

friendship had entirely healed. After each show, we would usually go our separate ways until we had to be back together. Part of that is just how one handles the rigors of touring life; you need a break from the bandmates. But the other part of it is that we still hadn't fully reconciled. Things were still frosty between us, but at the end of the day, we set that aside and tried to give the best show we could. The fact remains that Austen and I are business partners as well as friends. Sometimes those two things don't mesh well together. Sometimes, as Shep likes to say, we need to "clean out the basement" to remember why two friends decided to be business partners in the first place.

With that out of the way, let's get to the real update: Paige. If there's one criticism I heard about the first edition of *Pillow Talk* more than any other, it's readers complaining that I said next to nothing about Paige, despite the fact that we were definitely dating while I was finishing up writing. Let me make two points clear: First, *Pillow Talk* was always meant to be the story of how I found success doing something I loved. It's my story, but it's also the story of Sewing Down South. The ending of the book is the realization of a dream I've had since I was young: opening my own store. It just so happened that soon after I opened my store, I fell in love with Paige. Which brings me to the second point.

Under no circumstances was I going to write about a relationship that, at the time, I couldn't properly explain. I deeply hoped that Paige and I would still be together when the book came out, but I couldn't predict that. What's more, I needed time for myself, a moment to catch my breath, focus on the book, and work on me. If I learned anything from the process of writing this book, it was the twin lessons of humility and patience. I was trying to practice both while Paige and I started seeing each other. Not knowing where things would lead, I chose to hold off on talking about it publicly. Besides, I wanted her permission to talk about it.

Paige and I first met during season 4 of *Summer House*, which was filmed in 2019. Kyle Cooke, a regular on both *Summer* and *Winter House*, had invited Shep, Austen, and me to his birthday party, which was to be filmed (and shown in episode 10 of that season). At the party, I gravitated toward Paige immediately and we had a very quick moment together where we both went down a water slide. I was instantly smitten, even if we didn't talk the rest of the night. She was dating someone at the time, so nothing was going to happen anyway, but it was hardly the stuff of true love.

After that inauspicious encounter, we didn't see each other again until Austen and I had Paige on our Instagram Live during the pandemic. Once again, it wasn't exactly a romantic moment between us, but I found myself thinking about her more and more. Of course, when we came together again to film *Winter House* in January 2021, I had a girlfriend. It was a wild two weeks, but I distinctly remember that first night as being the moment when I found a new best friend. I had grabbed a couple mini bottles of prosecco and just chilled with her and Ciara Miller while they unpacked. There was nothing remarkable about the moment, except that for the first time in a long time I felt totally at ease and normal. There was an immediate connection between us, a kind of instant friendship. I started to tell them about me, the story that you've just read, that took me from a struggling law-school kid to cofounder of a successful home décor business. Prior to this I had always made excuses for my failings, but with Paige, I just let it all out there. You could say that she was my first reader—the story I told her would in time become the story of *Pillow Talk*.

After seventeen days filming *Winter House*—seventeen days of nearly nonstop drinking and partying, my memories of which are extremely foggy—I suddenly saw things very clearly. I knew my current relationship wasn't right for me, not because I was hoping to date Paige, but because I had started to get serious about what I wanted out of life. Later, in the spring, Paige visited Charleston with her brother, Gary, for his birthday, and I was able to show them the store before it opened, which means it was in a state of total chaos. While she was in town, we went to a club after several days of hanging out, where we got closer to each other and danced. At one point, as I was just rambling on about something, trying to hide my nervousness, Paige asked me: "Are you going to kiss me or not?" So I did what any gentleman would do: I grabbed her hand, led her outside, and kissed the girl. We stayed up that whole night just talking, strengthening that connection that first began a few months earlier. It was the spark we both needed, even if it didn't lead us to start dating immediately. She went back to New York shortly afterward but we stayed in touch throughout the summer. I was deep in the weeds of writing this book at the time, and perhaps for that reason, I was more concerned with coming to terms with my past in a way that I had never attempted before. It was an emotional time for me. I felt that whatever Paige and I had, if it was strong enough, would grow organically. Let's not forget that we lived in two different cities, a thousand miles apart. My heart soared when I thought about her, but I was skeptical that we could even make it work. My rational brain tried to keep expectations firmly on the ground.

The weeks passed. She dated; I dated. But always, in the background, she was there, and I was there with her. It was a slow-burn kind of beginning, but it was all going in the same direction. The times apart from each other started getting shorter and shorter. Then came the moment when she was filming *Summer House* that it happened. I was at a bachelor party in Canada, but I had talked to the *Summer House* producers about surprising Paige during the show's prom-themed party. It was actually kind of hilarious the lengths we went to to keep my arrival a surprise, since only a couple producers knew I was coming. They even gave me a code name: Cliff. I needed one because the production crew had to have all the equipment ready for everyone who was going to be on camera. So there were incredibly funny moments of some production person, looking at the guest list, asking, "Who the hell is Cliff?"

Meanwhile, I found myself getting ever more excited about the surprise. I mean, the trembling kind of excited. I couldn't remember feeling that way—at least in a long time. Then it hit me: I didn't want to be with anyone else. I wanted to be with Paige. I texted her my feelings, to which she instantly agreed. That was it. We were together. Of course, my surprise appearance at the party somewhat gave this away. Andy Cohen, who showed up for the party, even asked us point-blank if we were a couple. We both demurred. The cameras were rolling and we both wanted to be a couple together just for ourselves, just enjoying the moment before the inevitable reveal.

After *Summer House*, Paige came home to Delaware with me to meet my parents. Seeing her with my family was when I knew I was falling in love. My parents of course were ecstatic about Paige and how happy we were together. The only question that remained was whether we could survive filming a season of *Southern Charm* together.

Looking back, it's funny that I wasn't all that concerned about it. I just knew that we would be fine. I think the difference this time was that I wasn't so hell-bent on "protecting" our relationship from the cameras. Paige was no stranger to filming. She didn't need me to coach her through it. That took a great deal of pressure off of us. We could simply *be ourselves.* I suppose not being hooked on Adderall, nor dealing with the chaos of my professional life, also helped. I was simply in a better place this time around. And I experienced something that I hadn't in a long time: I had fun filming again. I got to work with my best friend and partner. We were a unit, but we also were able to let go and trust that the other would be just fine. I never had to worry about what Paige might say to me (or others) while the cameras were on. I never had to worry about keeping parts of our relationship hidden. I was finally able to let go and enjoy the ride. And what a great ride it's been. I don't want it to ever end.

And that's where I'll leave it. I hope readers now appreciate why I left out these parts of the story. Simply, they weren't ready to be told yet. I didn't know where they fit into the larger narrative at the time they were happening, but now I think I do, and I'm happy to end the book on this note. I know that I wouldn't be with Paige if I hadn't gone through everything I talked about in this book. If I was still on Adderall, if I was still flailing professionally, if I was still unable to admit my own faults, then I wouldn't be in the one place I never want to leave: with her. I had to get through all that to get to Paige. She's what I found waiting for me at the end. I couldn't ask for a better partner to go through this crazy, demanding life we have both chosen for ourselves. Our story together is just another sign—not that I needed any more—that living life on my terms is a decision that continually rewards me. I hope that it's also a sign for readers. Do the right thing and be patient; the happiness you seek will come along soon enough.

As for where our story goes from here? Well, I guess you'll have to read the next book.

ACKNOWLEDGMENTS

I was about halfway through writing this book when I realized that this stuff is hard work. I never could have finished without the help and support of so many people who believed in this project and in me. First, I want to thank my mom and dad—Marty and Craig Conover—for always encouraging me to follow my own path and for supporting me unconditionally. Your steadfast love is why I am where I am today. I also want to thank my little brother, Christopher, who never lost faith in me, who never doubted me, and who always knew I had it in me. You are one of the main reasons I continue to push myself.

I also never could have finished this book without my excellent team behind me. First, I want to thank Kirsten Neuhaus, my literary agent, who saw what this book could be before I did and never tired in trying to make it more than a dream. I want to thank my writing partner, Blake Dvorak, for helping me put my thoughts and story into discernable prose. Your eloquent way with words and our ability to connect on so many personal matters—not to mention your ability to keep the project moving forward despite my crazy schedule—are why I am so proud of what we accomplished together. And I want to thank my editor, Natasha Simons, who was able to take what Blake and I had created and make it better. I was truly blessed with an amazing writing and publishing team.

Of course, as readers are no doubt well aware of by now, I never could have gotten where I am today without my business partners, Jerry Casselano and Amanda Latifi. A chance call from you changed everything for me. You have never tried to make me into something I'm not and always listened to and dealt with my thoughts and designs and antics, even when some were completely crazy. You two aren't just business partners. You are family, and I can't wait to continue building our pillow kingdom.

I also want to thank the two people whose own stories made my own possible. First, thank you to Kory Keefer, my brother from another mother. We've been through it all: the good, the bad, and the ugly. We're still standing. And you were always by my side, even when we were thousands of miles apart. And thank you, Naomie, for letting me tell our story, flaws and all. Each of you gave your time to this project so that I didn't have to rely on my own memories, and it's a better book because of you.

I don't think there is enough room here to say how much I appreciate what Graham and Anna Heyward Hegamyer have done for me. From helping me find myself in the Bahamas to telling me when I was being the worst version of myself, you both have helped me through the toughest times and been there every step of the way. Thank you for always believing in me and staying by my side. I wouldn't be where I am today without you two. I love you both.

Whitney Sudler-Smith, Austen Kroll, Shep Rose—we've had a lot of ups, and a lot of downs. I appreciate you boys more than you know, and your friendship means everything to me.

To the team at Haymaker, especially Jessica Chesler, Aaron Rothman, and Josh Halpert, and the entire production crews past, present, and future: You've watched me grow from a young college graduate to pillow boss and lawyer. I appreciate everything you've done for me along the way. Through the highs and lows, breakups, failures, triumphs, I appreciate all of your hard work and effort that goes into everything you all do.

To Kathleen French and the team at NBC, thank you for always believing in me.

I want to thank Professor Meeks from the Charleston School of Law for helping me finish my thesis and graduate from law school. Despite battling cancer in the last months of her life, Professor Meeks worked with me, drinking coffee and discussing my future. A big thanks also to Marlene Urena, an administrative assistant at the school, who was my first friend on campus and became my law school "mom."

I want to give a shout-out to the staff of Sewing Down South, our Sew Crew: Kelly McGinty, Madison Carlson, Jack Gilchrist, Marissa Connors, Blair Wood, Gracie Birgnola, Dylan Staggard, Caitlin Guarisco, Maria Hoffman, Will Groark, and Lily Howard.

You all are the reason why the Sewing Down South store has become a destination for all Charlestonians and visitors. Your warm smiles brighten up the space and make coming to work so much fun. I couldn't be more proud of all of you.

I can't forget Alex Mims, without whom the store would be in ruins. Thank you from the bottom of my heart for the early mornings and late nights working and for teaching Jerry how to use power tools to get the store built out. Our vision came to life and you made it happen in just forty-five days.

To our friends at Harris Pillow, especially John Harris, Patrick Harris, Jenny Price, Bory, Blake, Aletha, Missy, Will, Daisy, and the entire crew down there: Thank you for being an integral part of the SDS story and giving us little guys a chance.

Thank you to Kevin Tighe II and Jayme Harper at Beachly for taking a leap of faith with Sewing Down South and me. You provided us with the largest business transaction in our young history, and our partnership has become a true friendship.

To Nick Woodhouse and the Authentic Brands Group/Thomasville crew, thank you for making me a part of your family and believing in our products and story. Our collaboration was the affirmation I needed to know we were on to something. Thank you for your continued friendship and business advice.

To the entire HSN family, especially Margoe Frazis and Judy Block, you all made my childhood dreams come true and put Sewing Down South on the map by putting our young company on air. I'll never forget the experience, and I'm indebted to you for taking a chance on us.

Finally, I want to thank all my supporters, who have been with me from day one. Sewing Down South exists because of your encouragement, your faith, and your love. You are the reason why I am able to do what I do. But the party's just starting. Let's see what happens.

Craig Conover is one of the stars of Bravo's *Southern Charm* and the cofounder and CCO of Sewing Down South. He is a graduate of the College of Charleston and the Charleston School of Law, and he currently resides in Charleston.